LEOPOLDO ALAS (CLARÍN)

an annotated bibliography

NOËL M. VALIS

Grant & Cutler Ltd
1986

© Grant & Cutler Ltd
1986
ISBN 0 7293 0236 9

314116

c ✓

I.S.B.N. 84-599-1691-X

DEPÓSITO LEGAL: V. 2.014 - 1986

Printed in Spain by Artes Gráficas Soler, S.A., Valencia

for

GRANT & CUTLER LTD
55-57 GREAT MARLBOROUGH STREET, LONDON W1V 2AY
and
27 SOUTH MAIN STREET, WOLFEBORO, NH 03894-2069, USA

CONTENTS

To my mother

INTRODUCTION

Clariniana: concentrated in that one word is the essence of both the scholarly and popular twentieth-century interest in the man Leopoldo Alas and his work. The large number of contributions which comprise the second part of this annotated bibliography points indisputably to an undiminished curiosity in a complex and often perplexing personality, whose work continues to yield perceptive scholarly studies and whose significant position in the world of late nineteenth-century Spanish letters has finally merited just recognition.

The user of this bibliographical guide may be surprised at the relative paucity of solid critical work on Leopoldo Alas until the late 1950s and early 1960s. There were, however, a number of factors which encouraged such neglect of the author of one of the two finest nineteenth-century Spanish novels, *La Regenta* (the other is of course Galdós's *Fortunata y Jacinta*).[1] During his lifetime (1852-1901), Leopoldo Alas provoked passionate devotion to his cause and equally committed hatred of his person and his work, an anti-Clarín rage which at times even vented itself upon his corpse: witness Luis Bonafoux's unforgiving and unforgiveable attacks on the dead Asturian writer (see B188). Such biased views obviously blinded many of Clarín's critics to the first-rate narrative qualities of his novels and short stories. There followed years of accumulated misunderstanding, indifference, and near oblivion, in which the Asturian was to be rescued at various times by Azorín, Sáinz Rodríguez, and Adolfo Posada, only to fall into the unsympathetic clutches of the Franco era. Even the centennial of Clarín's birth (1952), though it resulted in some homage numbers — notably, those of *Archivum* and *Insula* — in general, heralded a somewhat faltering and timid reevaluation of Alas's work. Add to this a scarcity of texts, of affordable and usable editions until 1966 —

---

[1]Mario Vargas Llosa in his *La orgía perpetua* declares *La Regenta* to be the best Spanish novel of the nineteenth century (Madrid: Taurus, 1975, p. 254).

there is still no complete edition of the works of Leopoldo Alas[2] –
and one then perceives how an entire series of circumstances con-
spired, unintentionally or not, to delay the now firmly held belief
in Clarín's literary eminence.

Because we now possess such an abundance of information, of
critical and noncritical books, monographs, articles, and reviews,
an annotated Clarín bibliography has become a necessity.[3] In this
guide, I have been inclined to place more emphasis on the secondary
sources for precisely that reason. By doing so, I do not mean to deny
the equally significant bibliographical development of primary sources
in Clarín's case. Indeed, as all Clarinistas know, what may amount to
thousands of Leopoldo Alas's journalistic pieces still remain buried
in now defunct and often obscure newspapers and magazines of the
period. The task of bringing this material to light, of cataloguing,
and possibly publishing it, requires a team of dedicated scholars in
order to do the job properly.[4]

For the present, I have attempted to catalogue those works of
Alas which did appear in the form of books, collections, anthologies,
translations, reprints, and the like. It is, I emphasize, a first step in
understanding, in bibliographical terms, the extent of Clarín's
productivity and of the enduring interest in his work. For conve-
nience, within the subsections A and B, items are numbered conse-
cutively. In Part A, I have listed Alas's works in chronological order
by date of publication. Works published in the same year are listed

---

[2]I now understand scholars at the University of Oviedo and others are planning
the publication of a six-volume edition of the *Obras completas* in time for the 1984-
85 celebration of *LR*'s centennial.

[3]Like all Clarín scholars, I am indebted to the bibliographical spade-work done
by Pedro Sáinz Rodríguez, Adolfo Posada, Marino Gómez-Santos, Francisco García
Pavón, Sergio Beser, Laureano Bonet, Jean-François Botrel, and, above all, José María
Martínez Cachero.

[4]I have since learned that Jean-François Botrel and Yvan Lissorgues have prepared
vols 4 and 5 of the forthcoming *Obras completas*, in which they publish LA's previously
uncollected criticism. I have been told that Lissorgues also incorporated therein his
indexes to LA's journalistic publications (see B664). (Most of Clarín's collected stories
and articles first appeared in this form.) Thus, there is no need for me to duplicate
their valuable contribution to Clarín scholarship.

alphabetically by title; and later editions of a work have been placed chronologically after the first edition. In Part B, secondary sources are arranged alphabetically by author. Anonymous articles are entered last. I have employed, when applicable, the sigla of the MLA International Bibliography (see Abbreviations); in other cases, I have spelled out the names of journals and newspapers. British style of dating has been followed. The reader will note that newspaper articles frequently bear no page numbers. When available to me, I have inserted them, but in any case, it should be easy for the researcher to locate these items with the information provided.

No bibliography is, by its very nature, complete. I have doubtless missed items which appeared prior to 1983 (I have also included post-1983 entries which have come to my attention); and I have on occasion omitted some references which until now have appeared in selected bibliographies in monographs and critical studies on Clarín. Those items, in most cases, either contained no mention of Alas or at most a footnote or two on the Asturian novelist. The Clarín scholar will encounter several items which, to my knowledge, have never before been cited (see, for example, B59, 79, 223, 485, 817, 987, 991, 1149-54, etc.). He will also note that I have clarified, when possible, some obscure or erroneous references which have appeared in previous studies on Leopoldo Alas. Entries B1086 and B1087, under Luis Ruiz Contreras, for example, have often been listed as 'anonymous'. Yet evidence exists which points to Ruiz Contreras as the indisputable author of 'Clarindustrial' and 'Los funerales de Clarín' (see Domingo Paniagua, *Revistas culturales contemporáneas*, I, Madrid, 1964; and Luis Granjel, *Biografía de Revista Nueva, 1899*, Salamanca, 1962). Walter Pabst's article (B897) receives its proper citation (*Die Neueren Sprachen*, 41, 1933), after residing many years in the dim and incorrect bibliographical reaches of *Narodna Starina*. And Augusto Martínez Olmedilla's piece (B745) is no longer cited as appearing in *ABC* (1931), but in *ABC* (4.1.31). An asterisk precedes any bibliographical entry which I was unable to examine myself.

Critical investigation of Leopoldo Alas's work continues. In preparation are six American theses: Roberto González-Casanovas' 'Diálogos de convivencia: el problema de la comunicación en cinco novelistas españoles (Cervantes, Galdós, Clarín, Unamuno y Pérez de Ayala)' (Harvard Univ.), Carrie Grady's 'Mythology in the Fiction of Clarín' (Univ. of Maryland), Nidia Mondéjar's '*La Regenta*: estudio semiótico de las máscaras en los monólogos interiores' (New York Univ.),

Ana-Ofelia Rodríguez's 'La animalización en *La Regenta*' (Washington Univ.- St Louis), Irène Simon's 'Fonction des couleurs dans *Le Rouge et le noir* et *La Regenta*' (Univ. of Arizona), and Lee Taylor's 'Personajes y temas en *La Regenta* de Leopoldo Alas "Clarín" y *O Crime do Padre Amaro* de Eça de Queiroz' (Univ. of Pennsylvania). In press is an Italian version of *Cuentos morales* (*Racconti morali*), by Elena Clementelli (Roma: Curcio). Gredos will be publishing María del Carmen Bobes Naves' *Teoría general de la novela: semiología de 'La Regenta'*. Mario Vargas Llosa is writing a preface to an edition of *La Regenta*. Ballet and stage versions of Clarín's masterpiece have been performed. In addition, an exhibit of Clariniana has been shown in Oviedo, Gijón, and Madrid in 1984; and the Fábrica Nacional de Moneda y Timbre issued a new bill depicting Clarín. Special issues devoted to *La Regenta* have been prepared by *Insula, Argumentos, Los Cuadernos del Norte* (all listed here). Frank Durand is preparing an anthology of critical essays on *La Regenta*, to be published in Taurus's series, 'El Escritor y la Crítica'. Add to that the 1984 international Clarín symposia in Barcelona and Oviedo, another at the University of Georgia in 1985, and the reader will have some idea of the fascination Leopoldo Alas continues to exert in the late twentieth century.

Grateful thanks are due to Professors Alan Deyermond, John Varey, Joseph Snow, Carolyn Richmond, José María Martínez Cachero, Stephen Miller, David Gies, Stephen Gilman, Vernon Chamberlin, Francisco García Pavón, John Dowling, Lee Fontanella, Robert Jackson, Antonio Fernández Insuela, Phillip Wolfe, David Billick, Antonio Ramos-Gascón, Eleanor Paucker, Hadassah Weiner, Lou Charnon-Deutsch, Monroe Z. Hafter, Sergio Beser, Mario Damonte, Flaviarosa Nicoletti Rossini, Candido Panebianco, Hensley Woodbridge, Gonzalo Sobejano, Dennis P. Seniff, Allen W. Phillips, Harriet Turner, Jean Bécarud, Franklin Proaño, José Manuel González Herrán, José Luis Gómez-Martínez, John Crispin, and Manuel Fernández Avello; and to the following institutions: the Biblioteca Nacional de Madrid, the Hemeroteca Municipal and the Ateneo de Madrid, the Library of Congress, the Centro Asturiano de Buenos Aires, the Centro Asturiano de Madrid, the Biblioteca de Catalunya, the libraries of the Consejo Superior de Investigaciones Científicas, the Instituto Internacional, the Universidad de Barcelona, the Universidad de Oviedo, and the Instituto de Estudios Asturianos. I most appreciated the long hours and hard work of the Interlibrary Loan Department

Introduction

of the University of Georgia Library and the support given me by the Department of Romance Languages of the University of Georgia in the form of summer research grants. Special thanks to Mrs María Rodríguez, who typed the manuscript. Responsibility for errors, omissions, and other editorial vagaries, of course, rests in my hands alone. I can only wonder what it would have been like to have had the use of a computer in the preparation of this bibliography.

Athens, Georgia, November 1984

ABBREVIATIONS

AGald	*Anales Galdosianos*
Archiv	*Archiv für das Studium der Neueren Sprachen und Literaturen*
ArH	*Archivo Hispalense*
BA	*Books Abroad*
BBMP	*Boletín de la Biblioteca Menéndez Pelayo*
BEPIF	*Bulletin des Études Portugaises et de l'Institut Français au Portugal*
BH	*Bulletin Hispanique*
BHS	*Bulletin of Hispanic Studies*
BIDEA	*Boletín del Instituto de Estudios Asturianos*
BRAE	*Boletín de la Real Academia Española*
CA	*Cuadernos Americanos*
CCLC	*Cuadernos del Congreso por la Libertad de la Cultura*
CCU	*Cuadernos de la Cátedra de Miguel de Unamuno*
CdD	*La Ciudad de Dios*
CH	*Crítica Hispánica*
CHA	*Cuadernos Hispanoamericanos*
CLS	*Comparative Literature Studies*
CMHLB	*Cahiers du Monde Hispanique et Luso-Brésilien*
CSIC	Consejo Superior de Investigaciones Científicas
DAI	*Dissertation Abstracts International* (previous to July 1969, called *Dissertation Abstracts*)
DHR	*Duquesne Hispanic Review*
DM	*The Dublin Magazine*
Ensayistas	*Los Ensayistas*
EstLit	*La Estafeta Literaria*

ETL	*Explicación de Textos Literarios*
HisJ	*Hispanic Journal*
Hispano	*Hispanófila*
HR	*Hispanic Review*
IDEA	Instituto de Estudios Asturianos
KRQ	*Kentucky Romance Quarterly*
LA	Leopoldo Alas
LBR	*Luso-Brazilian Review*
LR	*La Regenta*
MFS	*Modern Fiction Studies*
MLF	*Modern Language Forum*
MLJ	*Modern Language Journal*
MLN	*Modern Language Notes*
MLR	*Modern Language Review*
MLS	*Modern Language Studies*
NE	*Nueva Estafeta*
NRFH	*Nueva Revista de Filología Hispánica*
O.C.	*Obras completas*
PH	*La Palabra y el Hombre*
PMLA	*Publications of the Modern Language Association of America*
PP	*Philologica Pragensia*
PSA	*Papeles de Son Armadans*
PVR	*Platte Valley Review*
QIA	*Quaderni Iberoamericani*
RABM	*Revista de Archivos, Bibliotecas y Museos*
RCEH	*Revista Canadiense de Estudios Hispánicos*
REH	*Revista de Estudios Hispánicos* (Alabama)
RF	*Romanische Forschungen*
RFE	*Revista de Filología Española*
RHM	*Revista Hispánica Moderna*

RIB	*Revista Interamericana de Bibliografía / Inter-American Review of Bibliography*
RIE	*Revista de Ideas Estéticas*
RL	*Revista de Literatura*
RLC	*Revue de Littérature Comparée*
RO	*Revista de Occidente*
RomN	*Romance Notes*
Rpt.	reprinted
RR	*Romanic Review*
RyF	*Razón y Fe*
SAB	*South Atlantic Bulletin*
SAR	*South Atlantic Review*
SFr	*Studi Francesi*
SGym	*Siculorum Gymnasium*
SUH	*Su único hijo*
TAH	*The American Hispanist*
TB	*Tempo Brasileiro*
TLS	*Times Literary Supplement* (London)
Torre	*La Torre*
UDR	*University of Dayton Review*
UNAM	Universidad Nacional Autónoma de México
Univ.	University, Universidad, Université, Universität

A

PRIMARY MATERIAL

Aa   *Anthologies and Selections*

Aa1   Alas, Leopoldo, *Obras completas*, 4 vols (Madrid: Renaci-
miento, 1913-29). 4788 pp.
Consists of 4 vols: I, *Galdós* (Ab26); II, *Su único hijo* (Ac20); III,
Doctor Sutilis (Ad17); IV, *Doña Berta, Cuervo, Superchería* (Ad4).
The remainder of LA's works were not included in *O.C.*

Aa2   *Páginas escogidas*, ed. José Martínez Ruiz (Azorín) (Madrid:
Calleja, 1917). 394 pp. See also B780.
Divided into five sections ('El satírico'; 'El crítico'; 'El moralista';
'El novelista'; 'El cuentista'), this anthology contains selections from
LA's criticism, novel, and short stories.

Aa3   'Páginas escogidas de "Clarín" ', in B15, pp. 163-241.
As in Aa4, a selection made by his Falangist son Adolfo.

Aa4   'Páginas escogidas de Leopoldo Alas (Clarín)', in B16,
pp. 115-234.

Aa5   *Obras selectas*, ed. Juan Antonio Cabezas (Madrid: Biblioteca
Nueva, 1947). 1309 pp. 2nd ed., 1966, 1317 pp.
Rpts in their entirety, *LR* and *SUH*, and a generous selection of short
stories, criticism from *Solos, Palique, Ensayos y revistas*, and *Nueva
campaña*, as well as three *folletos literarios, Mis plagios, Un viaje a
Madrid*, and *Cánovas y su tiempo*. See also B238.
Reviews: 1. Baquero Goyanes, Mariano. *Revista de la Universidad
de Oviedo*, 8, Nos 45-46 (1947), 113-17.
2. Fernández Almagro, Melchor. *ABC* (12.10.47), 22.
3. Ledesma Miranda, [Ramón]. *Arriba*, 2a época (9.10.47), 3.

Aa6   **Páginas escogidas di Clarín*, ed. Franco Meregalli (Milano:
La Goliardica, 1956). 116 pp.

Aa7   *Leopoldo Alas (Clarín): cuento, ensayo, crítica*, ed. Salvador

Reyes Nevares, Colección Literaria Servet, El Mundo Moderno (México: Oasis, 1967). 125 pp.
An anthology of two short stories, and several pieces of criticism taken from *Nueva campaña*. See also B1019.

Aa8   *Selección de ensayos*. Ed. reservada a Los Amigos de la Historia (Geneva: Ferni, 1974). 317 pp. Rpt in 1976.
With a biobibliographical introduction by Federico Carlos Sáinz de Robles (pp. 7-19). Despite title of ed., selection also includes several short stories. See also B1103.

Aa9   *Alas, 'Clarín'*, ed. Benito Varela Jácome, Escritores de todos los tiempos, 6 (Madrid: EDAF, 1980). 383 pp.
B.V.J.'s study (pp. 13-169) gives an adequate outline of LA's life and works. The section on *SUH* is a rpt of B1251. Also devotes a few pp. to LA's fragment, 'Cuesta abajo', and reproduces some of this little-known work. Anthology (pp. 173-377) contains articles, extracts of theater, novels, and stories. With bibliography. See also B164, 732, 879-80, 1252.
Review: 1. V.M.R. *Triunfo* (17.5.80).

Ab   *Criticism*

Ab1   *El derecho y la moralidad (Determinación del concepto del derecho, y sus relaciones con el de la moralidad)* (Madrid: Casa Editorial de Medina, 1878). 162 pp.
LA's diss., which he dedicated to Francisco Giner de los Ríos. Originally published in *Revista Europea*, Nos 236-44 (1.9-27.10.78), 260-65; 292-97; 326-30; 360-64; 399-403; 437-43; 461-66; 487-95; 532-37.

Ab2   *Solos de Clarín* (Madrid: Alfredo de Carlos Hierro, 1881). vi+332 pp.
With a prologue by José Echegaray (pp. i-vi), in which E. confesses he is at a loss as to what to write in this introduction. LA's 'Prefacio a manera de sinfonía' (pp. 7-12) is rpt. in Ab32, pp. 55-60. See also B340.
The 2nd and 3rd ed. of *Solos* (1881) are reimpressions of the first. Contents: 'Prefacio a manera de sinfonía'; 'La crítica y los críticos'; 'Amador de los Ríos'; 'Marcelino Menéndez Pelayo'; 'Tamayo'; 'Del teatro'; 'El libre-examen y nuestra literatura presente'; 'Cavilaciones'; 'Castelar (*Recuerdos de Italia*)'; '*Consuelo* (Ayala)'; '*El nudo gordiano* (Sellés)'; '*Mar sin orillas* (Echegaray)'; 'La mosca sabia'; '*La opinión pública* (Cano)'; '*Theudis* (Castro)'; '*El frontero de Baeza* (Retes y Echevarría)'; '*El casino* (Cavestany)'; '*Soledad* (Blasco)'; '*Sobre quien viene el castigo* (Cavestany)'; '*Trece de febrero* (Díaz)'; 'Doctor Pértinax'; '*León Roch*, primera parte (Galdós)'; '*El niño de la bola* (Alarcón)'; '*El buey suelto* (Pereda)'; 'Un prólogo de Valera'; '*Pequeños poemas* (Campoamor)'; '*Marianela* (Galdós)'; 'De la comisión'; '*El tren directo* (Munilla)'; '*El Comendador Mendoza* (Valera)'; '*Tentativas dramáticas* (Valera)'; '*Doña Luz* (Valera)'; '*León Roch*, segunda parte (Galdós)'; '*De tal palo...* (Pereda)'; 'De burguesa a cortesana'; 'De burguesa a burguesa'; '*Don Gonzalo González de la Gonzalera* (Pereda)'; '*Gloria* (Galdós)'; 'Un lunático'; 'El diablo en Semana Santa'.

Ab3   *Solos de Clarín*. 4th ed. Con un prólogo de Don José Echegaray. Il. de Ángel Pons. (Madrid: Fernando Fe, 1891). 394 pp.
LA's 'Prólogo de la cuarta edición' (pp. 1-3) is rpt. in Ab32, pp. 86-88.

Ab4   *Solos de Clarín* (Madrid: Alianza, 1971). Prólogo de José Echegaray. 368 pp.

Ab5   *La literatura en 1881* (Madrid: Alfredo de Carlos Hierro, 1882). 202 pp.

LA wrote this book in collaboration with his friend, Armando Palacio Valdés. LA's contributions: 'Versicultura (Grilus Vastatrix)'; 'Madrileñas'; 'Palique'; 'Catalinaria'; 'Guía de forasteros'; 'Un tomo de tomo y lomo'; 'Revilla'; *'La desheredada* (Primera parte), novela de don Benito Pérez Galdós'; 'La lírica y el naturalismo (*Los buenos y los sabios,* poema de Campoamor)'; *'Enseñar al que no sabe* (Comedia en tres actos y en verso, por D. Miguel Echegaray)'; *'La justicia del acaso* (Drama en tres actos y en verso, por D. Emilio Ferrari)'; *'Lo que no ve la justicia* (Drama en tres actos y en prosa, de D. José F. Bremón)'; 'Don Juan Valera, en Francia'; *'Un viaje de novios* (Novela de la Sra. Doña Emilia Pardo de Bazán)'; *'Haroldo el Normando* (Leyenda trágica en tres actos y en verso, de Don José Echegaray)'.

Ab6   *Programa de elementos de economía política y estadística (Precedido del razonamiento necesario para dar a conocer, en breve, el plan y el método que se siguen).* Presentado para los ejercicios de oposición a la cátedra de esta asignatura vacante en la Universidad de Salamanca, por el Dr. Leopoldo Alas y Ureña (Madrid: Imp. de la Revista de Legislación, 1882). 111 pp. Originally published in *Revista General de Legislación y Jurisprudencia,* 60-61 (1882), 5-30; 254-76; 391-422; 161-85. LA's unsuccessful bid for a professorship at Salamanca. Exercises are dated Oviedo, 11 Aug. 1878.

Ab7   *Sermón perdido* (Madrid: Fernando Fe, [1885]). xix+358 pp. Printed four more times in 1885. The 'Epílogo que sirve de prólogo' (pp. v-xix) is rpt. in Ab32, pp. 60-68. Contents: 'Los poetas en el Ateneo'; *'Tormento'; 'Pedro Sánchez* (Novela por D. José María de Pereda)'; 'Tribunales (Sala de lo criminal en verso)'; 'Los señores de Casabierta'; '¡¿Mi caricatura!?'; 'Cartas a un poeta (Primera y última)'; *'La tribuna* (Novela original de Doña Emilia Pardo Bazán)'; *'Marta y María* (Novela por A. Palacio Valdés)'; 'Obras de Revilla'; 'La poética de Campoamor'; 'Camachología'; 'El genio (Historia natural)'; 'El poeta-buho (Historia natural)'; '¡Paso! '; 'Los actores'; 'Sobre motivos de un drama de Echegaray'; 'Discursos'; '¡Moralicemos! '; 'A Madrid me vuelvo'; 'Balaguer o los ideales'; 'Los Pirineos del arte (Sarah Bernhardt)'; *'El idilio de un enfermo* (Novela, por A.P. Valdés)'; 'Crónica literaria'; 'A Menéndez Pelayo'; 'Don Ermeguncio o la vocación (Del natural)'; 'Literatura de oficio'; 'De Profundis'; 'Un sabio más'; 'La siniestra corneja...'; 'Guillermo D'Acevedo'; *'Pedro Abelardo* (Poema de D. Emilio Ferrari)'.

Ab8   'Alcalá Galiano. El período constitucional de 1820 a 1823.

Causa de la caída del sistema constitucional. La emigración hasta 1833', in *Ateneo científico literario y artístico de Madrid. La España del siglo XIX*, II (Madrid: Librería de don Antonio San Martín, 1886), pp. 469-520.
An offprint was issued paginated 1-52.

Ab9 *Un viaje a Madrid, Folletos literarios*, I (Madrid: Fernando Fe, 1886). 84 pp.
On Menéndez Pelayo, Castelar, Campoamor, Núñez de Arce, and Fernanflor. The prologue, 'Folletos literarios' (pp. 5-13) is rpt. in Ab32, pp. 68-72.

Ab10 *Apolo en Pafos, Folletos literarios*, III (Madrid: Fernando Fe, 1887). 99 pp.
On poetry and the novel in Spain.

Ab11 *Cánovas y su tiempo (Primera parte), Folletos literarios*, II (Madrid: Fernando Fe, 1887). 104 pp.
A blistering, parodistic attack on the politician-statesman, Antonio Cánovas del Castillo. Contains the following sections: 'Cánovas, traseúnte'; ' "Intermezzo" lírico'; 'Cánovas, poeta'; 'Cánovas... "latente pensante" '; 'Cánovas, novelista'; 'Cánovas, historiador'; 'Cánovas, orador'; 'Cánovas, político'; 'Cánovas, pacificador'; 'Cánovas, prologuista'; 'Dos cartas'.

Ab12 *Nueva campaña (1885-1886)* (Madrid: Fernando Fe, 1887). 397 pp.
'Nueva campaña' (pp. 5-14) is rpt. in Ab32, pp. 72-78. Contains criticism which, like most of the other collected articles, first appeared in newspapers: 'Nueva campaña'; *'Los amores de una santa'*; *'El cantar del romero'*; ' ¡Seis bolas negras! '; 'Los grafómanos'; 'Carta a un sobrino disuadiéndole de tomar la profesión de crítico'; *'Blanca*. Historia inverosímil. Poema de M. del Palacio'; 'Alarcón'; 'Valera'; *'Las revoluciones.* Canto'; *'Lo prohibido*, Novela de Pérez Galdós'; 'Juan Fernández'; *'Sotileza'*; *'El cisne de Vilamorta*. Novela por Doña Emilia Pardo Bazán'; 'Poesías de Menéndez Pelayo'; *'Guerra sin cuartel*. Novela original de D. Ceferino Suárez'; *'Aguas fuertes*, por Armando Palacio Valdés'; 'Las *humoradas* de Campoamor'; 'Discurso de las armas y letras'; *'Los pazos de Ulloa'*; *'Riverita* de A. Palacio Valdés'; 'Las traducciones'; *'El patio andaluz*. Cuadros de costumbre por Salvador Rueda'; 'Mariano Cavia'; 'Temporada teatral'; 'Luis Taboada'; 'Impresionistas'; '¿Suscribirme?'; 'Palique'; 'A D. Tomás Bretón'; 'Consulta crítica'; 'Cosas viejas'; *'Sonetos* por Anthero de Quental'; 'Madrileña'; 'Nougués y el rey'; 'Críticos anónimos'; *'Numa Roumestan* de Alfonso Daudet'; 'Un drama de Renan. *Le Prêtre de Nemi*. Drame philosophique'.

Ab13 *Mis plagios. Un discurso de Núñez de Arce, Folletos literarios,*
IV (Madrid: Fernando Fe, 1888). 132 pp.
On the question of genres; and LA's defense against Bonafoux's charges
of plagiarism. Published simultaneously in *Revista de Asturias*, Nos 6-7
(15.4.88), 248-69.

Ab14 *A 0,50 poeta (Epístola en versos malos con notas en prosa
clara), Folletos literarios,* V (Madrid: Fernando Fe, 1889).
66 pp.
The notorious satire against poet Manuel del Palacio.

Ab15 *Celebridades españolas contemporáneas: Benito Pérez Galdós
(Estudio crítico-biográfico)* (Madrid: Ricardo Fe, 1889).
39 pp.
The 2nd ed. (1889) is a reimpression of the 1st. Rpt. in *Galdós, O.C.,*
I, pp. 7-38, Ab26; *Nosotros* (Buenos Aires), 34 (1920), 69-86 (slightly
cut); *Benito Pérez Galdós,* ed. Douglass M. Rogers (Madrid: Taurus,
1973), pp. 21-40; and *Krausismo: estética y literatura,* ed. Juan López-
Morillas (Barcelona: Labor, 1973), pp. 213-35. Also rpt. by Univ. Micro-
films International (Ann Arbor, Mich., 1977). 39 pp.

Ab16 *Mezclilla* (Madrid: Fernando Fe, 1889). 399 pp.
A varied collection of serious essays and improvisations, which LA calls
a *mezclilla,* "hecha con hilos de varios colores y clases'. Many of the
essays are on foreign critics. 'Advertencias' (pp. 5-9) is rpt. in Ab32,
pp. 78-80. Contents: 'Lecturas. Proyecto'; 'Baudelaire'; 'Una carta y
muchas digresiones'; *'La Montálvez';* 'Paul Bourget (Su última novela)';
'A muchos y a ninguno'; 'Palique'; *'Maximina* (Novela de Armando
Palacio)'; 'Palique'; 'Eduardo de Palacio (Fragmentos)'; 'Alfonso Daudet
(*Treinta años de París*)'; 'Palique'; 'Sobre motivos de una novela de
Galdós'; 'Palique'; 'Cartas de Julio Goncourt'; 'Frontaura'; 'Estilo fácil';
'La zarzuela'; 'España en Francia (*Le Naturalisme en Espagne,* por Alberto
Savine)'; 'Palique'; 'El testamento de Alarcón'; 'El teatro y la novela';
'Ripios aristocráticos (Venancio González)'; '¿Y la poesía?'; 'Cuestión
de palabras (Ad Quintilium Liberalis, a Quintilius el de *El Liberal*)'.

Ab17 *Museum (Mi revista), Folletos literarios,* VII (Madrid: Fernando
Fe, 1890). 88 pp.
'Mi revista' (pp. 5-14) is rpt. in Ab32, pp. 81-86. Contents: 'Mi revista';
'Poética de Campoamor'; 'Emilia Pardo Bazán y sus últimas obras';
'Libros recibidos'.

Ab18 *Rafael Calvo y el Teatro Español, Folletos literarios,* VI (Madrid:
Fernando Fe, 1890). 86 pp.

Personal reminiscences and echoes of LA's idealistic youth.

Ab19 *Discurso leído en la solemne apertura del curso académico de 1891 a 1892.* (Oviedo: Univ., 1891). 59 pp. Rpt. as *Un discurso, Folletos literarios*, VIII (Madrid: Fernando Fe, 1891). 107 pp.
On utilitarianism in education.

Ab20 *Ensayos y revistas, 1888-1892* (Madrid: Manuel Fernández y Lasanta, 1892). 434 pp.
Contents: 'Camus'; 'Lecturas. – Zola. – *La Terre*'; 'Zola y su última novela. – *L'Argent*'; '*Nubes de estío*. Novela de D.J.M. de Pereda'; 'Dos académicos'; 'Otro académico'; 'Cañete'; 'La novela novelesca'; 'Entre bobos anda el juego'; 'Nota bibliográfica (julio, 1889)'; 'Revista literaria (noviembre, 1889)'; 'Revista literaria (diciembre, 1889)'; 'Revista literaria (enero, 1890)'; 'Revista literaria (marzo, 1890)'; 'Revista literaria'; 'Revista literaria'; 'Revista literaria'; 'Revista literaria'; 'La novela del porvenir'; 'La juventud literaria'; 'Un libro de Taboada'; 'Ibsen y Daudet'.

Ab21 *Ensayos y revistas, 1888-1892* (New York: Clearwater Publishing Co., 1981). 434 pp.
Rpt of 1892 ed.

Ab22 *Palique* (Madrid: Victoriano Suárez, 1893). 342 pp.
Prologue (pp. vii-xxxi) is rpt. in Ab32, pp. 88-97. Contents: 'Prólogo'; 'El teatro. – Tenativas. – Galdós. – Echegaray, etc.'; 'Lope de Vega. – Juan Ruiz, etc.'; 'Castelar'; 'Renan'; 'Justicia de enero'; 'El teatro de Zorrilla'; 'El teatro ... de lejos. – Las tentativas de Pérez Galdós'; 'Posada y U.G. Serrano. – *La Dolores*'; 'Premio Cortina'; 'Silvela. – El P. Mir'; 'Heredia. – *Los trofeos*'; 'Introducción'; 'Bizantinismo'; 'A Gorgibus'; 'El retrato de Renan'; 'Lourdes y Zola'; 'Congreso de librepensadores'; 'Congreso pedagógico'; 'Bayoneta'; 'The Dangerous Life'; 'La educación del rey'; 'La coleta nacional'; 'Palique del palique'; 'Un candidato'; 'Diálogo edificante'; 'Preparativos del Centenario'; '¿Quién descubrió a América?'; 'Colón y Compañía'; 'La muiñeira'; 'Entre faldas'; 'El certamen de San Juan de la Cruz'; 'San Juan de la Cruz y la señorita Valencia'; 'Alarcón. – Últimos escritos'; 'Ramos Carrión'; 'Vital Aza'; 'D. Manuel Silvela'; 'Castro Serrano'; 'Fabié académico'; 'Un discurso de Cánovas'.

Ab23 *Palique*, ed. José María Martínez Cachero (Barcelona: Labor, 1973). 309 pp. Also Barcelona: Punto Omega 272, 1973. 314 pp.

Rpts the original ed., without, however, reproducing the original table
of contents. M.C.'s introduction (pp. 7-56) is a sturdy essay on the
literary world of LA's *paliques.* Provides a selected, annotated bibliography. See also B721.
Reviews: .1. Bonet, Laureano. *Ínsula,* No. 342 (May 1975), 12-13.
.2. Díez Borque, José María. *EstLit,* No. 540 (15.5.74), 1722-23.
.3. Kronik, John W. *HR,* 44 (1976), 299-301.

Ab24 *Crítica popular.* Con autógrafo del autor (Valencia: F. Vives
Mora, 1896). 124 pp.
Antonio Sotillo's 'Clarín (Semblanza literaria)' (pp. v-xvi), which gives
general impressions of LA's literary qualities, prefaces this vol. of essays
previously published in journals and newspapers. See also B1176.
Contents: 'Lecturas (Proyecto)'; 'Lecturas: Zola. *La Terre*'; 'El teatro
y la novela'; 'Revista literaria'; 'La prensa y los cuentos'; '¿Y la poesía?';
'El teatro de Zorrilla'.

Ab25 *Siglo pasado* (Madrid: Antonio R. López, 1901). 195 pp.
This posthumous work contains an introductory prologue by Juan
Alfonso Valdés (pp. 5-10). See also B1229. Contents: 'Romano'; 'La
contribución'; 'Renan'; 'No engendres el dolor'; 'Del Quijote'; 'Jorge,
diálogo, pero no platónico'; 'La leyenda de oro'; 'El arte de leer';
'Cartas a Hamlet. Revista de ideas'; 'El teatro en barbecho'; 'Roma
y Rama'.

Ab26 *Galdós, O.C.,* I (Madrid: Renacimiento, 1912). 366 pp.
Contents: 'Benito Pérez Galdós'; '*Gloria.* Primera parte'; 'Segunda
parte'; '*Marianela*'; '*La familia de León Roch.* Primera parte'; 'Segunda
parte'; '*La desheredada.* Primera parte'; 'Segunda parte'; '*Tormento*'; '*Lo
prohibido*'; 'Una carta y muchas digresiones'; '*Miau*'; 'El teatro ... de
lejos. Las tentativas de Pérez Galdós'; '*Realidad*'; 'Más sobre *Realidad*';
'*La loca de la casa,* en el teatro'; '*Ángel Guerra*'; '*Tristana*'; '*Torquemada
en la cruz*'; '*Torquemada en el purgatorio*'; '*Torquemada y San Pedro*';
'*Nazarín*'; '*Halma*'; '*El abuelo*'; 'Más sobre *El abuelo*'; 'Los *Episodios
Nacionales*'; '*Mendizábal*'; '*Luchana*'; '*La campaña del Maestrazgo*'; '*La
estafeta romántica*'; '*Vergara*'; '*Montes de Oca*'; '*Los Ayacuchos*'; '*Bodas
reales*'.

Ab27 *Leopoldo Alas: teoría y crítica de la novela española,* ed.
Sergio Beser (Barcelona: Laia, 1972). 302 pp.
S.B.'s 'Introducción' (pp. 9-21) provides an explanation for the
appearance of this noteworthy selection of criticism. Of special
interest are those essays on the novel which were gathering dust in
inaccessible newspapers and journals: 'Del estilo en la novela', 'Del

naturalismo', *'El sabor de la tierruca'*, and others.
Reviews: .1. Brown, G.G. *BHS*, 53 (1976), 353-54.
    .2. Díez Borque, José María. *CHA*, No. 279 (Sept. 1973),
    629-34.
    .3. ———. *EstLit*, No. 527 (1.11.73), 1512.
    .4. Jackson, Robert M. *MLN*, 90 (1975), 318-20.

Ab28 *Preludios de "Clarín"*, ed. Jean-François Botrel (Oviedo:
IDEA, 1972). 244 pp.
Rpts a generous selection of early Clarín articles previously buried in
the newspapers, *El Solfeo* and *La Unión* (1875-80). Also includes an
informative introduction by Botrel on LA's early years as a militant
journalist, his political and ideological, i.e., Krausist, commitments,
and his theory and practice of journalistic criticism (pp. xiii-lxxiii).
Reviews: .1. Cordero, Lorenzo. *Asturias Semanal*, No. 165 (29.7.72),
    4-5.
    .2. Cueto Alas, Juan. *Asturias Semanal*, No. 201 (7.4.73), 47.
    .3. Garmendia, Vincent. *BH*, 78 (1976), 416.
    .4. Jackson, Robert M. *MLN*, 90 (1975), 318-20.
    .5. Kronik, John W. *Hispania* (U.S.A.), 57 (1974), 1012-13.

Ab29 *Obra olvidada (Artículos de crítica)*, ed. Antonio Ramos-
Gascón (Madrid: Júcar, 1973). 264 pp.
In his 'Introducción' (pp. 11-33), R.-G. traces the evolution of LA's
thought and the justification for the texts selected in this anthology.
Divides the book into three sections: criticism of Spanish authors,
criticism of foreign writers, and articles of *crítica higiénica*.
Reviews: .1. Bonet, Laureano. *Ínsula*, No. 342 (May 1975), 12-13.
    .2. D'Auria, Riccardo. *Torre*, 23, Nos 87-88 (Jan.-June 1975),
    223-26.
    .3. Jackson, Robert M. *MLN*, 90 (1975), 318-20.

Ab30 *Clarín político. Leopoldo Alas (Clarín), periodista, frente a
la problemática política y social de la España de su tiempo
(1875-1901)*, I. Estudio y antología, ed. Yvan Lissorgues
(Toulouse: Institut d'Études Hispaniques et Hispano-Américaines, Univ. de Toulouse-Le Mirail, 1980). lxxxviii+377 pp.
A solid and useful contribution, giving us a fine sampling of LA's restless, yet perpetually engaged mind. These mostly unpublished texts are,
however, marred by an almost overwhelming subtext, i.e., a mass of
footnotes in which Y.L. extracts or even reproduces in their entirety
other Clarín pieces. Well-documented introduction analyses LA's attitude
to Castelar, *el posibilismo*, the War of 1898, socialism, and other matters.

Leopoldo Alas (Clarín)

See also B660.
Reviews: .1. Beyrie, Jacques. *CMHLB*, 38 (1982), 238-40.
.2. Bonet, Laureano. *Ínsula*, No. 418 (Sept. 1981), 1, 14.
.3. Botrel, Jean-François. *BH*, 83 (1981), 474-76.
.4. Valis, Noël M. *HR*, 51 (1983), 336-38.

Ab31 *Clarín político. Leopoldo Alas (Clarín), periodista, frente a la problemática literaria y cultural de la España de su tiempo (1875-1901)*, II. Estudio y antología, ed. Yvan Lissorgues (Toulouse: Institut d'Études Hispaniques et Hispano-Américaines, Univ. de Toulouse-Le Mirail, 1981). 225 pp. See also B657, 661, 663.
Continuation of Ab30, emphasizing LA's views on education, and on the roles of journalism and literature in society. Y.L. has sensibly reduced his scholarly apparatus this time. Sections include: 'Enseñanza y educación', 'Periodismo y cultura', and 'Literatura y sociedad'.
Reviews: .1. Belot, Albert. *CMHLB*, 40 (1983), 205-07.
.2. Richmond, Carolyn. *Ínsula*, No. 433 (Dec. 1982), 5.

Ab32 *Los prólogos de Leopoldo Alas*, ed. David Torres, Colección Nova Scholar (Madrid: Playor, 1984). 269 pp.
'Introducción' (pp. 7-10) and 'Presentación de los prólogos' (pp. 13-51). Gives mostly bibliographical information about the prologues and the books and authors for which they were written. Rpts prologues to Ab2, 3, 7, 9, 12, 16, 17, 22; Ad10; Ag1-5, 7-11, 13, 15-25; Ah67. See also B1211, 1212 bis.

Ac   *Novels*

Ac1   *La Regenta*, 2 vols, Biblioteca 'Arte y Letras' (Barcelona:
      Daniel Cortezo y Cía, 1884-85). 527; 592 pp. Rpt. by Maucci
      (Barcelona, 1908). I11. by Juan Llimona. Engravings by Gómez
      Polo.
      LA's first novel of provincial town life.

Ac2   **La Regenta*, 2 vols, folletín de *La Publicidad* (Barcelona, n.d.).
      Ortiz Aponte dates this ed. as c. 1902 (B890, p. 189). Beser and Bonet
      (B156, p. 194), however, note that serialization of *LR* began 15 Jan.
      1894, with No. 5283 of *La Publicidad*; but they do not appear to give
      concluding date. I have seen only vol. II (644 pp., divided into 80 Nos),
      located at the Biblioteca de Catalunya, Barcelona.

Ac3   *La Regenta*, 2 vols, 2nd ed. (Madrid: Fernando Fe, 1901).
      xix+523; 592 pp.
      'Prólogo' by Benito Pérez Galdós (pp. v-xix). P.G.'s admiration and
      enthusiasm for LA's novel are evident in this introduction. Title page
      is dated 1900; book cover, 1901. Delay in publication was due to P.G.'s
      slowness in finishing the prologue. See also B952.

Ac4   *La Regenta*, 2 vols (Buenos Aires: Emecé, 1946). 482; 521 pp.
      Contains Benito Pérez Galdós's prologue (pp. 9-21); and an anon. bio-
      bibliographical prologue (pp. 22-30).

Ac5   *La Regenta*, 2 vols, ed. Juan M. Lope and Huberto Batis,
      Colección 'Nuestros Clásicos' (México: UNAM, 1960).
      xxx+396; 459 pp. 2nd ed., 1972.
      J.M.L.'s contribution to the introduction is an appreciation of LA's
      life and works, while H.B.'s is an attempt to see the organic unity
      of *LR*. Without notes; includes a chronology, 'Leopoldo Alas (Clarín)
      y su época'.
      Review: .1. C.V. *Revista de la Universidad de México*, 15, No. 9 (1960-
           61), 31.

Ac6   *La Regenta*, 1 vol., ed. José María Martínez Cachero (Barcelona:
      Planeta, 1963). xciii+900 pp. 2nd ed., 1967.
      M.C.'s 'Introducción' (pp. ix-lxxvi) is a general study on LA's life and
      works. Contains a bibliography, notes, and an appendix on some of the
      controversy over *LR*'s initial appearance. Editor bases his text on the
      first ed. of 1884-85.
      Review: .1. Beser, Sergio. *BHS*, 43 (1966), 303-04.

Ac7   *La Regenta*, 1 vol. (Madrid: Alianza, 1966). 678 pp.
A popular ed. of *LR*. Latest printing seen is 16th (1984). See also
B592.
Review: .1. Anon. *TLS* (London) (12.1.67), 26.

Ac8   *La Regenta*, 1 vol. (Barcelona: Círculo de Lectores, 1968).
xv+660 pp. Rpt. 1973; 1975.
'Introducción' by Esteban Padrós de Palacios (pp. iii-xv). *LR*, writes
P., is not a doctrinal, but an objective novel.

Ac9   *La Regenta*, 1 vol., 'Sepan Cuantos', 225 (México: Porrúa,
1972). xix+519 pp. 2nd ed., 1977.
Jorge Ibargüengoitia tends to simplify in his introduction (pp. ix-xix).
Rpts Galdós prologue. Part of introd. rpt. in *Boletín Bibliográfico
Mexicano*, No. 301 (Nov.-Dec. 1972), 8-9.

Ac10 **La Regenta*, 2 vols, ed. Marina García (La Habana: Editorial
de Arte y Literatura, 1976). 404; 458 pp.
With Galdós prologue; Apéndice by Domingo Pérez Minik ('Revisión de
Leopoldo Alas, Clarín', see B955); and 'El autor y su época'.

Ac11 *La Regenta*, 1 vol., ed. Gonzalo Sobejano (Barcelona: Noguer,
1976). 932 pp.
An excellent ed. G.S. bases his text on the 2nd ed., and points out in
his notes the differences between the 1st and 2nd eds. He also corrects
the typographical and other errors of previous eds, helpfully annotates
the text, and includes Galdós's excellent prologue. See, in addition, G.S.'s
own fine introduction in which he discusses the naturalistic novel and
'la imaginación moral de *La Regenta*' (pp. 11-58). See B1166.
Reviews: .1. Richmond, Carolyn. *Ínsula*, Nos 392-93 (July-Aug. 1979),
   10.
.2. Rutherford, John. *BHS*, 55 (1978), 165-66.

Ac12 *La Regenta*, 2 vols, ed. Gonzalo Sobejano (Madrid: Castalia,
1981). 573; 537 pp. 2nd ed. corr., 1982; 3rd ed., 1983.
A revised, updated version of Ac11, with expanded, valuable annotations. The definitive ed. See also B1162.
Reviews: .1. Bly, Peter, *RCEH*, 8 (1984), 304.
.2. Caudel, Francisco. *Nuevo Hispanismo*, No. 1 (1982),
   241-44.
.3. Klein, Richard B. *Hispania* (U.S.A.), 66 (1983), 434-35.
.4. Rutherford, John. *BHS*, 60 (1983), 89-90.
.5. Valis, Noël M. *HR*, 51 (1983), 110-13.

Ac13   *La Regenta*, 1 vol. (Madrid: Akal, 1981). 844 pp.
With Galdós's prologue; and chronology.

Ac14   *La Regenta*, 2 vols, ed. facsímil, Colección Facsimilar
Asturiana (Gijón: Silverio Cañada, Editor, 1981). 527;
592 pp. With Galdós's prologue.
Review: .1. Méndez Riestra, Eduardo. *Los Cuadernos del Norte*
(Oviedo), 3, No. 12 (Mar.-Apr. 1982), 88-89.

Ac15   *La Regenta*, 2 vols, Colección Historia de la Literatura
Española 3-4 (Barcelona: Orbis, 1982). 352; 321 pp.

Ac16   *La Regenta*, 1 vol., Libro Amigo 904 (Barcelona: Bruguera,
1982). 798 pp. 2nd ed., 1983.
Popular paperback ed.

Ac17   *La Regenta*, 2 vols, ed. facsimilar (Oviedo: La Caja de
Ahorros de Asturias, 1983). 527; 592 pp. 2nd ed., 1984.
With a 'Nota previa' by Juan Cueto Alas (pp. ix-x); and Galdós
prologue.

Ac18   *La Regenta*, 2 vols, Biblioteca Júcar 76-77 (Barcelona: Júcar,
1983). 527; 590 pp. Ilus. de Juan Llimona. Grabados de
Gómez Polo.
With Galdós prologue.

Ac19   *La Regenta*. 1 vol., ed. Mariano Baquero Goyanes, Selecciones
Austral, 119 (Madrid: Espasa-Calpe, 1984). 743 pp.
Contains an introduction (pp. 9-59) and a 'Guía de Personajes', pp. 61-
117. The annotated list of characters and plot summaries of each chapter
are helpful additions.

Ac20   *La Regenta*, 2 vols, ed. Juan Oleza, Letras Hispánicas 182-83
(Madrid: Cátedra, 1984). 637; 586 pp.
In the Introduction to vol. 1 (pp. 11-104), J.O. discusses the novel's
naturalism, its structure and characterization, relying heavily on other
critics. The Introduction to the second vol. (pp. 11-45) situates *LR*
within the ideological confines of the young militant Clarín. With bibliography; and large blocks of notes which threaten at times to drown out
the text. See also B1432.

Ac21   *La Regenta*, 1 vol., Grandes Novelas de Amor de la Literatura
Universal 18 (Barcelona: Planeta, 1984). 540 pp.

Ac22   *La Regenta*, 1 vol. (Barcelona: Mundo Actual de Ediciones, 1984). 653 pp.

Ac23   *La Regenta*, 1 vol., ed. Carmen Fernández, Colección Pedagógica, 19 (San Sebastián: Haranburu Editor, 1984). 146 pp.
Introduction (pp. 9-25). Mutilated ed., intended for the classroom, with questions at the bottom of each page. Rpts a letter to José Quevedo (21.5.85); one to Martínez Vigil (11.5.85); one from Palacio Valdés (25.4.88); and another from Menéndez Pelayo (not dated).

Ac24   **La Regenta*, 2 vols (Barcelona: Círculo de Lectores, 1984). Introduction by Esteban Padrós de Palacios.

Ac25   *Su único hijo* (Madrid: Fernando Fe, 1891). 436 pp.
LA's second and last novel. Clarín's letters indicate he was still writing *SUH* in 1891 (see Af24, p. 260); and that the novel did not appear in bookshops until the spring of 1891 (Beser, B146, p. 522). Hence the date 1891 and not 1890, as is commonly given to *SUH*. See also Richmond, Ac33, pp. xii-xiii, for more details on this ed.

Ac26   **Su único hijo*, folletín de *La Publicidad* (Barcelona).
The serialization of *SUH* ran from 14 Oct. 1900 (No. 1657) until 13 Dec. 1900, according to Beser and Bonet (B156, p. 209).

Ac27   *Su único hijo*, *O.C.*, II (Madrid: Renacimiento, 1913). 371 pp.

Ac28   *Su único hijo*, Colección Pandora (Buenos Aires: Poseidón, 1944). 225 pp.

Ac29   *Su único hijo* (Madrid: Alianza, 1966). 276 pp. 2nd ed., 1969; 3rd ed., 1976; 4th ed., 1979; 5th ed., 1982.

Ac30   *Su único hijo* (Barcelona: Taber, 1968). 315 pp.
Introduction by Antonio Comas (pp. 7-18). Follows Baquero Goyanes and others in pointing out LA's parody of provincial pseudoromanticism.

Ac31   *Su único hijo* ([Estella] : Salvat, 1972). 216 pp.
Anon. introduction (pp. 7-8).

Ac32   *Su único hijo* (La Habana: Editorial de Arte y Literatura, 1977). 308 pp.
'Introducción' by Bernardo Marqués (pp. 7-14). Essentially a Marxist approach to *SUH*.

Ac33   *Su único hijo*, ed. Carolyn Richmond, Selecciones Austral, 67

(Madrid: Espasa-Calpe, 1979). lxxv + 388 pp.
An excellent, carefully-annotated ed. of *SUH*. C.R. in her introduction
(pp. xi-lxiii) stresses the ambiguous, transitional nature of the novel;
and also gives three useful appendices, in which she rpts 'Una medianía',
'Esperaindeo', and a fragment of Ch. XX of *LR*. With bibliography.
Reviews: .1. Anon. *Alerta* (Santander) (15.3.80).
    .2. Anon. *El Comercio* (Gijón) (29.3.80).
    .3. Anon. *Hoja Informativa de Literatura y Filología* (Fundación
    Juan March), No. 80 (Mar. 1980), 9.
    .4. Anon. *Lucha* (Teruel) (8.5.80).
    .5. Belarmino. *Región* (Oviedo) (28.4.80).
    .6. Cerezales, Manuel. *ABC* (13.3.80), 26 (erroneously signed
    'Pedro Rocamora').
    .7. Colón, Isabel. *NE*, No. 37 (Dec. 1981), 90.
    .8. Goñi, Javier. *El Norte de Castilla* (20.3.80).
    .9. Jackson, Robert M. *Hispania* (U.S.A.), 66 (1983), 296.
    .10. Martín Gaite, Carmen. *Diario 16* (31.3.80).
    .11. Matamoro, Blas. *CHA*, No. 370 (Apr. 1981), 218-19.
    .12. Salanova Matas, Ernesto. *El Noroeste* (16.3.80), 14.
    .13. Sobejano, Gonzalo. *HR*, 50 (1982), 496-99.
    .14. Soto, Apuleyo. *El Correo Español* (Bilbao) (4.3.80).
    .15. V.M.R. *Triunfo* (17.5.80).
    .16. Valis, Noël M. *HisJ*, 1, No. 2 (1980), 149.

Ac34 *Su único hijo*, Colección Libro Amigo, 954 (Barcelona:
      Bruguera, 1981). 288 pp. 2nd ed., 1982.

Ac35 *Su único hijo* (Barcelona: Júcar, 1984). 200 pp.

Ad   *Short Story Collections*

Ad1   *Pipá* (Madrid: Fernando Fe, 1886). 441 p. Rpt. three times in 1886.
Contents: 'Pipá'; 'Amor' è furbo'; 'Mi entierro'; 'Un documento'; 'Avecilla'; 'El hombre de los estrenos'; 'Las dos cajas'; 'Bustamante'; 'Zurita'.

Ad2   *Pipá*, ed. Antonio Ramos-Gascón (Madrid: Cátedra, 1976). 355 pp. 2nd ed., 1978; 3rd ed., 1980; 6th ed., 1983.
Contains a useful introduction (pp. 15-97) to LA's life and work, as well as to the stories found in the collection.
Review: .1. Martínez Torrón, Diego. *CHA*, No. 356 (Feb. 1980), 439-42.

Ad3   *Doña Berta, Cuervo, Superchería* (Madrid: Fernando Fe, 1892). 254 pp.

Ad4   *Doña Berta, Cuervo, Superchería, O.C.*, IV (Madrid: Renacimiento, 1929). 210 pp.

Ad5   *Doña Berta, Cuervo, Superchería*, Colección Hórreo-Serie Blanca, 16 (Buenos Aires: Emecé, 1943). 191 pp.
Contains Ramón Pérez de Ayala's essay, '"Clarín" y don Leopoldo Alas' (pp. 7-26). On LA as a thinker and educator in his life and works.

Ad6   *Superchería, Cuervo, Doña Berta* (Madrid: Taurus, 1970). 201 pp. 2nd ed., 1980.
Rpts Pérez de Ayala's ' "Clarín" y don Leopoldo Alas' (pp. 9-30).

Ad7   *El Señor y lo demás son cuentos* (Madrid: Manuel Fernández y Lasanta, [1892]). 339 pp.
Contents: 'El Señor'; ' ¡Adiós, Cordera! '; 'Cambio de luz'; 'El centauro'; 'Rivales'; 'Protesto'; 'La yernocracia'; 'Un viejo verde'; 'Cuento futuro'; 'Un jornalero'; 'Benedictino'; 'La Ronca'; 'La rosa de oro'.

Ad8   *El Señor y lo demás son cuentos*, Colección-Universal, 74-75 (Madrid: Calpe [Tip. Renovación], 1919). 223 pp.
Anon. introduction (pp. 5-6).

Ad9   *El Señor y lo demás son cuentos*, Colección Orbe (Buenos Aires: Sopena, 1941). 157 pp.

Ad10   *Cuentos morales* (Madrid: Imp. 'La España Editorial', 1896).

422 pp. Prologue (pp. v-viii) is rpt. in Ab32, pp. 98-99.

Contents: 'Prólogo'; 'El cura de Vericueto'; 'Boroña'; 'La conversión de Chiripa'; 'El número uno'; 'Para vicios'; 'El dúo de la tos'; 'Vario'; 'La imperfecta casada'; 'Un grabado'; 'El Torso'; 'Cristales'; 'Don Urbano'; 'El frío del Papa'; 'León Benavides'; 'El Quin'; 'La nochemala del diablo'; 'Ordalías'; 'Viaje redondo'; 'La trampa'; 'Don Patricio o el premio gordo en Melilla'; 'El sustituto'; 'El señor Isla'; 'Snob'; 'Flirtation legítima'; 'El caballero de la mesa redonda'; 'La tara'; 'González Bribón'; 'La Reina Margarita'.

Ad11 *Cuentos morales* (Madrid: Alianza, 1973). 287 pp.

Review: .1. J. *Asturias Semanal*, No. 212 (23.6.73), 46.

Ad12 *Las dos cajas; novela*, Biblioteca Mignon, 3 (Madrid: B. Rodríguez Serra, [1899]). 94 pp.

Ad13 *Zurita*, Biblioteca 'Clarín', 1 (Madrid: B. Rodríguez Serra, 1900). 75 pp.

Ad14 *El gallo de Sócrates (Colección de cuentos)* (Barcelona: Maucci, 1901). 213 pp.

Contents: 'El gallo de Sócrates'; 'El rey Baltasar'; 'Tirso de Molina'; 'El Cristo de la Vega ... de Ribadeo'; 'Un voto'; 'La médica'; 'El pecado original'; 'El sombrero del señor cura'; 'Dos sabios'; 'En la droguería'; 'Aprensiones'; 'En el tren'; 'La fantasía de un Delegado de Hacienda'; 'El entierro de la sardina'; 'Reflejo'.

Ad15 *El gallo de Sócrates y otros cuentos*, Colección Austral, 1547 (Madrid: Espasa-Calpe, 1973). 141 pp.

Despite small change in title, rpts same collection of stories as Ad14. Review: .1. Pazos, [Manuel R.]. *Archivo Ibero-Americano*, 2ª época, 34 (1974), 696.

Ad16 *Cuentos*, Colección Ariel, 2 (San José, Costa Rica: Imp. Alsina, 1914). 59 pp.

With an appreciation by Adolfo Posada (pp. 3-8). See B967. Contents: 'Boroña'; '¡Adiós, Cordera!'; 'El gallo de Sócrates'; 'El dúo de la tos'.

Ad17 *Doctor Sutilis, O.C.*, III (Madrid: Renacimiento, 1916). 338 pp.

A mix of previously published and unpublished stories. Contents: 'Doctor Sutilis'; 'La mosca sabia'; 'El doctor Pértinax'; 'De la comisión'; 'De burguesa a cortesana'; 'El diablo en Semana Santa'; 'Doctor Angelicus'; 'Los señores de Casabierta'; 'El poeta-buho'; 'Don Ermeguncio o la vocación'; 'Novela realista'; 'La perfecta casada'; 'El filósofo y la "Vengadora"';

'Medalla ... de perro chico'; 'Diálogo edificante'; 'Un candidato'; 'La contribución'; 'El Rana'; 'Versos de un loco'; 'Nuevo contrato'; 'Feminismo'; 'Manín de Pepa José'; 'Album-abanico'; 'Un repatriado'; 'Doble vía'; 'El viejo y la niña'; 'Jorge'; 'Sinfonía de dos novelas'.

Ad18 *El rey Baltasar* (Madrid: Imp. Clásica Española, 1918). 78 pp.
Also includes 'El frío del Papa' and 'Viaje redondo'.

Ad19 *Superchería; novela,* Colección Fémina, 1 (Madrid: Biblioteca Estrella, 1918). 150 pp.
Also contains 'Leopoldo Alas', by José Martínez Ruiz (Azorín) (pp. 7-21). A worthwhile introduction, in which M.R. notes LA's dual nature, the conflict between tradition and innovation in his writing, and his creative trajectory from the complex to the simple. See also B772.

Ad20 * *¡Adiós, Cordera!* (México, 1923).
Cited by Ortiz Aponte, B890, p. 191.

Ad21 *Pipá. La Novela Semanal,* 5, No. 194 (28.3.25) (Madrid: Prensa Gráfica, 1925). 62 pp.
Also contains a short anon. piece, ' "Clarín" (Leopoldo Alas)' (pp. 3-6).

Ad22 *Las dos cajas. La Novela Semanal,* 5, No. 220 (26.9.25) (Madrid: Prensa Gráfica, 1925). 60 pp.
Ill. by Ernesto Durias. 'Clarín', pp. 3-9, rpts Azorín's sketch in Ad19.

Ad23 *Avecilla. La Novela Mundial,* 1, No. 13 (10.6.26). 127 pp.
Ill. by Varela de Seijas. Also contains Luis Santullano's 'Carrocera, labrador' and a brief anon. introduction, 'Clarín' (pp. 3-4).

Ad24 *Pipá. El Cuento Azul,* 12 (Madrid: Prensa Moderna, n.d.). 62 pp.
A series published in 1929-30, according to Federico Carlos Sáinz de Robles, in *La promoción de 'El Cuento Semanal', 1907-1925* (Madrid: Espasa-Calpe, 1975), p. 91.

Ad25 *¡Adiós, Cordera! y otros cuentos* (Buenos Aires: Tor, 1939). 221 pp.
Introductory material by S.S., 'Vida y Obras de Leopoldo Alas (Clarín)' (pp. 5-9). Contains same stories as in Ad7, minus 'El Señor'.

Ad26 *¡Adiós, Cordera! y otros cuentos,* Colección Austral, 444 (Madrid: Espasa-Calpe, 1944). 150 pp. 8th printing, 1979.
Contains same stories as in Ad7, minus 'El Señor'.

Ad27 *Tres cuentos*, ed. Ernst Werner (Munich: Max Hueber, 1952). 36 pp.
Notes, 1-page introduction, and glossary by E.W. Contents: 'Un jornalero'; 'La rosa de oro'; 'La Ronca'.

Ad28 *Cuentos*, ed. José María Martínez Cachero (Oviedo: Gráficas Summa, 1953). 332 pp.
In his 'Nota liminar', M.C. gives the rationale behind the choice of short stories (pp. 5-8). In the prologue (pp. 9-23), Mariano Baquero Goyanes comments on LA's dualism, the contrast between satire and tenderness, in his short stories. As an intellectual writer, LA compares favorably with Pérez de Ayala and Aldous Huxley. See also B126.
Stories selected are: 'El cura de Vericueto'; 'La conversión de Chiripa'; 'El número uno'; 'El dúo de la tos'; 'Un grabado'; 'El Torso'; 'Don Urbano'; 'El frío del Papa'; 'El Quin'; 'La noche mala del diablo'; 'Viaje redondo'; 'La trampa'; 'El sustituto'; 'La Reina Margarita'; 'Bustamante'; 'El rey Baltasar'; 'El pecado original'; 'En el tren'; 'Manín de Pepa José'; 'Speraindeo'.
Reviews: .1. Anon. *Ateneo*, No. 41 (1.9.53).
.2. Alarcos Llorach, E. *BIDEA*, 8 (1954), 137-38.
.3. Caso González, José. *Archivum*, 3 (1953), 297-300.
.4. Entrambasaguas, Joaquín de. *RL*, 4 (1953), 256-57.
.5. Fernández Almagro, M. *ABC* (7.3.54), 57.
.6. Moreno Báez, Enrique. *Arbor*, 27 (1954), 480-81.
.7. Rico, Eduardo G. *La Nueva España* (Oviedo) (27.9.53), 8.

Ad29 *Doña Berta. La Novela del Sábado*, 1, No. 24 (Madrid: Tecnos, 1953). 62 pp.

Ad30 *Cuentos de Clarín*, ed. Laura de los Ríos de García Lorca (Boston: Houghton Mifflin, 1954). xxvi + 193 pp.
In her introduction, 'Leopoldo Alas y "Clarín" (1852-1901)', editor discusses the character of LA's personality and work, the types, themes and style of his stories, and points of contact with the Generation of 1898 (pp. xi-xxiv). A reader for students.
Stories: 'Cuento futuro'; 'Un viejo verde'; 'El Quin'; 'El entierro de la sardina'; 'La Reina Margarita'; 'Superchería'.

Ad31 *Cuentos escogidos*, ed. G.G. Brown (Oxford: Dolphin Book Co., 1964). 229 pp. 2nd ed., 1977.
Introduction (pp. 7-36) has an intelligent discussion of LA's short stories. G.G.B. stresses the fact that 'the attitudes expressed in Alas's short stories indeed remain virtually unchanged throughout his life. What does change is the manner in which Alas presents his ideas.'

His selection is intended as a chronological and representative edition of LA's stories.

Contains: 'La mosca sabia'; 'El diablo en Semana Santa'; 'De la comisión ...'; 'Zurita'; 'El caballero de la mesa redonda'; 'Superchería'; 'El Señor'; 'Viaje redondo'; 'El entierro de la sardina'; 'El gallo de Sócrates'.

Reviews: .1. Cheyne, G.J.G. *BHS*, 44 (1967), 134-35.
       .2. Hall, H.B. *MLR*, 63 (1968), 734-35.
       .3. Kronik, John W. *HR*, 35 (1967), 202-03.

Ad32 *Doña Berta y otras narraciones* (Barcelona [?]: Círculo de Lectores, [1964]). 232 pp.
Contents: 'Doña Berta'; 'Cuervo'; 'Superchería'; '¡Adiós, Cordera!'.

Ad33 *Dos cuentos: ¡Adiós, Cordera!. Pipá*, ed. Silvia Ferroni Clementi (Padova: CEDAM, 1967). 75 pp.
Introduction ('Rasgos biográficos y obra de Leopoldo Alas, "Clarín"', pp. 5-12), notes, and commentary by S.F.C.

Ad34 *Cuentos*, Cuadernos de Lectura Popular, 146 (México: Secretaría de Educación Pública, 1968). 79 pp.
Contents: '¡Adiós, Cordera!'; 'El Señor'; 'Cambio de luz'.

Ad35 *Doña Berta y otros relatos* (Estella: Salvat, 1969). 189 pp. Rpt. in 1971, 1972, 1978, 1982.
Prólogo de José María Martínez Cachero (pp. 9-16).
Contents: 'Doña Berta'; 'Zurita'; 'Mi entierro'; '¡Adiós, Cordera!'; 'El dúo de la tos'; 'El sustituto'; 'La imperfecta casada'; 'La conversión de Chiripa'; 'Dos sabios'; 'El entierro de la sardina'; 'El Rana'.

Ad36 'Avecilla', in Ae4, pp. 117-50.

Ad37 'El hombre de los estrenos', in Ae4, pp. 153-72.

Ad38 *¡Adiós, Cordera! , y lo demás son cuentos*, ed. Pascual Izquierdo (Madrid: Ediciones Generales Anaya, 1982). 255 pp. 2nd ed., 1983.
Ill. by Francisco Conesa. With Apéndice, pp. 233-53; and Bibliografía, pp. 254-55. Introductory, with brief comments on each of the stories.
Contents: '¡Adiós, Cordera!'; 'El dúo de la tos'; 'El Rey Baltasar'; 'La Reina Margarita'; 'Las dos cajas'; 'Benedictino'; 'El "Quin"'; 'El entierro de la sardina'; 'Pipá'; 'Mi entierro'; 'El sustituto'; 'La conversión de "Chiripa"'; 'Avecilla'.

Ad39 *Treinta relatos*, ed. Carolyn Richmond, Selecciones Austral, 114 (Madrid: Espasa-Calpe, 1983). 445 pp.

With a prologue, pp. 9-15; bibliography, pp. 16-22; introductions to each group of stories; and chronological ordering of the stories. Densely documented. Divides the *relatos* into four themes: 1. El escritor; 2. Las relaciones interpersonales; 3. La religiosidad; 4. La muerte. See also: B1030, 1035, 1040, 1042, 1044. Contents: 'Un documento'; 'Rivales'; 'La Ronca'; 'Vario'; 'Reflejo'; 'El dúo de la tos'; 'Un viejo verde'; 'El viejo y la niña'; 'La mosca sabia'; ' "Flirtation" legítima'; 'La Reina Margarita'; 'La imperfecta casada'; 'La perfecta casada'; 'Aprensiones'; 'Doctor Sutilis'; 'Amor' è furbo'; 'Benedictino'; 'Dos sabios'; 'Cristales'; 'El diablo en Semana Santa'; 'La noche-mala del diablo'; 'El frío del Papa'; 'Viaje redondo'; 'Cambio de luz'; 'El Señor'; 'Mi entierro'; 'El gallo de Sócrates'; 'El entierro de la sardina'; 'El caballero de la mesa redonda'; 'Doña Berta'.
Reviews: .1. Alfaro, José María. *ABC* (27.8.83), v.
.2. Amorós, Andrés. *ABC* (20.8.83), viii.
.3. Bonet, Laureano. (See B198).
.4. Thompson, Clifford R., Jr. *Hispania* (U.S.A.), 67 (1984), 474.

Ad40 * *¡Adiós Cordera!. Doña Berta* (Barcelona, 1982). 192 pp. Ilus. de Blanca López.

Ad41 *Adiós, Cordera y otros cuentos,* Los Clásicos 75 (Madrid: Emiliano Escolar Editor, 1983). 253 pp.
Introduction by José Sanroma Aldea (pp. 9-25) deals mostly with LA's life. Contents same as Ad7.

Ad42 * *Cuentos morales* (Barcelona: Bruguera, 1982). 317 pp.

Ad43 *Cuentos morales*, ed. facsimilar, Clásicos Populares Asturianos, 1. Gijón: Mases Ediciones, 1984). 422 pp.
With introductory material by Elías García Domínguez, 'Los cuentos de Clarín', pp. v-ix.

Ad44 *Una novela y ocho cuentos* (Barcelona: Planeta, 1983). 250 pp.
Contents: 'Doña Berta'; 'Avecilla'; 'Pipá'; 'Las dos cajas'; 'El cura de Vericueto'; 'El dúo de la tos'; '¡Adiós, Cordera! '; 'Cambio de luz'; 'El diablo en Semana Santa'.

Ae   *Plays*

Ae1   *Teresa* (Ensayo dramático en un acto y en prosa, original de D. Leopoldo Alas. Representóse en el Teatro Español de la noche del 20 de marzo de 1895) (Madrid: Imp. José Rodríguez, 1895). 36 pp.

LA's controversial dramatic experiment, which was recently performed once more on 30 Nov. 1984 by the Teatro Casona de Oviedo (Teatro Campoamor, Oviedo.)

Ae2   *Teresa* (Ensayo dramático en un acto y en prosa), 2nd ed. (Madrid: Imp. José Rodríguez, 1895). 36 pp.

Contrary to Romero, Ae4 (pp. 58-59), this 2nd ed. does exist.

Ae3   *Teresa* (Ensayo dramático en un acto y en prosa) (México: Eusebio Sánchez, 1895). 50 pp.

Ae4   *Teresa. Avecilla. El hombre de los estrenos*, ed. Leonardo Romero (Madrid: Castalia, 1975). 188 pp. 2nd ed., 1980; 3rd ed., 1981.

Contains a useful introduction, select bibliography, and appendices in which L.R. reproduces some contemporary criticism of *Teresa*'s opening night. Annotated. See also B1078.
Review: .1. Anon. *Asturias Semanal*, No. 354 (20-27.3.76), 30.

Af   Correspondence

I.   Published Correspondence

Af1   To Rafael Altamira: in B743, pp. 145-66.
Thirteen letters, dated from 1887 until possibly 1897-1901, detailing
LA's affection for Altamira, and his preoccupation with problems of
health, time, and money.

Af2   To Serafín and Joaquín Álvarez Quintero: in José Losada
de la Torre's *Perfil de los hermanos Álvarez Quintero* (Madrid:
Editora Nacional, 1945), p. 57.
Undated letter in which LA comments on their play, *La buena sombra*,
which opened on 4 Mar. 1898.

Af3   To Manuel Cañete: in José María de Cossío's "Correspondencias
literarias del siglo XIX en la Biblioteca de Menéndez y Pelayo",
BBMP, 12 (1930), 253-54.
LA agrees with Cañete that the play *La Pasionaria*, by Leopoldo Cano,
is a bad one. Date of letter is probably late Dec. 1883.

Af4   To Emilio Castelar: in B250, pp. 92-96.
Six letters in which LA declares his unswerving adhesion to Castelar
and his politics.

Af5   To Rufino José Cuervo: in *Rufino J. Cuervo. Cartas de su
archivo*, II (Bogotá: Imp. Instituto Gráfico Ltda, 1942), pp.
209-10. Also in *Literatura española de los últimos cien años
(desde 1850)*, ed. Rodolfo M. Ragucci (Buenos Aires: Editorial Don Bosco, 1962), p. 463.
LA offers to publicize R.J.C.'s dictionary of the Castilian language.

Af6   To José Victoriano de la Cuesta: in B662, pp. 385-86. Also
in Archives of Ateneo (Madrid).
In letters dated 2, 4.10.97, LA explains that he would like to give
his Ateneo course, 'Teorías religiosas en la filosofía novísima', during
the least cold period in Madrid.

Af7   To Sinesio Delgado: in B206, pp. 124-25.
Letter dated 17.12.89, in which LA humorously explains and justifies why he needs more money for the articles he publishes in *Madrid
Cómico*. Botrel also notes the existence of other letters to S.D., now
in the private archives of Fernando Delgado Cebrián.

Af8 To Fernando Fe: in *Clarín y sus editores (65 cartas inéditas de Leopoldo Alas a Fernando Fe y Manuel Fernández Lasanta, 1884-1893)*, ed. Josette Blanquat and Jean-François Botrel (Rennes: Univ. de Haute-Bretagne, Centre d'Études Hispaniques, Hispano-Américaines et Luso-Brésiliennes, 1981). 85 pp. 'Clarín y sus editores', pp. 3-5. An important series of letters, detailing LA's relationship, both literary and financial, with his two principal publishers. Letters give information on contractual arrangements between LA and his publishers; some of his unrealized projects; surprising changes in the conception of *SUH*; family life; etc. With helpful annotations. Review: .1. Lissorgues, Yvan. *CMHLB*, 38 (1982), 236-37.

Af9 To Manuel Fernández Lasanta: in Af8.

Af10 To Enrique Gómez Carrillo: in B506, pp. 105-09.
Gómez Carrillo published this letter from LA in a Guatemalan newspaper, *Diario de Centro América*, 'con algunos comentarios desagradables para 'Clarín', que éste había de atribuirme a mí más tarde ...'

Af11 To María Guerrero: in B554, pp. 140-59.
Seventeen letters dated from 1894 to 1896, on the subject of *Teresa* and its theatrical opening.

Af12 To José Martínez Ruiz (Azorín): in 'Azorín y sus amigos', *Revista* (Barcelona), 2, No. 68 (30.7-5.8.53), 2.
Rpt in B712, p. 172. Letter dated 16.4.1900, in which LA promises to help M.R. get onto the staff of *El Imparcial.*

Af13 To Fray Ramón Martínez Vigil: in B514, pp. 154-75.
Eleven letters to the Bishop of Oviedo, dated from 1885 to 1898. On *LR*'s morality, various recommendations, *Teresa*, and the death of LA's mother. One letter (11.5.85) also in Ac6, pp. lxxx-lxxxv; in Ah8, pp. 463-64; and in B239, pp. 44-47. Two in B229, pp. 141-47, 216-17; and two in B515, pp. 240-44. See also B56.

Af14 To Antonio Maura: in B1057, pp. 20-21.
A letter (12.5.98) on fraudulent elections held between Melquiades Álvarez and an unnamed Count, in 1898, Oviedo.

Af15 To Vicente Medina [y Tomás]: in Ag15, pp. 10-11.
A letter, dated 29.12.98, praising Medina's novel, *El rento.*

Af16 To Marcelino Menéndez y Pelayo: in B16, 234 pp.
Mutual respect, affection, and openness are revealed in this correspondence.

Each writer anxiously sought the other's opinion of his work. One letter (23.2.85) rpt. in B144, pp. 295-96.

Af17 To Marcelino Menéndez y Pelayo: in Enrique Sánchez Reyes's 'Centenarios y conmemoraciones', *BBMP*, 29 (1953), 108-14.
S.R. prints letters from LA to M. y P. which came to light after publication of the 1943 *Epistolario*, B16. LA discusses his difficulties with English and the writing of *SUH.*

Af18 To Segismundo Moret: in B662, pp. 382-85. Also in Archives of Ateneo (Madrid).
Two letters dated 22.7.97 and 3.8.97 in which LA discusses the title of a course on religion and philosophy that he was to give at the Ateneo the following year.

Af19 To Juan Ochoa Betancourt: in B399, pp. 171-76, and B394, pp. 147-49.
Three letters (28.9.96, 1.7.97, 4.8.97). On the loss of parents; Ochoa's novel, *Un alma de Dios*; and LA's lecture at the Ateneo. In B394, LA asks Ochoa to do a piece on *Teresa.*

Af20 To Juan Ochoa Betancourt: in B386, p. 321.
Letter reveals LA's affection for Ochoa.

Af21 To Narciso Oller: in B146, pp. 513-22.
Six letters from 1885 to 1891, revealing LA's unease, insecurity, and contradictoriness.

Af22 To Armando Palacio Valdés: in B514, pp. 50, 63-64.
Two letters (17.5.96, 19.12.92): on LA's ill-health; and the death of Tomás Tuero.

Af23 To Emilia Pardo Bazán: in B210, pp. 136-38.
Unpublished letter (1890?, wonders Bravo-Villasante). LA complains of his ill-health and nervousness, and wonders whether he will be able to complete *SUH.*

Af24 To Benito Pérez Galdós: in *Cartas a Galdós*, ed. Soledad Ortega (Madrid: Revista de Occidente, 1964), pp. 207-96.
A collection of seventy-two letters, dated from 1879 to 1901, many of them on the aesthetics of novel writing, Galdós's work, and LA's own distrust of himself as a novelist.

Af25 To Jacinto Octavio Picón: in B47, pp. 8-20.

An important series of letters for the insights it affords on LA's attitude toward critics of *LR*, on his own awareness of *LR*'s weaknesses, and for his relationship with Picón. One letter dated 3.10.85 is also reproduced in B45.

Af26   To Antonín Pikhart: in Zdeněk Hampejs's 'Cartas desconocidas de escritores españoles y catalanes a Antonín Pikhart', *PP*, 3 (1960), 151-52.
Letter in which LA alludes to Pikhart's translations of his work (see Ai2, Ai4). Characteristically, LA also cannot help correcting some of P.'s faulty Spanish grammar.

Af27   To Demetrio Pola Varela: in Ag19, p. 7.
A letter, dated 11.4.89, in which LA thanks Pola Varela for sending him his poetry and offers him kind words of encouragement.

Af28   To José Quevedo: in B480, pp. 241-80.
A series of twelve remarkable letters, previously published in truncated form by Posada (B973), illuminating LA's feelings about women and religion and his capacity for self-analysis.

Af29   To José Enrique Rodó: in B1060, p. 1260.
Letter (29.12.95) thanking Rodó for his article on the Asturian writer (see B1062).

Af30   To José Enrique Rodó: in B1061, pp. 96-98.
Letter (11.8.97) deals with LA's interest in the Uruguayans Pérez Petit and Rodó, as well as his conception of himself as a 'patriota ... intercontinental.'

Af31   To Bernardo Rodríguez Serra: in Ag12, pp. 145-46.
In a letter dated 18.1.01, LA happily agrees to write the prologue for Nicasio Mariscal's book, Ag12.

Af32   To José Yxart: in B153, pp. 385-97.
Seven letters, dated 1883, 1887, 1888, and 1891. The later correspondence tells us of LA's growing fatigue, ill-health, and profound dissatisfaction with his own work.

Af33   To José Zorrilla [y Moral]: in B28, pp. 47-49.
Two letters dated 2.4.85, 3.4.92: on Z.'s government pension; the publication of *LR*; Z.'s poem, 'Cádiz'.

Af34   To José Zorrilla [y Moral]: in B240, pp. 277-79.
Dated 20.11.85. LA calls Z. 'un rey de la poesía', unjustly treated

by the Academy in its denial of his pension; and attacks Suárez Bravo's *Guerra sin cuartel*, 'esa novela tonta y disparatada.'

II.   *Unpublished Correspondence*

Af35 *To José Martínez Ruiz (Azorín): two letters dated 15.1.97 and 16.4.1900.

Noted by Dionisio Gamallo Fierros, *Hacia una bibliografía cronológica en torno a la letra y el espíritu de Azorín* (Madrid: Dirección General de Archivos y Bibliotecas, 1956), pp. 11-12.

Af36 *To Jacinto Octavio Picón: in private archives of the Ortega family (Madrid).

According to Ramos-Gascón, Ad2, p. 42, in this correspondence LA discusses his publishing difficulties with the Marqués de Riscal, owner of *El Día*, who was unhappy about LA's 1883 articles, 'La crisis en Andalucía', and Clarín's naturalist bent in literary criticism.

Ag   *Prologues*

Ag1   Altamira [y Crevea], Rafael, *Mi primera campaña (Crítica y cuentos).* (Madrid: José Jorro, 1893), pp. i-xiii. Rpt. in Ab32, pp. 182-88; and in B743, pp. 169-76.
A very personal, deeply felt prologue, in which LA recalls the anguish and hard labor of earning one's living by the pen in Spain.

Ag2   Balart, Federico, *Poesías completas.* I, *Dolores* (Barcelona: Gustavo Gili, 1929), pp. 13-36. Rpt. in Ab32, pp. 202-17.
LA's 'Estudio crítico' was originally published in *Los Lunes de El Imparcial* (12, 19.2.94).

Ag3   *Balzac, Honoré de, *Cuentos droláticos*, trans. Querubín de la Ronda (Madrid: Imprenta de Ulpiano Gómez, 1883).
Rpt. in Ab32, pp. 140-41; and in B207, p. 83.

Ag4   Bobadilla, Emilio [pseud.: Fray Candil], *Escaramuzas* (Madrid: Fernando Fe, 1888), pp. vii-xxix. Rpt. in Ab32, pp. 145-58.
Fray Candil and LA were still on friendly terms when Clarín penned this prologue.

Ag5   Carlyle, Thomas, *Los héroes. El culto de los héroes y lo heroico en la historia*, 2 vols, trans. Julián G. Orbón (Madrid: Manuel Fernández y Lasanta, 1893), pp. 1-38 (I); 7-31 (II). Rpt. in Ab32, pp. 188-201.
LA concludes that the essence of 'la teoría del *heroísmo* está, a mi ver, en ... que las cosas *humanas* se traten de un modo *humano.* El héroe es el *hombre entero.*' See B572, for further discussion.

Ag6   *——, *Historia de la Revolución francesa* (Buenos Aires, 1946).
Cited by Gómez-Santos, B514, p. 234.

Ag7   Catarineu, Ricardo J., *Giraldillas (Versos)* (Madrid: Imp. y Lit. de los Huérfanos, 1893), pp. 7-9. Rpt. in Ab32, pp. 201-02.
A somewhat flippant prologue by LA, in which he appears to lack time (and inclination?) to do more.

Corzuelo, Andrés [pseud.]: See Matoses, Manuel.

Ag8   Gómez Carrillo, Enrique, *Almas y cerebros* (Paris: Garnier Hmns, 1898), pp. vii-xxii. Rpt. in Ab32, pp. 219-26.

One of the few instances in which a preface writer criticizes the work and tendencies he has presumably come to praise. Specifically, LA finds fault with Gómez Carrillo's *modernismo* and *cosmopolitismo* (read *snobismo afrancesado*).

Ag9 González Serrano, Urbano, *Goethe. Ensayos críticos*, 2a ed. corregida y aumentada (Madrid: Imprenta Económica de Luis Carrión, 1892), pp. v-xxiv. 3rd ed. (Madrid: Librería Internacional de Fernández Villegas y Cía, 1900), pp. 5-26. Rpt. in Ab32, pp. 163-72.

González Serrano's study enriches Spain's own literature, says LA. Beser, B149, p. 345, notes that this essay first appeared in *La Unión* (18.2.79).

Ag10 González Velasco, Eduardo, *Tipos y bocetos de la emigración asturiana tomados del natural* (Madrid: Imp. de la Revista de Legislación, 1880), pp. v-viii. Rpt. in Ab30, pp. 154-56; and in Ab32, pp. 101-03.

Appeared also in *La Revista de Asturias*, No. 11 (15.6.80), 171.

Ag11 Jhering, Rudolf von, *La lucha por el derecho*, trans. Adolfo Posada (Madrid: Librería de Victoriano Suárez, 1881), pp. v-lxxi. 2nd ed., 1921; 3rd ed. (Buenos Aires: Araujo, 1939). Rpt. in Ab32, pp. 103-32.

García San Miguel, B477, pp. 225-30, analyses LA's prologue.

Ag12 Mariscal, Nicasio, *La neurastenia en los hombres de estado (Reflexiones de medicina política)* (Madrid: B. Rodríguez Serra, 1901).

'Con un estudio crítico acerca del autor por Don Leopoldo Alas (Clarín)': on pp. 145-46, however, the publisher explains that LA died before he could write the study. Thus, we have a 'non-existent prologue'. Also contains a letter to Rodríguez Serra (Af31).

Ag13 Matoses, Manuel [pseud.: Andrés Corzuelo], *Del montón* (Madrid: Imp. de E. Rubiños, 1887), pp. 5-13. Rpt. in Ab32, pp. 141-45.

On Matoses's modesty and good taste.

Ag14 Medina [y Tomás], Vicente, *Poesía: obras escogidas* (Cartagena: Librería Bant, 1908), pp. 9-15.

LA's *juicio crítico* originally appeared in *La Vida Literaria* (Madrid) (20.7.99).

Ag15 ——, *El rento (Novela de costumbres murcianas)* (Cartagena: Tipografía La Tierra, 1907), pp. 10-11. Rpt. in Ab32, p. 256.
Uses a letter from LA, dated 29.12.98, as a prologue. See also Af15.

Ag16 Ochoa Betancourt, Juan, *Los Señores de Hermida* (Barcelona: Juan Gili, Librero, 1900), pp. 7-13. Rpt. in Ab32, pp. 227-31.
A warm tribute to one of LA's best friends.

Ag17 Pardo Bazán, Emilia, *La cuestión palpitante*, 2nd ed. (Madrid: Imp. Central, 1883), pp. ix-xx. Rpt. in Ab32, pp. 132-39.
Also: 4th ed. (Madrid: Imprenta de A. Pérez Dubrull, 1891), pp. 27-41.
Significant essay on what naturalism is not. See also Ai5.

Ag18 *Pérez Zúñiga, Juan, *Guasa viva* (Madrid, 1892). Rpt. in Ab32, pp. 181-82.
I have seen the 2nd ed. (Madrid: Administración del Noticiero-Guía, 1920), pp. 5-8. LA's humorous prologue is written in verse.

Ag19 Pola Varela, Demetrio, *Poesías líricas y La romería de Santa Marina (Zarzuela en dos actos)* (Llanes: Imprenta Las Novedades, 1902), p. 7. Rpt. in Ab32, p. 255.
Uses a letter from LA, dated 11.4.89, as a prologue (Af27).

Ag20 Posada, Adolfo, *Ideas pedagógicas modernas* (Madrid: Librería de Victoriano Suárez, 1892), pp. ix-xx. Rpt. in Ab32, pp. 172-81.
'Si hubiera en España muchos *pedagogos* como Posada', writes LA, 'el porvenir de la educación pública sería bien risueño.'

Ag21 Quevedo, José, *La batalla de Sao del Indio en la isla de Cuba ganada por el General Canella (Poema en bable)* (Oviedo: Imp. Uría, 1896), pp. i-iv.
Rpt. in *Asturias Semanal* (Oviedo), No. 390 (4-11.12.76), 42; and in Ab32, pp. 217-19. LA discusses the Asturian dialect, *el bable.*

Ag22 Rodó, José Enrique, *Ariel* (Valencia: F. Sempere y Cía, n.d. [1900?]), pp. vii-xiv.
LA's prologue first appeared in *Los Lunes de El Imparcial* (23.4.1900). Rpt. in Hugo D. Barbagelata's *Rodó y sus críticos* (Paris: Biblioteca Latino-Americana, 1920), pp. 39-49; in B15, pp. 195-201; in *Ariel* (Buenos Aires: Sopena, 1947), pp. 5-15; in *Ariel* (Madrid: Austral, 1948), pp. 11-22; in *Ariel* (New York: Las Américas, 1967), pp. 9-20; and in Ab32, pp. 231-37.

Ag23   Rueda y Santos, Salvador, *Cantos de la vendimia* (Madrid:
       Gran Centro Editorial, 1897), pp. 11-22. Rpt. in Ab32,
       pp. 158-63.
       LA's harsh but essentially just evaluation of S.R.'s poetry. See also B740.

Ag24   Tolstoy, Leo, *Resurrección* (Barcelona: Maucci, 1900). Rpt.
       in Ab32, pp. 237-46.
       I have seen the 1960 ed. (pp. 23-34: prologue). Beser and Bonet, B156,
       p. 209, also note that the prologue was published in *La Publicidad*
       (Barcelona) (29.4.1900).

Ag25 *Zola, Émile, *Trabajo*, 2 vols (Barcelona: Maucci, 1901). 320;
       288 pp. Rpt. in Ab32, pp. 246-55.
       LA also translated this Zola work.

Ah   *Reprints*

I.   *Stories*

Ah1   Alas, Leopoldo, '¡Adiós, Cordera!', in *Cuentos escogidos de los mejores autores castellanos contemporáneos*, ed. Enrique Gómez Carrillo (Paris: Garnier Hmns, 1894), pp. 2-17.

Ah2   '¡Adiós, Cordera!', in *Prosistas modernos*, ed. Enrique Díez-Canedo. Biblioteca Literaria del Estudiante, 4 (Madrid: Instituto-Escuela (Junta Para Ampliación de Estudios), 1922), pp. 196-213. 3rd ed., 1930 (pp. 229-46).

Ah3   '¡Adiós, Cordera!', in *Cuentistas españoles del siglo XIX*, ed. Federico Sáinz de Robles (Madrid: Aguilar, 1945), pp. 359-84.

Ah4   '¡Adiós, Cordera!', in *Asturias* (Buenos Aires), No. 339 (Apr. 1952), 18-21.

Ah5   '¡Adiós, Cordera!', in *Antología: prosas maestras castellanas*, ed. Clemente Cimorra. Colección Oro, 142-43 (Buenos Aires: Ed. Atlántida, 1952), pp. 201-06. Excerpt.

Ah6   '¡Adiós, Cordera!', in *Antología general de la literatura española*, II, 2nd ed., ed. Ángel and Amelia A. del Río (New York: Holt, Rinehart and Winston, Inc., 1960), pp. 390-94. 1st ed., 1953.

Ah7   '¡Adiós, Cordera!', in *Antología mayor de la literatura española*, IV, ed. Guillermo Díaz-Plaja (Barcelona: Labor, 1961), pp. 1191-96.

Ah8   '¡Adiós, Cordera!', in *Literatura española de los últimos cien años (desde 1850)*, ed. Rodolfo M. Ragucci (Buenos Aires: Editorial Don Bosco, 1962), pp. 73-76.

Ah9   '¡Adiós, Cordera!', in *La prosa española del siglo XIX*, III, ed. Max Aub (México: Antigua Librería Robredo, 1962), pp. 197-207.

Ah10   '¡Adiós, Cordera!', in *Presentación y antología de los siglos XVIII y XIX españoles*, II, ed. Lucía Dolores Bonilla and Juan Ventura Agudiez (New York: Las Américas Publishing Co., 1967), pp. 684-91.

Ah11 '¡Adiós, Cordera!', in *EstLit*, Nos 402-04 (15.9.68), 24-26.

Ah12 '¡Adiós, Cordera!', in *Literatura española*, II, ed. Diego Marín (New York: Holt, Rinehart and Winston, 1968), pp. 130-35.
With introduction (pp. 128-29).

Ah13 '¡Adiós, Cordera!', in *Cuentos del siglo XIX*, ed. José María Carandell. Moby Dick, Biblioteca de Bolsillo Junior, 13 (Barcelona: La Gaya Ciencia, 1972), pp. 97-115. 2nd ed., 1978.

Ah14 '¡Adiós, Cordera!', in *Literaturas e ideologías*, I, ed. Luis Yrache Esteban (Zaragoza: Editorial Librería General, 1977), pp. 370-73.

Ah15 '¡Adiós, Cordera!', in *Ocho siglos de cuentos y narraciones de España*, ed. Nancy C. Brooks, María T. Font and Teresa L. Chaves (New York: Regents Publishing Co., 1977), pp. 111-21.

Ah16 'Boroña', in *Asturias*, III, ed. Octavio Bellmunt y Traver and Fermín Canella y Secades (Gijón: Fototip. y Tip. de O. Bellmunt, 1900), pp. 505-07.

Ah17 'Boroña', in *Cuentistas asturianos (Antología y semblanzas)*, ed. Constantino Suárez (Españolito) (Madrid: Compañía Ibero-Americana de Publicaciones, 1930), pp. 99-106.

Ah18 'Boroña', in *Asturias (Publicación única de homenaje a Venezuela)*, ed. José Manuel Castañón (Venezuela, n.p., n.d.), pp. 75-78.

Ah19 'Cambio de luz', in *Cuentos españoles concertados (De Clarín a Benet)*, ed. Gonzalo Sobejano and Gary D. Keller (New York: Harcourt, Brace, Jovanovich, 1975), pp. 6-19.

Ah20 'La conversión de Chiripa', in *La Balesquida* (Oviedo), 2a época, No. 1 (June 1930), 46-51.

Ah21 'Cristales', in *Cuentos españoles* (see Ah19), pp. 28-33.

Ah22 'El cura de Vericueto', in *Cuentos españoles del siglo XIX*, ed. Consuelo Burell. Colección Novelas y Cuentos, 140 (Madrid: Emesa, 1973), pp. 204-47.

Ah23 'Dos sabios', in *Antología de cuentos españoles*, ed. John M. Hill and Erasmo Buceta (Boston: D.C. Heath, 1923), pp. 49-61.

Ah24 *'Dos sabios', in *Cuaderno de Lectura* (Madrid: Univ. Internacional 'Menéndez Pelayo', Sección de Lengua y Literatura, Curso para Extranjeros, 1955), pp. 93-114.

Ah25 'Dos sabios', in *El cuento*, ed. John A. Crow and Edward J. Dudley (New York: Holt, Rinehart and Winston, 1966), pp. 128-37.

Ah26 'El dúo de la tos', in *Literatura española*, II (see Ah12), pp. 136-39.

Ah27 *'En que, por fin, se presentan las verdaderas vírgenes locas, aunque tarde y con daño', in *Las vírgenes locas. Novela improvisada* (Madrid: F. Bueno y Compañía, 1886).
Ch. 5 of this collectively authored spoof. It is signed 'Flügel', but Martínez Cachero (B732) and Ruiz de la Peña (B1090) argue persuasively that the author is really LA. See also Ah34.

Ah28 'El gallo de Sócrates', in *Cuentos y narraciones en lengua española*, ed. Harriet de Onís (New York: Washington Square Press, 1961), pp. 67-71.

Ah29 'Un grabado', in *Los mejores cuentistas españoles*, I, ed. Pedro Bohigas (Madrid: Ed. Plus Ultra, 1958), pp. 417-25.

Ah30 'Un jornalero', in *Prosa moderna en lengua española (Antología)*, ed. Segundo Serrano Poncela (Río Piedras: Univ. de Puerto Rico, Ed. de La Torre, 1955), pp. 151-57.

Ah31 'Un jornalero', in *Perspectivas*, ed. Mary Ellen Kiddle and Brenda Wegmann (New York: Holt, Rinehart and Winston, 1974), pp. 67-74.

Ah32 'Un jornalero', in *Readings in Spanish Literature*, ed. Anthony Zahareas and Barbara Kaminar de Mujica (New York: Oxford Univ. Press, 1975), pp. 190-200.

Ah32bis 'Manín de Pepa José', in *Antología de narradores asturianos (1824-1877)*, I, ed. José María Martínez Cachero (Salinas, Asturias: Ayalga, 1982), pp. 105-20.

Ah33 'La noche-mala del diablo', in *Prosa española moderna y contemporánea*, ed. Joaquín de Entrambasaguas (Madrid): CSIC, 1943), pp. 123-28. 3rd ed., 1950.

Ah34 *'Un paraíso sin manzanas', in *Las vírgenes locas* (see Ah27). Ch. 6 of collective novel, orig. *Madrid Cómico*, 1886.

Ah35 'Protesto', in *Readings* (see Ah32), pp. 180-89.

Ah36 'Reflejo', in *Antología general*, II (see Ah6), pp. 388-90.

Ah37 'La Ronca', in *Cuentos españoles* (see Ah19), pp. 20-27.

Ah38 'Speraindeo (Capítulos olvidados de una novela inédita)', in *Nuestro Tiempo*, No. 30 (June 1903), 820-31. Chs I-II.

Ah39 'El sustituto', in *Representative Spanish Authors*, II, 3rd. ed., ed. Walter T. Pattison and Donald W. Bleznick (New York: Oxford Univ. Press, 1971), pp. 242-47.

Ah40 'El torso', in *First Spanish Reader*, ed. Everett Ward Olmsted and Edward H. Sirich (New York: Henry Holt and Co., 1924), pp. 99-114. 2nd ed., 1930.

Ah41 'Viaje redondo', in *Índice de Artes y Letras*, No. 108 (Jan. 1958), 5-6.
With a 'Breve nota sobre "Viaje redondo"'.

II. *Parts of Novels*

Ah42 "Leopoldo Alas (Clarín)', in *Prosateurs espagnols contemporains*, ed. Jean Sarrailh (Paris: Delagrave, 1938), pp. 21-27.
Description of the Casino of Vetusta, in *LR*.

Ah43 '*La Regenta*', in *Antología general*, II (see Ah6), pp. 378-88.
Excerpts from Chs III, XVI, XVII.

Ah44 ' "Clarín": *La Regenta* (1885)', in *Antología de la novela española*, ed. Francisco Ynduráin (Madrid: CSIC, 1954), pp. 171-85.
Excerpts from Ch. XVI.

Ah45 '*La Regenta*', in *Prosa moderna* (see Ah30), pp. 143-50.
Description of the Casino of Vetusta.

Ah46 '*La Regenta*', in *Antología mayor*, IV (see Ah7), pp. 1196-1200.
Excerpt from Ch. XVI.

Ah47 '*La Regenta*', in *A New Anthology of Spanish Literature*, II, ed. Richard E. Chandler and Kessel Schwartz (Baton Rouge): Louisiana State Univ. Press, 1967), pp. 174-91.
Excerpts from Chs I, XV.

Ah48 '*La Regenta*', in *Tesoro breve de las letras hispánicas*, Part V, ed. Guillermo Díaz-Plaja (Madrid: Emesa, 1968), pp. 185-93.
Excerpt from Ch. XVI.

Ah49 '*Su único hijo*', in *Cómo aman las españolas*, ed. P. Gómez Urquijo (Madrid: Mateu, [1918]), pp. 311-45.
Excerpt from Ch. X.

III. *Poetry*

Ah50 'A Menéndez Pelayo', in Enrique Sánchez Reyes, 'Poesías a Menéndez Pelayo', *BBMP*, 31 (1955), 215-18.

Ah51 'Poesías inéditas de Clarín', in *La Lectura*, 7 (June 1907), 162.
Rpts 'Soneto' and 'Sellado en hondo secreto'.

See also B511, 744, 1411.

IV. *Criticism*

Ah52 'Abajo los judíos', in *El Affaire Dreyfus en España 1894-1906*, ed. Jesús Jareño López (Murcia: Editorial Godoy, 1981), pp. 18-20.
Originally in *El Heraldo de Madrid* (31.1.98). Also in Ab30, pp. 137-41.

Ah53 'Al caer las hojas', in *La Revolución de 1868 (Historia, pensamiento, literatura)*, ed. Clara E. Lida and Iris M. Zavala (New York: Las Américas Publishing Co., 1970), pp. 482-83.

Ah54 *'La crítica y los críticos. A Jerónimo', in *Trozos escogidos de literatura castellana*, II, ed. Calixto Oyuela (Buenos

Aires: A. Estrada, 1897), p. 315. Also in Ah8, pp. 170-73.

Ah55 'La crítica y los críticos. A Jerónimo', in *Cumbres del idioma (Antología)*, nueva ed. refundida, ed. Rodolfo M. Ragucci (Buenos Aires: Don Bosco, 1963), pp. 614-16.

Ah56 'Filosofía y letras', in *El libro del año*, ed. Ricardo Ruiz y Benítez de Lugo et al (Madrid: Sucesores de Rivadeneyra, 1899), pp. 14-19.

Ah57 'Galdós', in *Prosateurs espagnols contemporains* (see Ah42), pp. 27-29.
From Ab15.

Ah58 'El hambre en Andalucía (1883)', in *Antecedentes y desarrollo del movimiento obrero español (1835-1888) (Textos y documentos)*, ed. Clara E. Lida (Madrid: Siglo XXI, 1973), pp. 441-51.
Rpts LA's articles VI, VIII, IX, and X, which appeared in *El Día*, in Feb. and Mar. 1883.

Ah58bis 'El hambre en Andalucía', in Ab30, pp. 157-60, 217-27.
Rpts articles numbered VIII, X, XV, and XXI.

Ah59 'El hambre en Andalucía (1883)', in *Historia de España en sus documentos. Siglo XIX*, ed. Fernando Díaz-Plaja (Madrid: Cátedra, 1983), pp. 391-98.
Rpts same articles as in Ah58, from LA's series.

Ah60 'El hambre en Andalucía', in B1077, pp. 139-71.
Rpts the entire series of twenty-two articles.

Ah61 'La idea de la muerte en Clarín. Trozos escogidos de sus *Ensayos y revistas*', in *Revista Popular* (Oviedo) (1.7.01), 4-5.

Ah62 'Un juicio sobre Menéndez y Pelayo', in Julio Cejador y Frauca, *Historia de la lengua y literatura castellana*, IX (Madrid: Tip. de la Revista de Archivos, Bibliotecas y Museos, 1918), pp. 174-75. Also in Ah8, pp. 173-74.

Ah63 'El libre examen y nuestra literatura presente', in *La Revolución de 1868* (see Ah53), pp. 387-96.

Ah64 'Palique', in B507, pp. 43-45 (1948 ed.); and in B712, pp. 169-72.
On Azorín's *Charivari*. Originally published in *Madrid Cómico* (8.5.97).

Ah65 'Palique', in Edelberto Torres, *Enrique Gómez Carrillo. El cronista errante* (México: Librería Escolar-Guatemala, C.A., 1956), pp. 90-91.
On G.C.'s *Esquisses* (from *Madrid Cómico*, 1892?).

Ah66 'Palique', in José Esteban, *Valle-Inclán visto por...* (Madrid: Las Ediciones de El Espejo, 1973), pp. 13-16.
Rpts article on Valle-Inclán's *Epitalamio* (*Madrid Cómico*, 25.9.97).

Ah67 'Palique' (Venancio González — *Ripios aristocráticos*)', in Antonio de Valbuena (Venancio González), *Ripios aristocráticos*, 3rd ed. (Madrid: Imp. de los Sres Viuda e Hijo de Aguado, 1887), pp. 11-16. Rpt. in Ab32, pp. 257-60.

Ah68 'Paliques. Palique del palique', in *EstLit*, Nos 402-04 (15.9.68), 22-23.

Ah69 'Un poeta menos', in Teodoro Cuesta, *Poesías asturianas* (Oviedo: Imp. de Pardo, Gusano y Cía, 1895), pp. 283-85.
Rpts his obituary on T.C. (*El Carbayón*, 5.2.95).

Ah70 '[Prólogo]', in *Literaturas e ideologías* (see Ah14), pp. 11-12.
Extract from the prologue to *Palique*.

Ai   *Translations*

I.   *Azerbaijani*

Short Story

'Rivales'

Ai1   *'Sopernik'. Trans. S. Gyseinova. In *Adabiiyat ve indzhesyemt* (8.7.67), 13.

II.   *Czech*

Short Story

' ¡Adiós, Cordera! '

Ai2   'S Bohem, Cordera! ' Trans. A. Pikhart. In *Lumǐr* (Praha), 23 (1895), 77-80.

'Doña Berta'

Ai3   *Doña Berta*. Trans. Eduard Hodoušek (Praha: Československý spisovatel, 1960). 83 pp.
Also contains a brief literary sketch of LA (pp. 77-81) and notes (pp. 82-83). See B587.

'Pipá'

Ai4   'Pipá'. Trans. A. Pikhart. In *Lumǐr* (Praha), 22 (1894), 321-33, 332-34, 344-47, 354-57.

III.   *English*

Criticism

'Prólogo', Ag17.

Ai5   'What Naturalism is Not'. Trans. George J. Becker. In *Documents of Modern Literary Realism*, ed. George J. Becker (Princeton: Univ. Press, 1963), pp. 266-73.

Novel

La Regenta

Ai6   *La Regenta.* Trans. John Rutherford (London: Allen Lane,
        1984). 734 pp. Also: Athens: Univ. of Georgia Press, 1984;
        and New York: Penguin Books, 1984 (ppr).
        An excellent translation. Introduction (pp. 7-17) stresses the modernity
        of *LR*'s complex psychology and *estilo latente*, or *style indirect libre*.
        With notes (pp. 717-34). See also B1094.
        Reviews: .1. Carr, Raymond. *TLS*, No. 4235 (1.6.84), 607.
                 .2. Mills, Robert P. *New York Times Book Review* (25.3.84),
                 20.
                 .3. Senna, Carl. *The Christian Science Monitor* (28.9.84).
                 .4. Seymour-Smith, Martin. *Financial Times* (London)
                 (11.2.84), 12.
                 .5. Vance, Birgitta J. *Hispania* (U.S.A.), 67 (1984), 672-73.

Su único hijo

Ai7   *His Only Son.* Trans. Julie Jones (Baton Rouge: Louisiana
        State Univ. Press, 1981). x + 256 pp.
        A worthwhile version of *SUH*. Based on her diss., B617.
        Reviews: .1. Bravo, María-Elena. *REH*, 17 (1983), 147-48.
                 .2. P[enelope] M[esic]. *Booklist*, 77 (1.2.81), 744.
                 .3. Valis, Noël M. *SAR*, 46, No. 4 (Nov. 1981), 76-78.

Short Story

'¡Adiós, Cordera!'

Ai8   '¡Adiós, Cordera!' Trans. Walter Brooks. In *Stories From
        Four Languages, Retold in English*, ed. Walter Brooks (New
        York: Kimball & Brentano's, 1905), pp. 203-11.

Ai9   'Adiós, Cordera!' Trans. Charles B. MacMichael. In *Short
        Stories from the Spanish*, ed. Charles B. MacMichael (New
        York: Boni and Liveright, 1920), pp. 97-116. Rpt., Girard,
        Kan.: Haldeman-Julius, 1923.

Ai10   'Adiós, Cordera!' Trans. Walter Brooks. In *Great Short
        Stories of the World*, ed. Barret H. Clark and Maxim Lieber
        (Cleveland: World; New York: Robert H. McBride, 1925),
        pp. 522-27. Later eds: London: Heinemann, 1926; New

York: Boni, 1931; Garden City, N.Y.: Garden City, 1938; Garden City, N.Y.: Halcyon, 1941.

Ai11 'Adiós, Cordera!' Trans. Charles B. MacMichael. In *An Anthology of Spanish Literature in English Translation*, II, ed. Seymour Resnick and Jeanne Pasmantier (New York: Frederick Ungar; London: John Calder, 1958), pp. 520-27. Translation was revised by editors.

Ai12 'Adiós, Cordera!' Trans. William E. Colford. In *Classic Tales from Modern Spain*, ed. William E. Colford (Great Neck, N.Y.: Barron's Educational Series, 1964), pp. 33-46.

Ai13 'Adiós, Cordera!' Trans. anon. In *World-wide Short Stories*, ed. Roger B. Goodman (New York: Glober, 1966), pp. 7-13.

'El doctor Pértinax'

Ai14 'Doctor Pertinax'. Trans. anon. In *The Humour of Spain*, ed. Susette M. Taylor (London: Walter Scott Ltd, 1894), pp. 291-300.

'Doña Berta'

Ai15 'Doña Berta'. Trans. Zenia DaSilva. In *Great Spanish Stories*, ed. Ángel Flores (New York: Modern Library, 1956), pp. 147-214.

'El dúo de la tos'

Ai16 'The Duet of the Coughs'. Trans. Bernard Dulsey. In *Arizona Quarterly*, 14 (1958), 21-28.

'El gallo de Sócrates'

Ai17 'The Cock of Socrates'. Trans. M.M. Lasley. In *Spanish Stories and Tales*, ed. Harriet de Onís (New York: Knopf, 1954), pp. 44-48. Also New York: Pocket, 1956.

'Un repatriado'

Ai18 'A Repatriate'. Trans. Howard R. Floan. In *Prairie Schooner*, 36 (1962), 125-29.

'El sustituto'

Ai19 'The Substitute'. Trans. Ángel Flores. In *Spanish Stories /
Cuentos españoles*, ed. Ángel Flores (New York: Bantam
Books, 1960), pp. 128-45.
A bilingual ed.

IV. *French*

Criticism

'Del naturalismo' (*La Diana*, 1.2-16.6.82)

Ai20 'Le Naturalisme'. Trans. Claire-Nicolle Robin. In B1055, pp.
97-136.

Short Story

'El rey Baltasar'

Ai21 'Le roi Baltasar'. Trans. Albert Moxhet. In *Marche Romane*,
15, No. 3 (1965), 111-19.

V. *German*

Novel

La Regenta

Ai22 **Die Präsidentin.* 2 vols. Trans. Egon Hartmann (Berlin: Buch-
verlag der Morgen, 1971). 404; 454 pp.
Epilogue and notes by F.R. Fries.

Short Story

' ¡Adiós, Cordera! '

Ai23 'Lebwohl, Cordera! ' Trans. K. Reiss. In *Die Tat* (Zurich)
(12 & 13.10.58), 7, 9.
Also includes 'Der Dichter Clarín', by K.R. (12.10.58), 7.

VI.   *Italian*

Novel

La Regenta

Ai24   *La Presidentessa*, 2 vols. Trans. Flaviarosa Nicoletti Rossini
(Torino: UTET, 1961). 537; 570 pp. 2nd ed., 1972.
See also B855.
Reviews: .1. Boni, Marco. *Convivium*, n.s., 31 (1963), 765.
　　　　　.2. Goytisolo, José Agustín. *Ínsula*, No. 173 (Apr. 1961), 12.

VII.   *Portuguese*

Short Story

' ¡Adiós, Cordera! '

Ai25   *'Adiós, Cordera! ' Trans. Edgard Cavalheiro. In *Maravilhas
do conto espanhol* (São Paulo: Editorial Cultrix, 1958).

VIII.   *Romanian*

Novel

La Regenta

Ai26   *Pasiunea Anei Ozores*, 2 vols. Trans. Dan Munteanu (Bucu-
reşti: Univers, 1972). xv + 420; 470 pp.
See also B833.

IX.   *Russian*

Short Story

' ¡Adiós, Cordera! '

Ai27   'Proschai, Kordera! ' Trans. R. Pokhlebkin. In *Proschai,
Kordera!* I11. (Moskva: Goslitizdat, 1956), pp. 5-15.
Includes introduction by S. Arkonada (pp. 3-4). See B78.

Ai28 'Proschchai, Kordera!' Trans. R. Pokhlebkin. In *Ispanskie povesti i rasskazy*, ed. R. Pokhlebkin (Moskva: Gosizdkhudlet, 1958), pp. 393-401.

'Boroña'

Ai29 'Kukuruznyi khleb'. Trans. M. Abegauz. In Ai27, pp. 33-38.

Ai30 'Kukuruznyi khleb'. Trans. M. Abegauz. In Ai28, pp. 425-29.

'Doble vía'

Ai31 'Dvoinym putem'. Trans. M. Abegauz. In Ai27, pp. 25-32.

Ai32 'Dvoinym putem'. Trans. M. Abegauz. In Ai28, pp. 419-24.

'El doctor Pértinax'

Ai33 'Doktor Pertinaks'. Trans. M. Abegauz. In Ai28, pp. 409-18.

'Protesto'

Ai34 'Oprotestovannyi veksel'. Trans. M. Abegauz. In Ai27, pp. 16-24.

Ai35 'Oprotestovannyi veksel'. Trans. M. Abegauz. In Ai28, pp. 402-08.

X.   *Serbo-Croatian*

Short Story

'¡Adiós, Cordera!'

Ai36 *'Adiós Cordera!' Trans. Josip Tabak. In *100 odabranih novela svjetske književnosti* [*Los cien cuentos escogidos de la literatura mundial*] (Zagreb: Stvarnost, 1968), pp. 155-61.

Aj   *Miscellaneous*

I.   *Translation*

Aj1   **Trabajo*, by Émile Zola, 2 vols (see Ag25).
LA translated the work and also wrote the prologue.

II.   *Films*

Aj2   *¡Adiós, Cordera!* (1966?). Spain. Written and directed by
Pedro Mario Herrero; produced by Alpe Films, S.L. Stars
Carlos Julia, María Gloria Romero, Carlos Estrada. Screenplay is deposited in Biblioteca Nacional (Madrid: Imp. Varicop,
n.d. [1966?]). 139 pp.

Aj3   *La Regenta* (1974). Spain. Directed by Gonzalo Suárez; produced by Emiliano Piedra. Stars Emma Penella, Keith Baxter,
Nigel Davenport, Adolfo Marsillach. Two versions of screenplay, by Juan Antonio Porto, are deposited in Biblioteca Nacional (Madrid: Carmen Moreno, Imp., 1972; 1974). 185 (1972);
213 pp. (1974).

III.   *Dramatic Adaptation*

Aj4   *La Regenta* (1983). Spain. Adapted and directed by Álvaro
Custodio. Presented 1-4.9.83 and 18-20.11.83 at the Teatro
Carlos III, San Lorenzo de El Escorial; and 3-4.12.83, at the
Teatro Campoamor, Oviedo. Dated 6.1.83. 73 leaves, type-
script.

IV.   *Dance Adaptation*

Aj5   *Los sapos de Vetusta* (1978?). Fantasía basada en *La Regenta*.
Ballet performed by the Laboratorio de Danza, Univ. de Oviedo,
30.6.78 (?).

B

SECONDARY MATERIAL

B1   A., *'Ensayos y revistas (1888-92)'*, *Revista Contemporánea*, No. 86 (30.5.92), 442.
A favorable review.

B2   ——., *'Solos de Clarín'*, *Revista Contemporánea*, No. 84 (30.10.91), 220-21.
A review.

B3   ——., *'Su único hijo'*, *Revista Contemporánea*, No. 83 (30.7.91), 221-22.
A generally favorable review, although A. deplores the naturalist bent in *SUH.*

B4   Abbot, James H., *Azorín y Francia* (Madrid: Seminarios y Ediciones-hora h, 1973), pp. 34-40.
Comments on the relationship between LA and Emilio Bobadilla ('Fray Candil') and between LA and Azorín.

B5   Acebal, Francisco, 'Los paisajes de Clarín', *Revista Popular* (Oviedo) (1.7.01), 12-13.
F.A. excuses himself for the brevity of the piece, since he was given only forty-eight hours to do it.

B6   Acebal González, José, & Jaime Alberti, 'Apuntes de derecho natural de Leopoldo Alas', *Los Cuadernos del Norte* (Oviedo), 2, No. 7 (May-June 1981), 43-49.
J.A. selects and introduces some notes taken by J.A.G. in LA's course on natural law given at the Univ. de Oviedo.

B7   Aggeler, William F., *Baudelaire Judged by Spanish Critics, 1857-1957* (Athens: Univ. of Georgia Press, 1971), pp. 4-5, 9-15, 22.
Notes LA's significance as an early admirer of Baudelaire and rpts extracts of his Baudelaire criticism.

B8   *Aguas Alfaro, J.J., ' "Clarín" creador de tipos clásicos', *El Universal* (Caracas) (28.8.58?).

B9   Agudiez, Juan Ventura, 'Emma Bovary – Ana Ozores o el símbolo del amor', *RR*, 54 (1963), 20-29.
Explains the differing sociological and ideological backgrounds to *LR* and *Mme Bovary* in the creation of the female protagonists and their attitudes toward love. A modified version of this article appears as Ch. VII in B10.

B10   ——, *Inspiración y estética en "La Regenta" de "Clarín"* (Oviedo: IDEA, 1970). 187 pp.
A rather diffuse study of *LR*'s ideological and thematic background and its significance as both a European and a Spanish novel.
Reviews: .1. E[lías] G[arcía] D[omínguez]. *BIDEA*, 24 (1970), 561-64.
.2. Fernández de la Vega, Oscar. *RIB*, 23 (1973), 99-100.
.3. * Giovacchini. *Comunicaciones de Literatura Española* (Buenos Aires), 2 (1973-74), 71-72.

B11   ——, 'La sensibilidad decadentista de Barbey d'Aurevilly y algunos temas de *La Regenta*', *RO*, 2a época, 33 (1971), 355-65.
One of the few studies to link LA's obsession with degeneration and evil to a definite French source of decadent motifs, Barbey d'Aurevilly.

B12   Alarcos Llorach, Emilio, 'Introducción literaria', in *Asturias*, by Francisco Quirós Linares et al (Madrid: Fundación Juan March; Barcelona: Noguer, 1978), pp. 103-10. Rpt. in B1382, pp. 36-50.
A lucid introduction to LA's life and work.

B13   ——, 'Notas a *La Regenta*', *Archivum*, 2 (1952), 141-60. Rpt. in his *Ensayos y estudios literarios* (Madrid: Júcar, 1976), pp. 99-118; in B144, pp. 227-45; and in B1382, pp. 68-91. Extracted in B1297, pp. 578-83.
A seminal essay on *LR*. A.L. gives a beautiful analysis of the two parts of the novel, their spatial and temporal differences.

B14   ——, 'Notas remozadas sobre *La Regenta*', *Argumentos* (Madrid), 8, Nos 63-64 (1984), 8-15.
Reelaborates his view of *LR* as published in B13.

——: See also Anon., B1328.

B15 Alas, Adolfo, ed., *Epistolario a Clarín: Menéndez y Pelayo, Unamuno, Palacio Valdés* (Madrid: Escorial, 1941). 241 pp.
A.A. ('Prólogo', pp. 9-11) describes his father as a defender of Christian civilisation. Vol. also contains 'Páginas escogidas de "Clarín"' (pp. 163-241). Of the correspondence, Unamuno's is the most fascinating, as he bares his soul to the maestro and complains of LA's treatment of his *Tres ensayos*. Palacio Valdés's letters are interesting for what they do not say, in particular the reasons for his absence from the opening night of *Teresa*. See also B1224.
Reviews: .1. Blecua, J.M. *Universidad* (Zaragoza), 19 (1942), 184-85.
   .2. Entrambasaguas, Joaquín de. *RFE*, 25 (1941), 405-18.

B16 ——, ed., *Epistolario: Marcelino Menéndez y Pelayo. Leopoldo Alas (Clarín)* (Madrid: Escorial, 1943). 234 pp.
In his 'Notas' (pp. 19-27), LA's son, a Franco supporter, denies his father was ever leftist in his thinking. Vol. also includes 'Páginas escogidas de Leopoldo Alas (Clarín)' (pp. 115-234). See also Af16, 17, B692.

B17 Alas, Genaro, 'La primera crítica de Clarín', *El Imparcial* (18.6.06).
A delightful anecdote of LA's critical tendencies at age seven.

Alas Mínguez, Leopoldo: See Benedetto, Antonio Di.

B18 Alas Pumariño, Armando de las, 'Se levantará en Oviedo el monumento a Clarín', *Asturias Gráfica* (Oviedo) (Sept. 1920), n. pag.
Author urges that a monument in honor of LA be erected in Oviedo.

Alberti, Jaime: See Acebal González, José.

B19 Alberto, Luis, 'La *Teresa* de "Clarín" (Carta abierta)', *La Gran Vía* (Madrid), 3, No. 98 (12.5.95), 314.
An admirer of LA's play. See also B1212.

B20 Alfaro, José María, '*La Regenta* recobrada', *ABC* (23.12.79), 25.
In *LR*, 'un libro de desengaños', the theme of *el tedio* still needs to be explored more thoroughly.

B21 Alonso, Luis Ricardo, '*La Regenta*: Contrapunto del ensueño

y la necesidad', *Los Cuadernos del Norte* (Oviedo), 5, No. 23 (Jan.-Feb. 1984), 3-9.
The dream/reality conflict provides the thematic key to the novel's action.

B22   Alonso Bonet, Joaquín, *La poesía de Asturias* (Oviedo: IDEA, 1950), pp. 10-11.
Categorizes *LR* as a poetic creation, native to Asturias.

B23   Alonso Cortés, Narciso, 'Armonía y emoción en Salvador Rueda', *Cuadernos de Literatura Contemporánea*, 7 (1943), 36-48.
A.C. believes LA was a decisive, i.e., negative influence on Salvador Rueda's thwarted poetic reform.

B24   ———, ' "Clarín" y el *Madrid Cómico*', *Archivum*, 2 (1952), 43-61.
An informative overview of LA's significant role in *Madrid Cómico*.

B25   ———, 'Crítica belicosa', *El Norte de Castilla* (Valladolid) (14.11.52).
Notes how much time and effort LA wasted on literary disputes and ephemeral criticism.

B26   ———, *Jornadas. Artículos varios* (Valladolid: Imp. de E. Zapatero, 1920), pp. 68-73, 191.
Reviews the literary polemic between LA and Manuel del Palacio.

B27   ———, *Zorrilla, su vida y sus obras*, 2nd ed. (Valladolid: Librería Santaren, 1943), pp. 830-33, 848-51, 854-55.
I have not seen the 1st ed. (1916). Reproduces a letter from Zorrilla to LA and a *palique* on the subject of Z.'s government pension.

B28   ———, 'Zorrilla y "Clarín" ', in *Amigos de Zorrilla (Colección de artículos dedicados al poeta)* (Valladolid: Imp. Castellana, 1933), pp. 47-49.
Comments on LA's lifelong admiration for Zorrilla and reproduces letters from LA to Z. See Af33.

B29   Alperi, Víctor, *Asturias vista por los asturianos* (Salinas, Asturias: Ayalga Ediciones, 1976), pp. 24-26, 28-30, 73, 88-89.
Mostly quotations from LA's work.

B30 Altamira [y Crevea], Rafael, ' "Clarín" y Palacio Valdés en Italia', *La Justicia* (11.4.88). Rpt. in B743, pp. 166-69.
Signed by 'Fedón' (Altamira), this article is a refutation of G.A. Cesareo's analysis of *LR* (see B267).

B31 ——, 'D. Leopoldo Alas (Clarín)', in his *Tierras y hombres de Asturias* (México: Revista Norte, 1949), pp. 123-29.
Remembers LA as an Asturian above all. See also the 'Prólogo', pp. 11-14, in which R.A. explains why only one article on LA appears in the book.

B32 ——, 'Leopoldo Alas', *Anales de la Universidad de Oviedo*, 1 (1901-02), 371-80.
Summarizes the intellectual and literary versatility of LA's work.

B33 ——. 'Leopoldo Alas', *Revista Crítica de Historia y Literatura Españolas, Portuguesas e Hispanoamericanas*, 6 (Aug. 1901), 219-30.
A moving obituary of his friend.

B34 ——. 'Leopoldo Alas – I. El literato. II. El profesor', in his *Cosas del día* (Valencia: F. Sempere y Cía, 1907 [prol.]), pp. 82-99.
Rpt. in B723, pp. 23-33. Essentially repeats what R.A. says in B32 and 33.

B35 ——, 'Los "Paliques" (Fragmento)', *Revista Popular* (Oviedo) (1.7.01), 12.
The *paliques* are important to the intellectual and moral history of LA.

B36 Álvarez, Blanca, 'Ana', *Los Cuadernos del Norte* (Oviedo), 5, No. 23 (Jan.-Feb. 1984), 58-59.
Ana Ozores as 'una maestra del erotismo' similar to Justine.

B37 Álvarez, Carlos Luis, 'Clarín va a misa', *Los Cuadernos del Norte* (Oviedo), 2, No. 7 (May-June 1981), 109-13.
LA's sense of compassion and humor derive from his own suffering and doubts about faith and existence.

B38 Álvarez, Faustino F., 'Polémica asturiana en torno a la película "La Regenta" ', *Asturias Semanal*, No. 292 (11.1.75), 24-25.
A series of interviews conducted by author indicate that most people thought the film betrayed the spirit of the novel.

B39   Álvarez Buylla, Adolfo, 'Alas sociólogo', *Revista Popular* (Oviedo) (1.7.01), 16-17.
Emphasizes that LA was a sociologist in both theory and practice.

B40   ——, *Discurso leído en la solemne apertura del curso académico de 1901-1902.* (Oviedo: Univ., 1901). 32 pp.
An obituary. Praises LA as an educator.

B41   ——, 'Leopoldo Alas', *Anales de la Universidad de Oviedo*, 1 (1901-02), 357-71. Rpt. in B723, pp. 15-22.
Discusses LA's position as an intellectual and an educator.

B42   ——, 'Leopoldo Alas. Sus ideas pedagógicas y su acción educadora', *Boletín de la Institución Libre de Enseñanza*, 25 (1901), 263-74.
Extracts some of B41.

B43   Álvarez-Buylla, Benito [pseud.: Silvio Itálico], 'Anécdota conocida (de los tiempos viejos)', *La Balesquida*, 2a época, No. 3 (1933), 23.
Recounts a story of LA's love for gambling and his renowned wit.

B44   Álvarez Sereix, Rafael, 'Leopoldo Alas y su folleto *Un viaje a Madrid*', *Revista Contemporánea*, No. 62 (30.6.86), 628-33.
A review-article, in which LA is considered the best and most fearless critic of the day.

B45   Amorós, Andrés, 'Una carta inédita de Clarín', *ABC* (13.6.81), III. Rpt. in B47, p. 15; and in B183, pp. 26-27.
Letter to Picón, dated 3.10.85. On *LR* and the kind of reviews it was receiving.

B46   ——, 'Contra Clarín. (Algunas citas)', *Argumentos* (Madrid), 8, Nos 63-64 (1984), 48-49.
Reviews the negative opinions of Blanco García, Ladrón de Guevara, Hurtado and González Palencia, and others as representative of the critical incomprehension of LA's work.

B47   ——, 'Doce cartas inéditas de Clarín a Jacinto Octavio Picón', *Los Cuadernos del Norte* (Oviedo), 2, No. 7 (May-June 1981), 8-20.
Also rpts J.O.P.'s 1885 review of *LR* (see B961).

Andrenio [pseud.]: See Gómez Baquero, Eduardo.

B48 Andreu Valdés, Martín, 'Breve apunte para el centenario de "Clarín"', *BIDEA*, 6 (1952), 149-58.
Remarks on LA's struggle between grace and free will.

B49 Antón del Olmet, Luis, & José de Torres Bernal, *Los grandes españoles: Palacio Valdés* (Madrid: Imp. de Juan Pueyo, 1919), pp. 53-63, 80-83.
On LA's lifelong friendship with Palacio Valdés and their role in the Bilis-Club.

Aparicio Díaz, José: See Anon., B1326.

B50 Aramburo y Machado, Mariano, '*El gallo de Sócrates*', in his *Literatura crítica* (Paris: Sociedad de Ediciones Literarias y Artísticas, n.d.), pp. 81-91.
A review-article on LA's collection of short stories, which M.A.M. sees as a primary source of his religious ideas.

B51 Aramburu, Félix de, 'Eternos discípulos', *Revista Popular* (Oviedo) (1.7.01), 7.
A very short piece by one of LA's admirers and former professors.

B52 *——, *La Extensión Universitaria en Gijón de 1902 a 1903* (Gijón, 1903).

Aramís [pseud.]: See Bonafoux, Luis.

B53 Aranguren, José Luis L., 'De *La Regenta* a *Ana Ozores*', in his *Estudios literarios* (Madrid: Gredos, 1976), pp. 177-211.
Views *LR* as primarily a novel of sensuality and tedium, in which Ana's quest for freedom stands out. An article of provocative insights.
Review: .1. Romero Márquez, Antonio. *Ínsula*, Nos 368-69 (July-Aug. 1977), 37.

B54 Araujo-Costa, Luis, ' "Clarín"', *ABC* (13.5.47).
A commentary on Posada's biography (see B973).

B55 *——, 'Zorrilla, Arriaza y "Clarín". Un autógrafo, una auto-crítica y un corazón sincero', *El Español*, No. 225 (15.2.44), 4.

B56 Arboleya Martínez, Maximiliano, 'Alma religiosa de "Clarín". Datos íntimos e inéditos', *La Revista Quincenal* (Barcelona), 8 (10.7.19), 328-49. Rpt. in *Renovación Social* (Oviedo), 3, Nos 46-49 (1926); and in B723, pp. 43-59.

An interesting, personal essay on the question of LA's religious beliefs.

B57 ——, *De la acción social. El caso de Asturias* (Barcelona: Luis-Gili, 1918), pp. 30-31.
Teresa is not socialist, but religious in intention.

B58 Arcadio [pseud.], 'Yo fui el monaguillo en la boda de Clarín. D. Rafael Loredo nos habla del célebre escritor', *Voluntad* (Gijón) (18.6.52), 8.
A biographical tidbit.

B59 Arce, Evaristo, 'Claves para una vida secreta de Clarín', *La Nueva España* (Oviedo) (23.4.1978), 28.
An interview with the expressionistic painter Jaime Herrero, who executed a series of paintings called 'Claves para la vida secreta de "Clarín"' and who offers a relativist perspective of LA.

B60 ——, *Oviedo y los ovetenses* (Salinas, Asturias: Ayalga Ediciones, 1977), pp. 32-37; 80-81; 133-34.
Not much here, except for examples of Oviedo as the literary Vetusta.

B61 *Archivum* (Oviedo), 2 (1952). 231 pp. Rpt. 1963.
Probably the best homage vol. dedicated to LA. Contents: Ad5; B13, 24, 120, 347, 368, 454, 469, 561, 744, 798, 1202.
Reviews: .1. *Rossi, Giuseppe Carlo. *Idea* (Roma) (5.4.53), 4.
       .2. Villa Pastur, Jesús. *La Voz de Asturias* (20.12.52), 3.

B62 *Arciniega, R., 'Un gran novelista silenciado', *El Universal* (Caracas) (13.11.58).

B63 Argüelles, Juan Benito, 'Nómina de personajes de *La Regenta*', *Los Cuadernos del Norte* (Oviedo), 5, No. 23 (Jan.-Feb. 1984), 10-18.
Identifies characters and notes their first appearance in the novel.

B64 *Argumentos* (Madrid), 8, Nos 63-64 (1984).
See the following, written in commemoration of *LR*'s centennial: B14, 46, 137, 182, 239, 309, 389, 401, 583, 643, 1032, 1090, 1254.

B65 Arias, Pedro G., 'A "Clarín" (En el primer centenario de su nacimiento)', *Asturias* (Madrid), No. 13 (Apr. 1952), 12-13. A poem.

B66 Arias Argüelles-Meres, Luis, 'Clarín', *La Nueva España* (Oviedo) (14.6.81).
Rpt. in B183, pp. 14-15. On LA's development as a writer within a hostile and insensitive environment.

B67 Arias de Velasco, J[esús], 'Crónica de Asturias', *Nuestro Tiempo*, 1 (1901), 722-23.
Comments on two talks LA gave for the Extensión Universitaria of Oviedo.

B68 Arimón, Joaquín, 'A Clarín', *El Liberal* (4.4.95). Rpt. in B731, pp. 470-73.
Even after purchasing a copy of *Teresa*, J.A. still thinks it is a bad play.

B69 ——, 'Mis paliques', *El Liberal* (24.4.95).
Rpt. in B731, pp. 475-77. Another polemical piece against LA and *Teresa.*

B70 ——, 'Mis paliques. La autopsia de Clarín', *El Liberal* (6.7.95).
A favorable review of B700.

B71 ——. 'Mis paliques. La clave del enigma', *El Liberal* (2.6.95).
LA is suddenly attacking Núñez de Arce, says J.A., because Núñez did not help him defend *Teresa* against his enemies.

B72 ——, 'Mis paliques. Un juicio respetable', *El Liberal* (21.5.95).
J.A. quotes from Blanco García's negative view of LA (see B161) in order to insult Clarín.

B73 ——, 'Mis paliques. El segundo entierro de *Teresa*', *El Liberal* (20.6.95).
On *Teresa*'s failure in Barcelona.

B74 ——, 'Mis paliques. Una solución', *El Liberal* (13.6.95).
An attack on the supposed lies in LA's work.

B75 ——, 'Mis paliques. *Teresa*, en Barcelona', *El Liberal* (17.6.95).
Accuses LA of having had a claque at the Barcelona première.

B76 ——, 'Teatro Español. *La niña boba. Teresa*', *El Liberal* (21.3.95).
Rpt. in B731, pp. 464-65. *Teresa* is a thoroughly bad, sterile effort on the Spanish stage, says J.A.

B77   ——, 'Y vuelta con "Clarín" ', *El Liberal* (15.4.95).
Further attacks on *Teresa.*

B78   Arkonada, S., 'Leopoldo Alas', in *Proshchai, Kordera!*
(Ai27), pp. 3-4.

B79   Arpe, C. José de, 'A un tal Corzuelo', *Barcelona Cómica*,
4, No. 124 (11.11.91), 7, 10.
Criticizes the pro-Clarín *bombos* by Andrés Corzuelo in *El Globo.*
See also Ag13; B80, 186.

B80   ——, 'Dos palabras a guisa de palos', *Barcelona Cómica*,
4, No. 127 (2.12.91), 3, 6.
Continues his harsh view of Corzuelo (see also B79, 186).

B81   ——, 'Un libro de Clarín', *Revista de España*, 138 (1892),
503-06.
A review of *Doña Berta, Cuervo, Supercheria.*

B82   Arroyo de López-Rey, Justa, '*La Regenta* de Clarín:
justicia, verdad, belleza', in *Homenaje a Casalduero (Crítica
y poesía)*, ed. Rizel Pincus Sigele and Gonzalo Sobejano
(Madrid: Gredos, 1972), pp. 325-39.
One of the worst studies on *LR* in recent years. Author appears to be
imitating Casalduero's hermetic, mosaic style, an approach which is
probably inapplicable to LA. Commonplaces are expressed in over-
blown language, bizarre statements are made with little relationship
to LA, and actual errors of scholarship slip in. LA, for example, did
not translate Zola's *L'Œuvre*, but *Travail*; and it is critically extrava-
gant to label *Teresa* as the culminating point of LA's later period.

B83   Artigas Ferrando, Miguel, & Pedro Sáinz Rodríguez, ed.,
Epistolario de Valera y Menéndez y Pelayo (Madrid:
Compañía Ibero-Americana de Publicaciones, 1930).
See 'Índice onomástico' for references to LA.

B84   Asensio, Jaime, 'El motivo del "alarde" en *La Regenta*,
de Clarín', *RABM*, 77 (1974), 597-600.
Analyses the *alarde* which occurs in Ch.XVI as an example of the
interpenetration of life and literature.

B85   Ashhurst, Anna Wayne, 'Clarín y Darío: una guerrilla literaria
del modernismo', *CHA*, No. 260 (Feb. 1972), 324-30.

Recounts the *anti-modernista* stance of LA and Darío's defense. See B601, for a superior account of the same dispute.

B86 ——, *La literatura hispanoamericana en la crítica española* (Madrid: Gredos, 1980), pp. 132-69.
Reviews LA's generally unfavorable attitude toward Latin-American writers. The section on LA-Rodó contains excerpts of unpublished correspondence between the two men.

B87 *Asterisco [pseud.], ' "Clarín", maestro de maestros', *Proa* (León) (24.11.49).

B88 *Astur Fernández, Néstor, 'El asturianismo de "Clarín" ', *El Progreso de Asturias* (La Habana) (Oct. 1952).

B89 ——, ' "Clarín" ', *Asturias* (Buenos Aires), No. 339 (Apr. 1952), 9. *Rpt. in *Oviedo*, 1952 ed. (cited by Martínez Cachero, B714, p. 93).
A sonnet.

B90 ——, 'Palique de "Clarín" y de "Vetusta" ', *Los Cuadernos del Norte* (Oviedo), 2, No. 7 (May-June 1981), 120-22.
An abridged version of a lecture given in Buenos Aires in 1964.
Also rpts his 1952 sonnet, 'Clarín' (B89).

B91 *Asturias* (Buenos Aires: Centro Asturiano de Buenos Aires), No. 339 (Apr. 1952).
Homage vol. Sums up talk on LA by Augusto Barcia Trelles; rpts extracts from *LR* and *Solos*; and ' ¡Adiós, Cordera! ' Articles: B89, 276, 341, 526, 545, 923.

B92 *Asturias* (Madrid: Centro Asturiano de Madrid), No. 13 (Apr. 1952).
Vol. dedicated to LA. Contents: B65, 230, 512, 611, 975, 1178, 1261.

B93 *Asún, Raquel, 'El proyecto cultural de *La España Moderna* y la literatura (1889-1914). Estudio de la revista y de la editorial', unpubl. diss., Univ. de Barcelona, 1979.
Contains chapter on the LA-Lázaro Galdiano dispute.

B94 Aub, Max, *Discurso de la novela española contempóranea* (México: El Colegio de México, Centro de Estudios Sociales, 1945), pp. 27-29.

LA's small novelistic production hampers a proper critical perspective of his work.

B95　Aullón de Haro, Pedro, Javier Huerta Calvo et al., *Historia breve de la literatura española en su contexto* (Madrid: Playor, 1981), pp. 526-30.
Introductory material.

B96　Avecilla, Ceferino R., 'El centenario de Leopoldo Alas y la sombra de su hijo', *España Libre* (New York), 15, No. 1 (2.1.53), 6.
Urges his readers not to forget either LA's son, assassinated during the Spanish Civil War, or Clarín himself.

Avello [pseud.]: See Fernández Rodríguez-Avello, Manuel.

Avello, Manuel F.: See Fernández Rodríguez-Avello, Manuel.

B97　Avilés Fernández, Miguel et al, 'La España de Galdós y Clarín', *La Restauración*, No. 16, 'Nueva Historia de España' (Madrid: EDAF, 1974), pp. 126-31.
Follows Tuñón de Lara's ideas of LA (see B1216).

B98　Avrett, Robert, 'The Treatment of Satire in the Novels of Leopoldo Alas (Clarín)', *Hispania* (U.S.A.), 24 (1941), 223-30.
A somewhat superficial approach to a rather complex technique in LA.

B99　Ayala, Francisco, ' "Clarín", en su tiempo y en el nuestro', *El País* (13.6.81), 11. Rpt. in B183, pp. 18-19; and in his *Palabras y letras* (Barcelona: Edhasa, 1983), pp. 275-77.
Points out LA's deep sense of insecurity, his vacilations and doubts as an artist and man. His restless nature made him continually dissatisfied as a result.

B100　Ayesta, Julián, 'Estilo de Clarín: La corriente germánica en la literatura', *El Español*, No. 121 (17.2.45), 6.
LA's work shows signs of a suggestive vagueness and mysteriousness, which are Germanic in character.

Azorín [pseud.]: See Martínez Ruiz, José.

B101　Bacas, Evan G., 'Estudio del estilo y lenguaje en las narraciones de Leopoldo Alas, "Clarín" ', unpubl. diss., Univ.

de Madrid, 1961. An abstract appears in the *Revista de la Universidad de Madrid*, 10, No. 40 (1961), 836-37.
A stylistic study. LA's characters possess a language which mirrors their social class, profession, and personality.

B102 Bacilus [pseud.], 'Letras de molde', *Revista Cómica*, No. 98 (21.3.89), 6.
Favorably reviews B292 and especially likes Cortón's judgment of LA.

B103 ——, 'Letras de molde', *Revista Cómica*, No. 121 (29.8.89), 3, 6.
A polemical piece against LA and for Luis Bonafoux.

B104 Bailar, Sarah Frances, 'The Short Stories of Leopoldo Alas (Clarín)', unpubl. M.A. thesis, Univ. of Southern California, 1927. 56 pp.
Comes to the unsurprising conclusion that LA was an outstanding short-story writer.

B105 Baker, Clayton, 'Echegaray and his Critics', unpubl. diss., Indiana Univ., 1969. 254 pp. Abstracted in *DAI*, 30 (1969-70), 1162-A.
Examines attitudes of three major critics – LA, Manuel de la Revilla, and Azorín – toward Echegaray. LA is considered a benevolent critic of the playwright.

B106 Balart, Federico, 'Correspondencia particular. A Sr. D. Leopoldo Alas', *El Imparcial* (22.12.90).
F.B. attempts to rectify some of LA's judgments on the poet's conception of art. Contrary to what LA says, F.B. does not deny the serious purpose of art.

B107 ——, 'Correspondencia particular. II. Sr. D. Leopoldo Alas', *El Imparcial* (5.1.91).
Continues the argument over art's purpose.

B108 *Balbín Victorero, Luis, *De cómo desfigura el Sr. Arboleya las grandes figuras* (Covadonga: Edit. Covadonga, 1927). 31 pp.

B109 Balseiro, José Agustín, 'Leopoldo Alas (Clarín)', in his *Novelistas españoles modernos* (New York: Macmillan, 1933), pp. 348-81.
An 8th ed. was published by the Univ. de Puerto Rico press,

Universitaria, in 1977 (pp. 293-318). Unlike other early twentieth-century critics (e.g., Hurtado y Palencia, Northup), J.B. understood quite well the literary magnitude of LA. He sees *LR* as both a collective and an individual portrait of *lo español*; and *SUH*, though inferior to *LR*, as the expression of 'la voz interior y humana.' A study still worth reading.

B110 Bandera, Cesáreo, 'Respuesta a García Sarriá', *HR*, 46 (1978), 515-17.
A letter in which C.B. criticizes what he terms García Sarriá's tendency to simplify and ignore the complexity of LA's *opus*. See also B480, 481.

B111 ——, 'La sombra de Bonifacio Reyes en *Su único hijo*', *BHS*, 46 (1969), 201-25. Rpt. in B723, pp. 212-37.
An excellent analysis of the symbolic meaning implicit in what C.B. calls Bonifacio's antiheroic voyage through life and dubious paternity.

B112 Baquero Goyanes, Mariano, 'Alas, Leopoldo (Clarín)', in *Enciclopedia de la cultura española*, I (Madrid: Nacional, 1963), pp. 134-35.
A compact, well-written article. Signed M.B.G.

B113 ——, ' "Clarín", creador del cuento español', *Cuadernos de Literatura*, 5 (1949), 145-69. Extracted in B1297, pp. 607-13.
Gives a descriptive analysis of various types of Clarín stories. B.G. concludes that, unlike the dry, impersonal Maupassant, LA is an impassioned interpreter of life.

B114 ——, ' "Clarín", novelista', *Insula*, No. 76 (15.4.52), 1, 9-10.
LR is essentially a psychological novel, immersed in a pre-Proustian inner time and multiple images of the past and present.

B115 ——, ' "Clarín", novelista olvidado', *Revista de la Universidad de Oviedo*, [7] (1946), 137-45.
Uses the 1943 ed. of *Doña Berta, Cuervo, Supercheria* as a point of departure to reevaluate mainly the short stories of LA.

B116 ——, ' "Clarín" y la novela poética', *BBMP*, 23 (1947), 96-101.
A good discussion of what LA meant by the term, 'novela poética'. B.G. believes 'Doña Berta' is the best example.

B117 ——, *El cuento español en el siglo XIX* (Madrid: CSIC, 1949), pp. 328-41, 462-75, 531-36.

Situates LA's short stories within the categories of the religious and humoristic; and notes the role of the child, mainly in 'Pipá'. See also the index for other references.

B118 ——, 'Los "cuentos largos" de "Clarín"', *Los Cuadernos del Norte* (Oviedo), 2, No. 7 (May-June 1981), 68-71.
Relying on Judith Leibowitz' theory of the *novella*, M.B.G. discusses 'Doña Berta', 'Pipá', 'Las dos cajas', and other works as *novellas* and not as short stories in their structure.

B119 ——, 'Una edición de *Obras selectas* de Clarín', *Revista de la Universidad de Oviedo*, 8, Nos 45-46 (Sept.-Dec. 1947), 113-17.
A review-article. B.G. notes LA's intellectual flexibility and modernity. See Aa5.

B120 ——, 'Exaltación de lo vital en *La Regenta*', *Archivum*, 2 (1952), 189-219. Rpt. in his *Prosistas españoles contemporáneos* (Madrid: Rialp, 1956), pp. 127-72; and B723, pp. 157-78.
An early, still important, study of *LR* as the psychological conflict between *lo intelectual* and *lo vital.*

B121 ——, 'Introducción', *La Regenta* (see Ac18), pp. 9-59.

B122 ——, 'La literatura narrativa asturiana en el siglo XIX', *Revista de la Universidad de Oviedo*, 9, Nos 49-50 (Jan.-Apr. 1948), 81-99.
Considers LA, Palacio Valdés, and Juan Ochoa as the best representatives of Asturian humor and gentleness in writing.

B123 ——, 'Una novela de "Clarín": *Su único hijo*', *Anales de la Universidad de Murcia*, 10 (1951-52), 125-71. Rpt. as a pamphlet (Murcia: Universidad de Murcia, 1952), 55 pp.; and in his *Prosistas españoles contemporáneos*, pp. 33-125.
A fundamental essay on *SUH*. B.G. describes it as 'la novela más fríamente narrada de todo nuestro siglo XIX', in which satire and the grotesque predominate to create a caricaturized vision of an inauthentic and pseudoromantic Spain.
Reviews: .1. Helman, Edith. *HR*, 22 (1954), 81-84.
.2. Muñoz Cortés, M. *Archiv*, 189 (1953), 399.

B124 ——, 'La novela española en la segunda mitad del siglo XIX', in *Historia general de las literaturas hispánicas*, V

ed. Guillermo Díaz-Plaja (Barcelona: Barna, 1958), pp. 120-25.
Introductory pages.

B125 ——, *La novela española vista por Menéndez Pelayo* (Madrid: Nacional, 1956), pp. 200-02.
Prints excerpts from Menéndez Pelayo's correspondence, in which he gives his opinion of *SUH* and *LR*.

B126 ——, 'Prólogo', *Cuentos* (see Ad28), pp. 9-23. Rpt. in B723, pp. 245-52.

B127 ——, 'Valle-Inclán y lo valleinclanesco', in his *Temas, formas y tonos literarios* (Madrid: Prensa Española, 1972), pp. 220, 239.
Refers to el *pre-valleinclanismo* of Clarín's stories.

——: See also Anon., B1325.

B128 Baragaño, Manuela, '*La Regenta*, por primera vez en escena', *El Alcázar* (19.11.83).
On the actors' enthusiasm and energy as they prepare for *LR*'s stage adaptation (see Aj4).

B129 Barbáchano, Carlos, '*La Regenta* y el cine', *Los Cuadernos del Norte* (Oviedo), 5, No. 23 (Jan.-Feb. 1984), 77-81.
Rightly tears apart the vulgarized 1974 film version of *LR* (see Aj3).

B130 Barbero, Teresa, 'La Regenta', *EstLit*, No. 555 (1.1.75), 36-37.
A psychological analysis of Ana Ozores as a repressed individual, suffering from 'infantilismo psíquico'.

B131 Barcelo Jiménez, Juan, *Vida y obra de Federico Balart* (Murcia: Imp. Provincial, 1956), pp. 66-67, 192-93, 198-99.
Refers to the sometimes polemical relationship between LA and Balart. See also B106, 107.

B132 Barinaga y Ponce de León, Graziella, *Estudio crítico bio-gráfico de Emilio Bobadilla (Fray Candil)* (La Habana: Carasa y Cía, 1926), pp. 45-46.
On Fray Candil's quarrel with LA.

B133 Barja, César, *Libros y autores modernos: siglos XVIII y XIX*

(Los Angeles: Campbell's Book Store, 1933), pp. 367-76. 2nd ed. (New York: Las Américas, 1964), pp. 367-76. An introduction to LA's work.

B134 Barra, Eduardo de la, *El endecasílabo dactílico: crítica de una crítica del crítico Clarín* (Rosario: Est. Cromo-Litográfico de J. Ferrazini y Cía, 1895). 85 pp.
A response to LA's attack against Rubén Darío and his use of the hendecasyllable.

B135 *Barrio, Ana, 'Las colaboraciones de Clarín a *La Ilustración Ibérica*', unpubl. M.A. thesis, Univ. of Toulouse, 1975.

B136 Barroso Gil, Asunción, Alfonso Berlanga Reyes et al, *Introducción a la literatura española a través de los textos: siglos XVIII y XIX* (Madrid: Ediciones Istmo, 1980), pp. 311-39.
Elementary commentaries on *LR* and *SUH*, with special emphasis on an analysis of 'El Rana'.

B137 Barutell, Teresa, 'Retrato de Ana Ozores', *Argumentos* (Madrid), 8, Nos 63-64 (1984), 34-37.
A sketch of Ana's inner and outer life, relying heavily on other critics.

Batis, Huberto: See Lope, Juan M.

B138 Bauzá, Hugo F., 'El espiritualismo de "Clarín"', in *Estudios literarios*. Departamento de Letras: Trabajos de alumnos en los cursos de seminario, lectura y comentario de textos y clases prácticas, I (La Plata: Univ. Nacional, 1966), pp. 43-48.
Other than saying that LA has a 'mentalidad dialéctica', author offers little else.

B139 Bécarud, Jean, '*La Regenta* y la España de la Restauración', *CCLC*, No. 69 (Feb. 1963), 49-57. Rpt, rev., as a book, *"La Regenta" de Clarín y la Restauración* (Madrid: Taurus, 1964), 42 pp.; and in *De La Regenta al "Opus Dei"* (Madrid: Taurus, 1977), pp. 11-30.
A study of the interaction between the individuals and the specific social structure found in *LR*.
Review: .1. Pino, Juan del. *ArH*, 2a época, No. 123 (Jan.-Feb. 1964), 91-92.

B140 ——, 'Una segunda lectura de *La Regenta*', *Ínsula*, No. 451 (June 1984), 5.
LR does not fit into any predetermined classification.

B141 Bell, Aubrey F.G., *Contemporary Spanish Literature* (New York: Knopf, 1925), pp. 75-80.
A.B. believes *LR* is a flawed masterpiece, weighted down by an excessive materialism.

B142 Bello, Luis, 'Si Clarín volviera', *El Imparcial* (18.6.06).
A member of the Generation of 1898 looks at LA, one of an earlier generation.

B143 Benedetto, Antonio Di, 'Presentación', in Leopoldo Alas Mínguez' *África entera tocando el tan-tan* (Madrid: Altalena, 1981), pp. 9-11.
Influence of LA on his great grandnephew's often acerbic and absurdist stories.

Benet Goitia, Juan: See Chacel, Rosa.

Berlanga Reyes, Alfonso: See Barroso Gil, Asunción.

B144 Beser, Sergio, ed., *Clarín y "La Regenta"* (Barcelona: Ariel, 1982). 320 pp.
Introducción, pp. 9-93. S.B. situates *LR* within its literary and historical circumstances; discusses how short-story techniques are adapted and exploited; analyses the complexity of LA's naturalism; and comments on the use of literature and literary types in *LR*. Occasionally repetitive, but useful. Bibliography, pp. 89-93, needed updating. Contents: Af16, B13, 281, 334, 337, 826, 862, 952, 1146, 1161, 1268, 1283.
Review: .1. Sánchez Arnosi, Milagros. *Ínsula*, No. 434 (Jan. 1983), 9.

B145 ——, 'La crítica de Leopoldo Alas y la novela de su tiempo', in *Homenaje a Jaime Vicens Vives*, II (Barcelona: Univ., 1967), pp. 57-66. Extracted in B1297, pp. 613-19.
LA's criticism of the novel is illustrative of the empirical approach and can be divided into three different phases.
Review: .1. C[arlos] S[eco] S[errano]. *Índice Histórico Español*, 13 (1967), 142.

B146 ——, 'Documentos clarinianos', *Archivum*, 12 (1962), 507-26.
S.B. publishes six letters to Narciso Oller; and an obituary by Emilio Bobadilla. See Af21, B172.

B147 ——, 'En torno a un cuento olvidado de Leopoldo Alas', *CHA*, No. 231 (Mar. 1969), 526-48.
Examines and rpts an unfinished short story, 'Kant, perro viejo'.

B148 ——, 'Introducción', in *Leopoldo Alas: teoría y crítica de la novela española* (see Ab27), pp. 9-21.

B149 ——, *Leopoldo Alas, crítico literario* (Madrid: Gredos, 1968). 371 pp.
S.B. first worked on this theme in his M.A. thesis, 'Crítica literaria de Leopoldo Alas', Univ. de Barcelona, 1958 An excellent study of LA's criticism and his concept of the critic. Author underlines the degree to which the critical vision is paramount in LA's work, and how much of it is European in scope, though always in reference to things Spanish. Bibliography.
Reviews: .1. Brown, G.G. *BHS*, 47 (1970), 362-63.
.2. Davis, Gifford. *RR*, 62 (1971), 153-54.
.3. Debicki, Andrew P. *BA*, 43 (1969), 563.
.4. Dowling, John. *Hispania* (U.S.A.), 53 (1970), 149-50.
.5. Fernández de la Mora, Gonzalo (see B378).
.6. Godoy Gallardo, Eduardo. *Mapocho* (Santiago, Chile), No. 19 (Fall, 1969), 187-89.
.7. Jackson, Robert M. *MLN*, 86 (1971), 306-09.
.8. Kronik, John W. *HR*, 39 (1971), 329-34.
.9. LeBouill, J. *BH*, 71 (1969), 697-99.
.10. López-Morillas, Juan. *CLS*, 9 (1972), 234-37.
.11. Mathias, Julio. *EstLit*, No. 463 (1.3.71), 486.
.12. Mayoral, Marina. *CHA*, No. 230 (Feb. 1969), 458-63.
.13. Mayoral, Marina. *RO*, 2a época, No. 83 (1970), 97-103.

B150 ——, 'Leopoldo Alas o la continuidad de la Revolución', in *La Revolución de 1868 (Historia, pensamiento, literatura)*, ed. Clara E. Lida and Iris M. Zavala (New York: Las Américas, 1970), pp. 397-411.
Looks for examples of LA's enthusiasm toward the Revolution of 1868. Two elements appear repeatedly in LA's political articles: a questioning of the role of the masses in the Revolution and a search for the reasons why the Revolution ultimately failed.

B151 ——, 'El lugar de "Sinfonía de dos novelas" en la narrativa de L. Alas', in *Hispanic Studies in Honour of Frank Pierce*, ed. John England (Sheffield: Dept. of Hispanic Studies, Univ., 1980), pp. 17-30.

A significant article showing through previously unavailable correspondence with his publishers how LA's conception of *SUH* and 'Una medianía' underwent quite radical changes in structure. See also Af8, B1036.

B152 ——, '*Regenta (La)*', in *Diccionario literario*, IX, 2nd ed.,ed. González Porto-Pompiani (Barcelona: Montaner y Simón, 1967-68), pp. 72-73. 1st ed., 1959.
Remarks on the conflict between the individual (Ana) and society (Vetusta).

B153 ——, 'Siete cartas de Leopoldo Alas a José Yxart', *Archivum*, 10 (1960), 385-97.
Indicates parallels between LA and Yxart, who were born in the same year. See also Af32.
Review: .1. M[arco] R[evilla], J[oaquín]. *Índice Histórico Español*, 6 (1960), 550-51.

B154 ——, ' "Sinfonía de dos novelas." Fragmento de una novela de "Clarín" ', *Ínsula*, No. 167 (Oct. 1960), 1, 12. Rpt. in B723, pp. 238-44.
A noteworthy analysis of the unfinished sequel to *SUH*, 'Una medianía'.

B155 ——, '*Su único hijo*', in *Diccionario literario*, IX, 2nd ed. (see B152), pp. 877-78.
Bonifacio offers a parallel to Ana Ozores, but 'sin ninguno de sus atractivos'.

B156 —— & Laureano Bonet, 'Índice de colaboraciones de Leopoldo Alas en la prensa barcelonesa', *Archivum*, 16 (1966), 157-211.
An annotated index of LA's contributions to *Arte y Letras*, *La Ilustración Ibérica*, *La Publicidad*, *La Ilustración Artística*, *Pluma y Lápiz*, and *La Saeta*.

B157 Bianchini, Angela, 'L'eroica città', in her *Cent'anni di romanzo spagnolo 1868-1962* (Torino: Edizioni RAI Radiotelevisione Italiana, 1973), pp. 227-39.
Notes the leitmotifs of the city, the seasons, the tower, and the church in *LR*, as well as the sense of fatalism in the passing of the seasons.

B158 Biervliet d'Overbroeck, Malcolm D. van, 'The Early Polemics of José Martínez Ruiz', *Hispano*, No. 77 (Jan. 1983), 45-60.

Rpts, pp. 49-51, Dionisio de las Heras' public quarrel with Azorín (see B578) over the latter's conduct toward LA.

B159 Blanch, Antonio, '*La Regenta*, vigoroso relato de dos impotencias', *RyF*, No. 209 (May 1984), 537-42.
LR's characters as an example of the Spanish bourgeoisie's social and individual frustration and its shrinking from leadership and reform.

B160 Blanco Aguinaga, Carlos, Julio Rodríguez Puértolas, & Iris M. Zavala, *Historia social de la literatura española (en lengua castellana)*, II (Madrid: Castalia, 1978), pp. 152-57.
Emphasizes that LA, like Galdós, writes '*desde* la burguesía, pero *contra* esa misma burguesía.'

B161 Blanco García, Francisco, *La literatura española en el siglo XIX*, II, 3rd ed. (Madrid: Sáenz de Jubera, 1910), pp. 546-47, 603-04.
The now classic example of critical lopsided benightedness on the part of an Augustinian cleric who thought *LR* 'en el fondo rebosa de porquerías, vulgaridades y cinismo', and *SUH*, a 'monstruoso feto, verdadera pelota de escarabajo.'

B162 Blanquat, Josette, 'Clarín et Baudelaire', *RLC*, 33 (1959), 5-25.
A good comparative article on LA's attitudes toward, and interpretation of, Baudelaire.
Reviews: .1. Fongaro, A. *SFr*, 4 (1960), 176-77.
.2. M[arco] R[evilla], J[oaquín]. *Índice Histórico Español*, 5 (1959), 106.
.3. Martínez Cachero, José María. *BIDEA*, 13 (1959), 469-72.

B163 ——, 'L'Hommage de Clarín à un prélat asturien', *BH*, 68 (1966), 216-52.
Author studies LA's religious sensibility as expressed in an article dedicated to Father Ceferino González y Díaz Tuñón.

B164 ——, 'La Sensibilité religieuse de Clarín. Reflets de Goethe et de Leopardi', *RLC*, 35 (1961), 177-96.
J.B. analyses the unfinished story, 'Cuesta abajo', as an example of LA's obsession with the Virgin Mary and the maternal figure.
Reviews: .1. G[roult], P[ierre]. *Les Lettres Romanes*, 17 (1963), 283.
.2. López Jiménez, Luis. *RFE*, 48 (1965), 458-59.

B165 —— & Jean-François Botrel, 'Clarín y sus editores', in *Clarín y sus editores* (see Af8), pp. 5-7.

B166 *Blasco Ibáñez, Vicente, Unpublished correspondence to LA (16.2.95, 1900?, 17.1.01): in private archives of Don Gamallo Fierros (Madrid).
According to Paul Smith, *Vicente Blasco Ibáñez: an Annotated Bibliography*, Research Bibliographies and Checklists, 14 (London: Grant and Cutler, 1976), p. 34, 'BI asks Alas for opinion on *Arroz y tartana*; thanks him for letter concerning *Entre naranjos*; thanks him for his praise in "Palique" in *El Heraldo de Madrid*."

B167 Bobadilla, Emilio [pseud.: Fray Candil], 'A Clarín (Punto final)', *Madrid Cómico*, No. 469 (13.2.92), 6-7.
Fray Candil responds to LA's offer to duel with him. One of several literary quarrels LA sustained.

B168 ——, '¡Adiós, Anciano!', *Madrid Cómico*, No. 467 (30.1.92), 6-7.
An anti-Clarín attack. See also B167, 179, 180.

B169 ——, 'Baturrillo', *Madrid Cómico*, No. 242 (8.10.87), 3, 6.
Praises *Nueva campaña* and *Apolo en Pafos*.

B170 ——, 'Baturrillo', *Los Madriles*, No. 45 (10.8.89), 6-7.
On *A 0,50 poeta*.

B171 ——, *Capirotazos (Sátiras y críticas)* (Madrid: Fernando Fe, 1890), pp. 145-46, 298-99.
Reviews *A 0,50 poeta* and *Un discurso de Núñez de Arce*.

B172 ——, 'Clarín', *Madrid Cómico*, No. 25 (22.6.01), 199.
An obituary, rpt. in B146, pp. 524-26. Despite his quarrel with LA, E.B. still admires his work.

B173 ——, 'Clarín, histérico (Estudio patológico)', in his *Triquitraques* (Madrid: Fernando Fe, 1892), pp. 49-54.
Subjects LA to a satiric, psychological profile modeled on Lombroso.

B174 ——, *Escaramuzas* (Madrid: Fernando Fe, 1888), pp. 133-42, 206-08, 258-61.
Reviews favorably *Cánovas y su tiempo*, *Nueva campaña*, and *Apolo en Pafos*; and compares LA with Quevedo.

B175 ——, '*Estudios críticos* (Por U. González Serrano)', in *Triquitraques* (see B173), pp. 165-73.
E.B. does not agree with González Serrano's favorable judgment of *Un discurso.*

B176 ——, 'Un nuevo libro de Clarín', *Madrid Cómico*, No. 307 (5.1.89), 6-7.
On *Mezclilla.*

B177 ——, 'Riña de gallos', in *Triquitraques* (see B173), pp. 109-14.
Refers to the quarrel between LA and Pardo Bazán and between LA and critic Luis Alfonso of *La Época.*

B178 ——, '*Su único hijo* (Por Leopoldo Alas)', in *Triquitraques* (see B173), pp. 193-214. Rpt. in *Crítica y sátira*, II (La Habana: Univ., 1964), pp. 161-81.
SUH is an anemic, tedious novel, which imitates *Mme Bovary.* Also attacks LA's syntax.

B179 ——, 'La última palabra (A Clarín)', *Madrid Cómico*, No. 471 (27.2.92), 7.
A short piece, in which E.B. states that if LA wants a duel, he can have one.

B180 ——, 'Veleidades de Clarín', *Madrid Cómico*, No. 464 (9.1.92), 6.
More anti-Clarín.

B181 Bobes Naves, María del Carmen, 'Los espacios novelescos en *La Regenta*', *Los Cuadernos del Norte* (Oviedo), 5, No. 23 (Jan.-Feb. 1984), 51-57.
On physical, social and psychological space and its metaphorical, metonymic, and iconic relationship with the main characters.

B182 ——, 'Significado y función de los personajes secundarios, en la novela cumbre de Leopoldo Alas', *Argumentos* (Madrid), 8, Nos 63-64 (1984), 22-26.
Secondary characters in *LR* serve as a counterpoint to the protagonists and as emblems of realism.

B183 *Boletín de Información Municipal del Excmo Ayuntamiento de Oviedo*, No. 6 (June 1981).
Homage to Clarín on the 80th anniversary of his death. Contains the

Ayuntamiento's minutes of 2 July 1887 and 20 June 1891, in which LA participated; the declaration of a 'Jornada Clariniana' on 13 June 1981, along with words of homage by Manuel F. Avello; assigns names of characters from *LR* to streets; and rpts 1981 newspaper articles on LA. Contents: B45, 66, 99, 302, 391, 393, 540, 724, 917, 1043, 1165, 1250, 1314, 1319, 1345, 1369, 1370.

B184 Bonafoux [y Quintero], Luis [pseud.: Aramís], 'Algunas palabritas...', in his *Coba* (Madrid: Imprenta Popular, 1889), pp. vii-xiii.
Mockingly suggests Oviedo put up a statue to LA, Aramís' arch-enemy, to whom *Coba* is dedicated (pp. v-vi).

B185 ——, 'Clarín, folletista', in his *Literatura de Bonafoux* (Madrid: Tip. de Manuel Ginés Hernández, 1887), pp. 228-36.
Apparently first published in **El Español* (Apr. 1887). On *Cánovas y su tiempo*, a silly work, says Aramís.

B186 ——, 'Corzuelo incapaz...', in his *Huellas literarias* (Paris: Garnier, 1894), pp. 7-11.
Andrés Corzuelo's praise of *SUH* is most unfortunate, says B., since the novel is really very poor. See also Ag131, B79, 80.

B187 ——, '*Doña Berta, Cuervo, Superchería*', in *Huellas literarias* (see B186), pp. 119-27.
Another nasty attack on LA's writing.

B188 ——, 'Explosión de un traductor', in his *Bilis* (Paris: Sociedad de Ediciones Literarias y Artísticas, 1908), pp. 265-70. Rpt. in B208, pp. 183-88, by Botrel, who notes that the article first appeared in *El Heraldo de París*, No. 33 (22.6.01), 1-2.
In this obituary, Aramís maintains his enmity toward Clarín. See also B326.

B189 ——, 'Más sobre don Leopoldo', in *Coba* (see B184), pp. 182-85.
Attacks LA, whom Aramís calls 'D. Leopoldo I El Egregio', for his bad writing. Aramís is convinced LA is 'una de las grandes calamidades de la patria'.

B190 ——, 'Novelistas tontos. Don Leopoldo Alas (a) Clarín', in *Literatura de Bonafoux* (see B185), pp. 218-27.
Apparently first published in **El Español* (Apr. 1887). *LR* is absurd and silly. It is here that L.B. first accuses LA of plagiarism.

B191 *——, 'Suscripción', *La Campaña* (Paris) (29.4.1900). Rpt.
in B208, pp. 178-79.
L.B.'s mocking attack on LA's economic difficulties.

B192 *——, 'Suscripción', *El Heraldo de París*, No. 5 (18.11.1900).
Rpt. in B208, p. 180.
Another satiric attack on LA's pecuniary problems.

B193 ——, *Yo y el plagiario Clarín. Tiquis-miquis de Luis Bonafoux*
(Madrid: Administración, 1888). 74 pp. Rpt. in *Huellas lite-*
rarias (see B186), pp. 357-415.
The now infamous piece on LA's supposed plagiarism of Flaubert in
LR and 'Zurita', and of Fernanflor in 'Pipá'.

B194 Bonet, Laureano, 'Clarín ante la crisis de 1898', *RO*, 2a
época, 25 (1969), 100-19.
An interesting article on LA's sometimes ambiguous attitudes toward
the disaster of 1898. L.B. comments on LA's pragmatic Republicanism
and his emphasis on a cultural Hispanism, rather than on administrative or colonial ties between Spain and Cuba.

B195 ——, ' "Clarín" en imágenes múltiples: una antología de
José María Martínez Cachero', *Ínsula*, Nos 392-93 (July-
Aug. 1979), 10.
A favorable review-article of B723.

B196 ——, ' "Clarín" entre el romanticismo y el modernismo:
una nueva edición de *Su único hijo*', *Ínsula*, No. 406 (Sept.
1980), 1, 11-12.
Reviews favorably Richmond's ed. (see Ac33); and gives an interesting
discussion of LA's *fin de siècle* tendencies and how they anticipate
el modernismo.

B197 ——, ' "Clarín", periodista: un estudio y antología de
Yvan Lissorgues', *Ínsula*, No. 418 (Sept. 1981), 1, 14.
Review-article on Ab30, in which L.B. judiciously points out that
'ante un escritor es erróneo mantener una frontera discriminatoria
entre obras mayores y obras menores.'

B198 ——, 'Clarín y el espíritu de la modernidad: una antología
de Carolyn Richmond', *Ínsula*, No. 446 (Jan. 1984), 1, 15.
Review-article on Ad39.

B199 ——, 'Clarín y la función de la crítica', *Ínsula*, No. 342 (May 1975), 12-13.
A review-article on *Obra olvidada* (see Ab29) and the 1973 ed. of *Palique* (see Ab23). Author believes these editions are especially good because they illustrate 'el último Clarín' in his criticism.

B200 ——, *De Galdós a Robbe-Grillet* (Madrid: Taurus, 1972), pp. 47-50, 53-57, 79-94.
Discusses LA's position on the utility of the narrative form, the question of verisimilitude, and the notion of 'la novela teatral'.

B201 ——, ed., 'Introducción', in *Emile Zola: el naturalismo* (Barcelona: Península, 1972), pp. 7-24.
LA's work on naturalism is cited throughout most of this introduction to Zola's essays.

B202 ——, 'La música como voz callada en *La Regenta*: un rastreo léxico', *Los Cuadernos del Norte* (Oviedo), 5, No. 23 (Jan.-Feb. 1984), 64-69.
Examples of the *fin de siècle* literary use of music as a means to express and stimulate ineffable, subjective states of mind and mood.

——: See also Beser, Sergio.

B203 Boring, Phyllis Z., 'Some Reflections on Clarín's *Doña Berta*', *RomN*, 11 (1969-70), 322-25.
Points out parallels between *Doña Berta* and Maupassant's *Une vie*; and between Doña Berta and Don Quijote.

B204 Botrel, Jean-François, 'Clarín, el dinero y la literatura', *Los Cuadernos del Norte* (Oviedo), 2, No. 7 (May-June 1981), 78-82.
Citing from LA's correspondence with his publisher, M. Fernández Lasanta and others, J.F.B. discusses LA's love-hate relationship with money as a symbol of both his independence and dependence as a writer. See also Af8.

B205 ——, ed., 'Introducción', in *Preludios de "Clarín"* (see Ab28), pp. xiii-lxxiii. Extracted in B1297, pp. 619-22.

B206 ——, 'Producción literaria y rentabilidad: el caso de "Clarín"', in *Hommage des hispanistes français à Noël Salomon* (Barcelona: Laia, for Société des Hispanistes Français, 1979), pp. 123-33.

An extremely interesting article on LA's worth in the literary market-place. See also Af7, B204.

B207　——, 'Un prólogo olvidado de Clarín', *Los Cuadernos del Norte* (Oviedo), 2, No. 7 (May-June 1981), 83.
Rpts prologue to *Cuentos droláticos*, Ag3.

B208　——, 'Últimos ataques de Bonafoux a "Clarín" ', *Archivum*, 18 (1968), 177-88.
Discusses and rpts some of Bonafoux's later attacks on LA, published in *La Campaña* and *El Heraldo de París*. See also B188, 191, 192.

——: See also Blanquat, Josette.

B209　Bouma, Frederick John, 'The Structure of the Short Stories of Leopoldo Alas, Clarín', unpubl. diss., Univ. of Illinois at Urbana-Champaign, 1969. 182 pp. Abstracted in *DAI*, 30 (1969-70), 3449-A.
Analyses the beginnings; expositions and entanglements; and climaxes, dénouements, and endings of LA's stories. Concludes that LA's use of these elements is basically conventional, and that he was primarily interested in his characters.

B210　Bravo-Villasante, Carmen, *Vida y obra de Emilia Pardo Bazán* (Madrid: Revista de Occidente, 1962), pp. 136-38, 176-79.
Relates the reasons for LA's quarrel with Pardo Bazán, and believes that despite the break, he still admired her work. See also Af23.

B211　Brent, Albert, *Leopoldo Alas and "La Regenta". A Study in Nineteenth Century Spanish Prose Fiction*, Univ. of Missouri Studies, 24, No. 2 (Columbia, 1951), 135 pp.
Originally a diss., 'Leopoldo Alas and the Novel from 1875 to 1885 (A Critical Analysis of *La Regenta*)' (Princeton Univ., 1949, 234 pp.). Of limited usefulness. H.B. Hall observes it is more expository than critical; and both Hall and Helman note the oversimplification in analysing *LR* as an autobiographical novel of frustration.
Reviews:　.1. Avrett, Robert. *MLJ*, 39 (1955), 330.
　　　　　.2. Bull, William E. *Hispania* (U.S.A.), 35 (1952), 255-56.
　　　　　.3. Hall, H.B. *BHS*, 29 (1952), 122-23.
　　　　　.4. Helman, Edith F. *HR*, 20 (1952), 347-50.
　　　　　.5. R.G. *CHA*, No. 38 (Feb. 1953), 219-20.
　　　　　.6. Santullano, Luis. *Ínsula*, No. 76 (Apr. 1952), 4.

B212 Brown, Donald F., 'Successive Variations on the Theme of the Priest in Love', *TAH*, 4, Nos 34-35 (Mar.-Apr. 1979), 8-10.
Goes over old ground discussing Fermín's relationship with his mother in *LR*.

B213 Brown, G.G., 'Introduction', in *Cuentos escogidos* (see Ad31), pp. 7-36.

B214 *——, 'The Novels and *cuentos* of Leopoldo Alas', unpubl. diss., Univ. of Oxford, 1963.

B215 Bryan, T. Avril, 'Un estudio de la religión en *La Regenta*', *Humanitas* (Nuevo León), 15 (1974), 435-44.
A rather superficial study, which offers nothing new.

B216 Bull, William Emerson, 'Clarín: an Analytical Study of a Literary Critic', unpubl. diss., Univ. of Wisconsin, 1941. 264 pp.
A rather distorted view of LA as a conservative writer. W.E.B. presents the critic in isolation from his times and judges him from a 1940 perspective. Parts of the diss. were published as articles (see B217, 218, 219, 220).

B217 ——, 'Clarín and his Critics', *MLF*, 35 (1950), 103-11.
Gives examples of contemporary and later critical opinions of LA's significance.

B218 ——, 'Clarín's Literary Internationalism', *HR*, 16 (1948), 321-34.
This article inaugurated, though with a somewhat questionable approach, the series of studies dedicated to LA's relations to non-Spanish writers. W.E.B. uses 'quantitative analysis' to indicate Clarín's knowledge of foreign literature, but does not really evaluate the relationship.
Review: .1. Santullano, Luis. *Ínsula*, No. 76 (Apr. 1952), 4.

B219 ——, 'The Liberalism of Leopoldo Alas', *HR*, 10 (1942), 329-39.
LA is really a conservative, says W.E.B.

B220 ——, 'The Naturalistic Theories of Leopoldo Alas', *PMLA*, 57 (1942), 536-51.
Apparently also printed as *'Las teorías naturalistas de Leopoldo

Alas', *Europe* (Paris), Nos 14-16 (Apr.-June 1941); but I have been unable to locate this. W.E.B. notes LA's reservations on the subject of naturalism. He concludes that Clarín is really a realist writer, and not a naturalist.

B221 Bull, William E., & Vernon A. Chamberlin, *Clarín: the Critic in Action*, Oklahoma State Univ. Publications, 60, no. 9 (Stillwater, 1963). 64 pp.
Authors discuss LA's differing critical treatment of his peers and beginners, as an example of his personal approach to literary criticism and of his dual personality. One notes in this book a tendency to distort and downplay LA's worth as a critic.
Reviews: .1. Gramberg, Eduard J. *Hispania* (U.S.A.), 48 (1965), 178.
.2. Kronik, John W. *Hispano*, No. 25 (Sept. 1965), 57-62.
.3. Pattison, Walter T. *HR*, 34 (1966), 192-93.

B222 Bustillo, Eduardo, 'Los teatros', *La Ilustración Española y Americana*, 39, No. 12 (30.3.95), 198-99. Rpt. in B734, pp. 270-72.
On *Teresa*, which E.B. calls a character play.

Buylla, Adolfo: See Álvarez Buylla, Adolfo.

B223 Buylla, José, 'Concepto del derecho en D. Leopoldo Alas', *Renacimiento Latino*, 1, No. 1 (Apr. 1905), 56-61.
One of LA's former students reconstructs his concept of the law: 'El derecho es una actividad en todos los sentidos. No hay objeto alguno con que pueda relacionarse la idea del derecho, que no sea jurídico.'

B224 Cabal, C., 'Esta vez era un hombre de Laviana', *BIDEA*, 7 (1953), 178-85, 189-97, 220-33.
On the friendship of Tomás Tuero, Palacio Valdés, and LA.

B225 *Cabezas, Juan Antonio, 'Centenario de Clarín', in *Oviedo*, 1951 ed., p. 3.
Cited by Martínez Cachero, B714, p. 95.

B226 *——, 'Centenario de Clarín', *Revista Oviedo* (San Mateo) (1951), 53.

B227 ——, 'El centenario de "Clarín"', *España* (Tánger) (3.3.52), 3.
Reviews some recent publications of 1952, which reaffirm J.A.C.'s judgment that LA is a 'provinciano universal'.

B228 ——, ' "Clarín", con aspiraciones políticas en la Restauración canovista', *ABC* (6.4.75).
Reviews the LA - Castelar correspondence and relationship; and LA's disillusionment with Restoration politics.

B229 ——, *"Clarín", el provinciano universal* (Madrid: Espasa-Calpe, 1936). 244 pp. 2nd ed. (1962), 229 pp.
The standard, though not definitive, biography.

B230 ——, ' "Clarín" en su paisaje', *Asturias* (Madrid), No. 13 (Apr. 1952), 9.
Extract from B229.

B231 ——, 'Clarín, un provinciano universal', *El Sol* (Madrid) (13.6.35), 5.
Reflections on the Clarinian landscape of Guimarán; LA's spiritual restlessness c. 1890.

B232 ——, 'Clarín vivo', *BIDEA*, 29 (1975), 461-74.
Discusses the reasons for writing a biography of LA.

B233 ——, ' "Clarín", vivo. La casa de Guimarán y Oviedo. Su vida y su crisis moral', *Índice de Artes y Letras*, No. 51 (15.5.52), 5-6.
Biographical details.

B234 ——, 'Cómo nació la primera biografía de "Clarín". Memorias de "El Provinciano Universal" ', *Los Cuadernos del Norte* (Oviedo), 2, No. 7 (May-June 1981), 98-103.
Tells how he researched for the Clarín biography, and about the curious events surrounding its publication.

B235 ——, 'Cosas de Clarín', *ABC* (27.1.46).
Anecdotes about LA's irascible temperament.

B236 ——, 'Estanislao Sánchez-Calvo: un filósofo y filólogo olvidado', *El Español*, No. 204 (21.9.46), 4.
LA was an astute and appreciative critic of Sánchez-Calvo's work.

B237 ——, 'El fusilamiento de Leopoldo Alas', *Asturias Semanal*, No. 353 (13-20.3.76), 23-25.
On the execution of LA's son in 1937.

B238 ——, 'Prólogo biográfico', in *Obras selectas* (see Aa5), pp. vii-xlvii.

A condensed version of B229.

B239   ——, '*La Regenta* y sus enemigos', *Argumentos* (Madrid), 8, Nos 63-64 (1984), 44-47.
On the initial local reaction to *LR*. Rpts LA's letter (11.5.85) to Martínez Vigil. See Af13.

B240   Cabo Martínez, María Rosa, 'La amistad entre Clarín y Zorrilla', *BIDEA*, 35 (1981), 277-79.
Rpts a letter from LA to Z. found in the Casa de Zorrilla de Valladolid. See Af34.

B241   Canals, Salvador, 'Después de la lectura. "Clarín" y el martirio de *Teresa*, o berrinches mal reprimidos', *El Diario del Teatro*, No. 92 (7.4.95), 1; No. 94 (21.4.95), 1. Rpt. in *El año teatral, 1895-6* (Madrid: Est. tip. de El Nacional, 1896), pp. 102-04; and in B734, pp. 260-70.
Criticizes the play for its ideological defects.

B242   ——, 'En Asturias. Colmena intelectual', *El Español* (29.1.1900).
Discusses the Asturian intellectual community: Altamira, Sela, Aramburu, Buylla, LA.

B243   ——, 'El ensayo de "Clarín"', *El Diario del Teatro*, No. 84 (21.3.95), 1. Rpt. in *El año teatral, 1895-6* (Madrid: Est. tip. de El Nacional, 1896), pp. 97-101; and in B734, pp. 256-60.
On *Teresa* and its fatal flaw as a thesis play.

B244   [Canals, Salvador], 'Polémicas literarias. Un cuento ruidoso de la Pardo Bazán y un estrepitoso drama de "Clarín"', *Nuevo Mundo*, 2, No. 67 (18.4.95), 14.
Comments on LA's lamentable effort to defend *Teresa* against his enemies.

B245   Cándido [pseud.], 'Aparece un humorista', in *El asesinato de Clarín y otras ficciones* (see B877), pp. 9-10.
The Asturian Francisco G. Orejas' irony and intellectual humor in his stories reveal the strong influence of LA.

B246   Canella y Secades, Fermín, *Historia de la Universidad de Oviedo y noticias de los establecimientos de enseñanza*

de su distrito, 2nd ed. (Oviedo: Imprenta de Flórez, Gusano y Cía, 1903), pp. 244-45, 258, 729.
Comments on the great outpouring of grief after LA's death.

B247 *Cañete, Manuel, '[Carta literaria?]', *Diario de la Marina* (La Habana) (30.5.85).
Contains harsh words on *LR*.

B247 bis Cañizal de la Fuente, Luis, 'Antonio Gala trasplanta una situación de *La Regenta*', *Ínsula*, No. 406 (Sept. 1980), 3, 14.
Points out Gala's complex iconoclastic-admiring attitude toward *LR* when he incorporates part of it – the mother-son relationship – into *Los buenos días perdidos* (1976).

B248 Cantelly, Juan, 'Anecdotario del autor y sus personajes – Clarín en Oviedo – Hace 43 años de su muerte y 60 que nació *La Regenta* – El secreto y el pateo histórico de *Teresa*', *El Español*, No. 89 (8.7.44), 5.
On the reactions provoked by *LR* and *Teresa*.

B249 Caramés, Francisco, 'Enalteciendo a "Clarín"', *Libertad* (5.5.31), 3-4.
Recounts the inauguration of a monument dedicated to LA in the Parque de San Francisco, Oviedo.

B250 Cardenal Iracheta, M., 'Seis cartas inéditas de "Clarín" a Castelar', *BBMP*, 24 (1948), 92-96.
On LA's support of Castelar's political position. See Af4.

B251 Cardwell, Richard A., *Juan R. Jiménez: the Modernist Apprenticeship 1895-1900* (Berlin: Colloquium Verlag, 1977), pp. 53-54, 69, 70, 74-75, 89-90, 92, 147, 194, *et passim.*
On LA's role as a critic and disseminator of French literary ideas during J.R. Jiménez's youth.

B252 Carenas, Francisco, '¿Anticlericalismo en *La Regenta* de Clarín?', *Norte* (Amsterdam), 10, No. 1 (1969), 1-7.
LA's satire of individual abuses in the church does not constitute an anticlerical stance in *LR*, since it does not strike at the heart of the problem, the question of religious belief itself. F.C. appears to be faulting *LR* because it does not conform to the critic's vision of an authentic anticlerical point of view.

B253 Carnicer, Ramón, 'La etapa de Leopoldo Alas en la Universidad de Zaragoza', *Ínsula*, Nos 284-85 (July-Aug. 1970), 27.
Discusses some of the documents contained in the 'Expediente de D. Leopoldo García Alas, catedrático de derecho', found in the archives of the Univ. de Zaragoza.

B254 Carreño, Orlando, ' "Clarín", el escritor y el público', *Los Cuadernos del Norte* (Oviedo), 5, No. 23 (Jan.-Feb. 1984), 48-50.
Goes over old ground, using the sociology-of-literature approach to LA.

B255 Carretero, Tomás, 'Don Leopoldo Alas', *Madrid Cómico*, No. 25 (22.6.01), 199.
An obituary.

B256 Casar, Eduardo, 'Realismo y crítica literaria: los Solos de Clarín', *Plural*, 2a época, 8, No. 93 (1979), 22-28.
Indicates parallels between LA's perception of applied esthetics and Hegel's.

Cascales Muñoz, José: See León Sánchez, Manuel.

B257 Casielles, Ricardo, 'Mi dolor', *Revista Popular* (Oviedo) (1.7.01), 17.
A poetic composition dedicated to LA.

B258 Castañón, Luciano, 'Bibliografía de novelas asturianas', *BIDEA*, 24 (1970), 83-103.
Cites *LR*, *SUH*, 'Doña Berta' (pp. 86-87).

B259 ——, 'Referencias a la vaca en la literatura asturiana, sus nombres', *Archivum*, 22 (1972), 211-23.
Includes '¡Adiós, Cordera! ' (pp. 211-12).

B260 Castro, José P., 'Un epistolario y unas cartas: Menéndez Pelayo, Martínez Vigil, la Universidad de Oviedo', *BBMP*, 27 (1952), 7-29.
Discusses LA's role in Menéndez Pelayo's political career.

B261 Cavia, Mariano de, 'El desquite de doña Berta', *El Imparcial* (30.12.10).
Humorously refers to 'Doña Berta' and her fatal accident in the congested streets of Madrid.

B262 Caviglia, John Lawrence, 'Flaubert and Leopoldo Alas: an

Essay in Comparative Anatomy', unpubl. diss., Indiana
Univ., 1970. 232 pp. Abstracted in *DAI*, 31 (1970-71),
6047-A.

Compares the use of symbolic geography found in *LR* to the same
use in *La Tentation de Saint Antoine, Salammbô*, and *Mme Bovary*.

B263   Cayuela, Arturo María, 'Efectivamente ... (A propósito del
centenario de "Clarín")', *Cristiandad* (Barcelona), Nos 201-
02 (Aug. 1952), 302-03.

Attacks LA as an anti-Christian author.

B264   Cejador y Frauca, Julio, *Historia de la lengua y literatura
castellana*, IX (Madrid: Tip. de la Revista de Archivos,
Bibliotecas y Museos, 1918), pp. 263-70.

Gives an overview of LA's writings.

B265   ——, 'El modelo del casticismo', *El Imparcial* (13.8.06).

On LA's regret over the anticlerical position of his youth.

Cela, Camilo José: See Chacel, Rosa.

B266   Cesareo, G.A., 'Rassegna delle letterature straniere (spagnuola).
Due libri di versi di José Zorrilla – Un dramma di José
Echegaray – Un volume di critica di Leopoldo Alas', *Nuova
Antologia di Scienze, Lettere ed Arti* (Roma), 3rd series, 19
(16.2.89), 829-40.

Favorably reviews LA's essays in *Mezclilla*, though the critic believes
Clarín places too much emphasis on French literature.

B267   ——, 'Rassegna delle letterature straniere (spagnuola). Il
naturalismo nel romanzo spagnuolo', *Nuova Antologia di
Scienze, Lettere ed Arti* (Roma), 3rd series, 14 (16.3.88),
323-39.

G.A.C. criticizes two weaknesses he finds in *LR*: the lack of unity
and proportion; and the vacillating, undefined characters (see also
B30).

B268   ——, 'Rassegna di letteratura straniere (spagnuola). Una
novella in versi di don R. de Campoamor – La poesia
d'alcove in Ispagna – Critica e critici – Leopoldo Alas –
Strenne illustrate', *Nuova Antologia di Scienze, Lettere ed
Arti* (Roma), 3rd series, 12 (16.12.87), 740-53.

A mostly positive evaluation of LA as a critic.

B269 Chacel, Rosa et al, 'Encuesta sobre *La Regenta*', *Ínsula*, No. 451 (June 1984), 1, 8-9.

Respondents are: R.C., Camilo José Cela, Gonzalo Torrente Ballester, Lourdes Ortiz, Juan García Hortelano, Miguel Delibes, Juan Benet Goitia, Carmen Martín Gaite, Jesús Fernández Santos, and Francisco García Pavón. Questions asked: when did you first read *LR* and what struck you most about it; and what is *LR*'s significance today?

Chamberlin, Vernon A.: See Bull, William E.

B270 Champsaur, Baltasar, 'Clarín y la enseñanza laica', *Revista de España*, 137 (1891), 291-306.

B.C. criticizes *Un discurso* for what he considers a grave misunderstanding and rejection of lay education on LA's part.

B271 ——, '*Su único hijo* por Leopoldo Alas', *Revista Contemporánea*, No. 84 (30.12.91), 615-32.

Beyond the long plot summary of *SUH*, there are some interesting, though at times negative, remarks by a contemporary of LA.

B272 Chandler, Richard E., & Kessel Schwartz, *A New History of Spanish Literature* (Baton Rouge: Louisiana State Univ. Press, 1961), pp. 220-22, 547-49. 3rd ed., 1967.

Introductory pages on LA as novelist and critic.

B273 Charnon-Deutsch, [Mary] Lou[ise], 'El espacio ficticio en *Doña Berta*', in *Estructura y espacio en la novela y en la poesía*. Seminario Ricardo Gullón (Sacramento, Calif.: Hispanic Press, 1980), pp. 113-23.

On the complexity of literary space and its relationship with the personality of Doña Berta as the projection or extension of that space.

B274 ——, 'The Short Fiction of Leopoldo Alas, "Clarín"', unpubl. diss., Univ. of Chicago, 1978, 219 pp. Abstracted in *DAI*, 39 (1978-79), 2314-A.

Analyses the structural features of ninety of LA's short stories.

B275 Cigarroa, Barbara Judith, 'The Conceptual Transformation of the Characters and Events of *La Regenta* in *Fortunata y Jacinta*', unpubl. senior honors thesis, Harvard Univ., 1978. 50 pp.

Galdós's reading of *LR* evidently stimulated his major work. Sees

Fortunata as 'Ana turned inside out' and the themes of both novels as antithetical.

B276 Cimorra, Clemente, 'Es hora de decir ...', *Asturias* (Buenos Aires), No. 339 (Apr. 1952), 6.
Says that it is time to judge LA as one of the masters.

B277 Ciplijauskaité, Biruté, 'Don Fermín, ¿anti-modelo de don Magín?', in *Actas del VII Congreso de la Asociación Internacional de Hispanistas*, ed. Giuseppe Bellini (Roma: Bulzoni Editore, 1982), pp. 307-15.
Contrastive study based on Harold Bloom's idea that writers assimilate their literary heritage of the past generation with the express desire of avoiding it. Hence, Miró's don Magín, who seems to be the complete opposite of don Fermín.

B278 ——, *La mujer insatisfecha. El adulterio en la novela realista* (Barcelona: Edhasa, 1984), pp. 43-98.
A comparative analysis of *LR*, *Madame Bovary*, *Anna Karenina*, and *Effi Briest*, focussing on: the motif of escape; autobiographical elements; structure; authorial perspective; the character of the adulteress; the don Juan type; and the deceived husband.

B279 ——, 'El narrador, la ironía, la mujer: perspectivas del XIX y del XX', in *Homenaje a Juan López-Morillas. De Cadalso a Aleixandre: estudios sobre literatura e historia intelectual españolas*, ed. José Amor y Vázquez and A. David Kossoff (Madrid: Castalia, 1982), pp. 129-49.
Uses *LR* (pp. 137-41) as an example of how LA's compassion for Ana as a victim of society comes through indirectly by using irony mainly against the male characters.

B280 Clavería, Carlos, ' "Clarín" y Renán', in his *Cinco estudios de literatura española moderna* (Salamanca: CSIC, 1945), pp. 31-45.
Emphasizes LA's own subjective interpretation of Renan and his spiritual eclecticism.

B281 ——, 'Flaubert y *La Regenta*', *HR*, 10 (1942), 116-25. Rpt. in *Cinco estudios* (see B280), pp. 11-28; in B144, pp. 165-83; and B723, pp. 179-93. Extracted in B1297, pp. 572-77.
Concentrates on parallels between the female protagonists of *LR*

and *Mme Bovary*, their boredom, romanticism, and inability to see reality as it is.

B282 ——, 'Una nueva carta de Clarín sobre *Teresa*', *HR*, 18 (1950), 163-68.
In a letter to Luis París, LA talks of his lifelong interest in theater and of his desire to write new, experimental drama. C.C. transcribes only two paragraphs of the letter.

B283 ——, '*La Teresa*, de "Clarín" ', *Ínsula*, No. 76 (15.4.52), 1, 4. Rpt. in B723, pp. 101-04.
Discusses the public's inability to comprehend LA's play.

B284 Clocchiatti, Emilio, ' "Clarín" y sus ideas sobre la novela', *Revista de la Universidad de Oviedo*, 9, Nos 53-54 (May-Aug. 1948), 5-28; 10, Nos 57-58 (Sept.-Dec. 1948), 41-78; 10, Nos 59-60 (Jan.-Dec. 1949), 37-72. Rpt. as *Leopoldo Alas "Clarín": su crítica y estética* (Québec: Ediciones La Crítica, 1949). 218 pp.
A general, not particularly incisive, study of LA's relationship with his contemporaries and his conception of the novel.

B285 ——, 'Miguel de Unamuno y sus cartas a Clarín', *MLJ*, 34 (1950), 646-49.
On Unamuno's religious affinities with LA and his disappointment over LA's failure to criticize *Paz en la guerra* and to appreciate *Tres ensayos*.

B285 bis Comas, Antonio, 'Introducción', in *Su único hijo* (see Ac30), pp. 7-18.

B286 Conde Gargollo, Enrique, ' "Clarín", universitario', *Ínsula*, No. 167 (Oct. 1960), 12, 16.
On LA's love of teaching and his efforts to obtain a university position.

B287 Cordero, Lorenzo, 'Clarín, político', *Asturias Semanal*, No. 165 (29.7.72), 4-5.
Contains a review of *Preludios de Clarín* (see Ab28) and an interview with its editor, J.-F. Botrel.

B288 ——, 'Gonzalo Suárez: la película de *La Regenta* conservará fresco el vientecillo de Vetusta', *Asturias Semanal*, No. 249 (9.3.74), 16-18.

Interview with Suárez, the director of the film.

B289   Correa, Gustavo, 'El Bovarysmo y la novela realista española', *AGald*, 17 (1982), 25-32.
Reviews Jules de Gaultier's notion of *bovarysme* in several Galdós novels and *LR*.

Correa Calderón, E.: See Lázaro Carreter, F.

B290   Correa Rodríguez, P[edro], 'Clarín (Leopoldo Alas y Ureña)', in *Gran Enciclopedia Rialp*, V (Madrid: Rialp, 1981), pp. 735-36. Also in 1971 ed.
Introductory material.

B291   *El Correo de Asturias* (Oviedo) (12.6.16).
A homage issue.

B292   Cortón, Antonio, ' ¡Sépase quién es "Clarín"! ', in his *Pande-monium (Crítica y sátira)* (Madrid: Victoriano Suárez, 1889), pp. 549-69.
A harsh anti-Clarín satire on the supposedly ungrammatical, obscene *LR*.

B293   Cossío, Francisco de, 'Evolución literaria', *ABC* (9.11.73), n. pag.
A dreadful article, replete with errors of fact and of judgment. See B1091, for a reply to Cossío.

B294   Cossío, Pedro, 'Cuestión gramatical', *Revista Nacional de Literatura y Ciencias Sociales* (Montevideo), No. 53 (10.8.97), 73.
Refers to LA's judgment of Latin-American literature and the use of gallicisms in it.

Cristóbal, Manuel [pseud.] : See Granell, Manuel, B544.

B295   Cruz Rueda, Ángel, 'La amistad con Tuero y Clarín', in his *Armando Palacio Valdés. Su vida y su obra*, 2nd ed., aumentada (Madrid: Saeta, 1949), pp. 68-76.
Gives biographical details on LA, his friendship with Palacio Valdés and Tomás Tuero, and their experiences in Madrid.

B296   *Los Cuadernos del Norte* (Oviedo), 2, No. 7 (May-June 1981).
Homage issue. Contents: B6, 37, 47, 90, 118, 204, 207, 234, 390, 494, 656, 729, 797, 925, 1026, 1105, 1109, 1163, 1243, 1286.

Reviews: .1. Anon. *ABC* (29.7.81), 27.
.2. Anon. *Ínsula*, No. 419 (Oct. 1981), 3.
.3. Lissorgues, Yvan. *CMHLB*, 38 (1982), 247-49.

B297 *Los Cuadernos del Norte* (Oviedo), 5, No. 23 (Jan.- Feb. 1984).
Issue devoted to *LR*. Contents: B21, 36, 63, 129, 181, 202, 254, 335, 575, 695, 732, 853, 1033, 1094, 1195, 1208, 1284.

B298 Cuéllar, José de, *Dioses caídos (Clarín, Pardo Bazán, Galdós)* (Madrid: Imp. de la Viuda e Hijos de la Riva, 1895). 31 pp.
The title is indicative of the contents.

B299 Cuenca, Carlos Luis de, *Alegrías (Versos)* (Madrid: Est. tip. Sucesores de Rivadeneyra, 1900), pp. 35-41.
A poem, 'Gramática', dedicated to LA. Theme is one of LA's favorite complaints: bad grammar.

B300 ——, 'Leopoldo Alas (Clarín)', *La Ilustración Española y Americana*, 45, No. 23 (22.6.01), 371.
An obituary.

B301 Cueto Alas, Juan, 'La cuarta persona del singular. El humor literario: dos ejemplos asturianos', *El Urogallo*, 3, No. 16 (1972), 83-90.
An interesting article, which discusses how LA adopts the point of view of God (the fourth person singular) to display his self-directed, intellectual humor and to comment on the universe.

B302 *——, 'Desde la cuarta persona del singular', *El País* (13.6.81), 31. Rpt. in B183, pp. 21-22.
Argues that LA's ironic, critical stance – 'la cuarta persona del singular' – may have made him, today, 'una figura poco fascinante entre la intelectualidad'.

B303 ——, *Los heterodoxos asturianos* (Salinas, Asturias: Ayalga, 1977), pp. 249-52, 266-67, 282-85.
On LA's Krausist and anticlerical tendencies.

B304 ——, 'El humorismo ovetense', in *VI y VII Ciclo de conferencias sobre Oviedo* (Oviedo: Gráficas Summa, 1973), pp. 119-32.
Cites LA as one of the principal humorists of Oviedo.

B305 ——, 'Nota previa', in *La Regenta* (see Ac17), pp. ix-x.

B306 ——, 'Pedro Olea: intentaré ser fiel a "Clarín" ', *Asturias Semanal*, No. 181 (18.11.72), 20-22.
The director P. Olea explains his version of the film, *LR*.

B307 ——, 'La provincia como espectáculo', *El País* (26.1.84).
How Oviedo is, in reality, a reflection of the fictional Vetusta.

B308 ——, '*La Regenta*, la dictadora y la esfera espantosa', *Triunfo*, 35, No. 11, 6ª época (Sept. 1981), 8-12.
Argues that the provincial morality found in *LR* served as *la moral dominante* of the Franco era.

B309 Custodio, Álvaro, '*La Regenta* en la escena', *Argumentos* (Madrid), 8, Nos 63-64 (1984), 50-52.
A.C. explains why he chose to adapt *LR*; and discusses some of the problems attached to turning a long and complex novel into a play. See Aj4.

B310 D.E.P., 'Juan Ochoa', *El Español*, 2 (30.4.99).
An obituary, in which author cites LA's words on Ochoa, published in *El Imparcial*, and prints a letter from Pereda to LA, dated 2 Apr. 1898.

B311 Damonte, Mario, 'Funzione dei riferimenti musicali, in *La Regenta*', in *Miscellanea in omaggio a C. Guerrieri-Crocetti* (Genova: Fratelli Bozzi, 1971), pp. 137-79.
Concludes that the musical references in *LR* demonstrate a sociological, realistic, and autobiographical function.

B312 Darío, Rubén, 'La crítica', in his *España contemporánea, O.C.*, XIX (Madrid: Mundo Latino, n.d.), pp. 295-301.
Darío treats LA far more generously here than LA treats Darío in his *paliques*.

B313 ——, 'Pro domo mea', in his *Escritos inéditos recogidos de periódicos de Buenos Aires y anotados*, ed. E.K. Mapes (New York: Instituto de las Españas, 1938), pp. 50-51.
First published in *La Nación* (30.1.94). Darío says: 'Clarín debe procurar conocer lo que vale de las letras americanas'.

B314 *Davies, G.J., 'Leopoldo Alas (Clarín), his Work and his Contemporaries', unpubl. diss., Univ. of Leeds, 1938.

B315 Davies, Martha Leveritt, 'Clarín's Novelistic Criticism and *La Regenta*', unpubl. diss., Indiana Univ., 1972. 167 pp. Abstracted in *DAI*, 33 (1972-73), 5717-A.

Because LA does not follow his own novelistic theory in the creation of Ana Ozores, he does not succeed in making her the protagonist of the novel.

B316 Davis, Dwight M., 'The Attitude of Leopoldo Alas (Clarín) toward Spanish Letters (Does he Despair of Spanish Letters?)', unpubl. M.A. thesis, Univ. of Oklahoma, 1932. 111 pp.

Concludes that LA, despite harsh criticism, did not despair.

B317 Davis, Gifford, 'The Critical Reception of Naturalism in Spain Before *La cuestión palpitante*', *HR*, 22 (1954), 97-108.

LA 'was better informed than most, more dynamic, and more unorthodox' in his reception of naturalism.

B318 ——, 'The Literary Relations of Clarín and Emilia Pardo Bazán', *HR*, 39 (1971), 378-94.

In a chronological summary, author traces the downward course of the LA-Pardo Bazán literary friendship and, in so doing, reveals the sharply distinctive personalities of the two.

Review: .1. Anon. *Thesaurus*, 29 (1974), 561-62.

Delibes, Miguel: See Chacel, Rosa.

B319 Delogu, F.M., 'Note su Leopoldo Alas (Clarín). 1852-1901', *SGym*, n.s., 14 (1961), 212-19.

Describes LA as an innate poet, possessed of a critical intelligence, and, under certain circumstances, as possibly even an existentialist. Above all, he is a Christian writer.

B320 Dendle, Brian J., *The Spanish Novel of Religious Thesis (1876-1936)* (Princeton: Dept of Romance Languages, Princeton Univ.; Madrid: Castalia, 1968), pp. 41-43.

LA's 'charges are directed against the lack of religion in the Vetustans, not against Christianity itself'.

B321 *Díaz, Luis Felipe, 'Irony and Ideology in *La Regenta* of Leopoldo Alas', unpubl. diss., Univ. of Minnesota, 1983.

B322 Díaz Dufóo, Carlos, 'Teresa', *Revista Azul* (México), 3, No. 16 (18.8.95), 241-42.

Rpt. in Ae4, pp. 185-88. The public, says D.D., could not accept the social realism of *Teresa.*

Díez-Echarri, Emiliano: See Anon., B1327.

B323 —— & José María Roca Franquesa, 'Leopoldo Alas ("Clarín")', in their *Historia de la literatura española e hispanoamericana* (Madrid: Aguilar, 1960), pp. 1111-15.
An overview of LA as novelist, short story writer, and critic. Considers *LR* an 'estudio de almas'.

B324 Díaz Estévanez, Maximino, 'Don Leopoldo en su cátedra de Derecho Natural. Final de una conferencia', *Revista Popular* (Oviedo) (1.7.01), 5-7.
Notes taken by one of LA's disciples.

B325 ——, 'Non omnis moriar', *Revista Popular* (Oviedo) (1.7.01), 18-20.
LA's teachings will live through his disciples from the Univ. de Oviedo.

B326 Díaz Miranda, Eulogio, 'La explosión del envidioso Bonafoux', *Semanario Pintoresco* (Avilés), 1, No. 10 (4.8.01), 5-6.
In this article taken from *El Heraldo de Asturias* (La Habana), the author attacks Bonafoux's wretched anti-Clarín obituary (see B188) and defends LA.

B327 Díaz-Plaja, Guillermo, *Modernismo frente a Noventa y Ocho*, 2nd ed. (Madrid: Espasa-Calpe, 1966), pp. 46-52.
On LA's *anti-modernismo.*

B328 Dicenta, José Fernando, ' "Aramís" contra "Clarín" (1888)', in his *Luis Bonafoux (La víbora de Asnières)* (Madrid: CVS-Videosistemas, 1974), pp. 87-134.
A rather superficial treatment of the LA-Bonafoux feud.

B329 Domínguez Bordona, J., 'Centenario del autor de *Pepita Jiménez.* Cartas inéditas de Valera', *Revista de la Biblioteca, Archivo y Museo* (Madrid), 3, No. 12 (Oct. 1926), 437, 438-40.
In two letters to Narciso Campillo (13.10.87, 22.10.87), Valera defends LA's talent: 'Yo no he leído *La Regenta*; pero aunque sea pésima *La Regenta*, la crítica de Leopoldo Alas no pierde por ello.'

B330 Donald [pseud.], '*La Regenta*, novela de "Clarín", en la pantalla', *Blanco y Negro*, No. 3270 (4.1.75), 63-64.
The film version, says this reviewer, is a dignified and respectful adaptation of LA's novel, but 'la intención crítica, dura, aguda, fustigante de "Clarín" se echa un tanto de menos.'

B331 Don Cualquiera [pseud.], 'Después de leído a Clarín', *La Justicia* (13.4.95). Rpt. in B731, pp. 461-62.
Teresa is a rotten play, says Don C.

B332 ——, 'Éxitos y fracasos', *La Justicia* (22.3.95). Rpt. in Ae4, pp. 175-78.
Teresa is an unequivocal failure as a play.

B333 Dorwick, Thalia, 'El amor y el matrimonio en la obra creacional de Clarín', unpubl. diss., Case Western Reserve Univ., 1973. 302 pp. Abstracted in *DAI*, 34 (1973-74), 5165-A.
Discusses two kinds of love present in LA's work: sensual and sentimental love.

B334 Durand, Frank, 'Characterization in *La Regenta*: Point of View and Theme', *BHS*, 41 (1964), 86-100. Spanish version in B144, pp. 249-70.
An excellent article. Demonstrates how LA, by using the omniscient point of view, is able to give the reader 'both extensive and intensive views of the characters and the city'.

B335 ——, 'El crimen religioso y ético de Ana de Ozores', *Los Cuadernos del Norte* (Oviedo), 5, No. 23 (Jan.-Feb. 1984), 19-24.
How Ana sins against convention and reacts against the disfigurement of morality.

B336 ——, 'A Critical Analysis of Leopoldo Alas's *La Regenta*', unpubl. diss., Univ. of Michigan, 1962. 188 pp. Abstracted in *DA*, 23 (1962-63), 3896.
A thorough study of the themes, narrative techniques, form, and style of *LR*. A number of articles taken from this fine diss. have been published separately (see B334, 337, 338).

B337 ——, 'Leopoldo Alas, "Clarín": Consistency of Outlook as Critic and Novelist', *RR*, 56 (1965), 37-49. Spanish version in B144, pp. 97-115.

LR provides a world view which is consistent with LA's negative but reformist attitudes as a critic.

B338 ——, 'Structural Unity in Leopoldo Alas's *La Regenta*', *HR*, 31 (1963), 324-35.

Illustrates how the thematic and structural emphases on both Vetusta and Ana Ozores are well integrated to form a unified conception of the novel.

B339 E., ' "Las dos cajas" ', *Revista Contemporánea*, No. 116 (30.9.99), 447-48.

A favorable review of the short story.

B340 Echegaray, José, 'Cuatro palabras a manera de prólogo', in *Solos de Clarín* (see Ab2, 3, 4), pp. i-vi.

B341 Echevarría, María de las Nieves, 'Responso a Leopoldo Alas', *Asturias* (Buenos Aires), No. 339 (Apr. 1952), 10-12. Rpt. in *Oviedo* (1952 ed.), n. pag.

A somewhat wandering appreciation of LA's influence and *LR*. Reprint cited by Martínez Cachero, B714, p. 96.

B342 *Echeverría Ezponda, María Dolores, 'Análisis literario de la obra narrativa de Clarín', unpubl. diss., Univ. Complutense de Madrid, 1975. Abstracted in *Revista de la Universidad Complutense*, 24 (1974-75), 68.

A semiological approach.

B343 Endress, Heinz-Peter, '*La Regenta* von Leopoldo Alas Clarín und *Madame Bovary*: von der Anklage des Plagiats zum Nachweis der Originalität', in *Beiträge zur vergleichenden Literaturgeschichte (Festschrift für Kurt Wais zum 65. Geburtstag)* (Tübingen: Max Niemeyer Verlag, 1972), pp. 225-46.

Reviews criticism on the question of Flaubert's influence on LA and uses the theater scene in *LR* to suggest differences between *LR* and *Mme Bovary*.

B344 Entralgo, Elías, *Una vocación y un temperamento: desde Emilio Bobadilla hasta después de Fray Candil* (Discurso de ingreso como miembro correspondiente en la Academia Nacional de Artes y Letras, leído el 26 de junio de 1958) (La Habana, 1958), pp. 46-53.

On the LA-Bobadilla literary relationship.

B345   Entrambasaguas, Joaquín de, ' "Clarín", redivivo', in his *El
       año literario (1953)* (Madrid: CSIC, 1954), pp. 88-89.
       On publications commemorating LA's centennial.

B346   ——, 'Notas bibliográficas: Menéndez y Pelayo, Unamuno,
       Palacio Valdés, Epistolario a Clarín', *RFE*, 25 (1941), 405-
       18.
       A review-article on the correspondence, B15.

B347   ——, 'Una semblanza de Menéndez y Pelayo, por "Clarín" ',
       Archivum, 2 (1952), 23-32.
       Comments on the portrait of Menéndez y Pelayo which LA drew in
       Un viaje a Madrid.

B348   Eoff, Sherman H., 'In Quest of a God of Love', in his *The
       Modern Spanish Novel* (New York: New York Univ. Press,
       1961; London, Peter Owen, 1962), pp. 51-84. Spanish
       version: 'En busca de un dios de amor', in *El pensamiento
       moderno y la novela española* (Barcelona: Seix Barral, 1965),
       pp. 59-90.
       A provocative comparative study on 'the heaviness of the material
       world and the failure of love as a means of liberation' in *LR* and
       Mme Bovary.

       Epistolario de Valera y Menéndez y Pelayo: See Artigas
       Ferrando, Miguel, and Pedro Sáinz Rodríguez.

B349   Esbrí, José M., 'Carta de despedida a Clarín', *Los Madriles*,
       No. 51 (21.9.89), 5, 7.
       A response to two articles by LA on Esbrí (*Los Madriles*, Nos 49-
       50, 1889).

       Españolito [pseud.] : See Suárez, Constantino.

B350   Espina, Antonio, *El cuarto poder. Cien años de periodismo
       español* (Madrid: Aguilar, 1960), pp. 259-62.
       A rather unfavorable view of LA's worth as critic and novelist.

       ——: See also Nueda, Luis.

B351   Espinosa Rodríguez, Ciro, *En torno a la crítica de Leopoldo
       Alas (Clarín)* (La Habana: Imp. Oscar Echevarría, 1931).
       12 pp.
       LA's criticism marks the transition between the old and the new criti-
       cism in Spain.

B352 ——, *Leopoldo Alas (Clarín) como ensayista* (La Habana: Imp. Oscar Echevarría, 1910). 15 pp.
An essay of little interest to anyone.

B353 ——, *Leopoldo Alas (Clarín): matices de su personalidad literaria* (La Habana: Imp. Oscar Echevarría, 1930). 15 pp.
Not much substance here.

B354 ——, *Leopoldo Alas (Clarín) y la novela en España del romanticismo al realismo* (La Habana: Imp. Oscar Echevarría, 1928). 15 pp.
Very poorly done criticism; mostly just extracts quotations from previous critics.

B355 Esquer Torres, Ramón, 'Las luchas del siglo XIX: el P. Blanco García y Leopoldo Alas "Clarín" ', *Boletín de la Sociedad Castellonense de Cultura*, 38 (1962), 241-55.
Author publishes some extremely interesting correspondence between Blanco García and Rafael Álvarez Sereix, in which the Augustinian father's anti-Clarín bias is quite apparent.

B356 Estévanez [pseud.], 'Leopoldo Alas', *El Imparcial* (11.6.01).
Gives details of LA's last hours.

B357 Estruch Tobella, Joan, 'La *Teresa* de Clarín, un intento fracasado de renovación del teatro español', *Segismundo*, 17, Nos 37-38 (1983), 99-111.
Makes a valiant attempt to reevaluate *Teresa* positively as a technically and thematically innovative play. E.T. attributes its failure principally to the actors', critics', and public's inability to understand such innovation.

B358 El Estudiante [pseud.: E. Rivas?], 'Miscelánea', *Revista Cómica*, 1, No. 1 (6.5.87), 6-7.
Attacks *LR*, as 'una traducción mal hecha de *Mme Bovary*'.

B359 Un Ex-Alumno [pseud.], 'Clarín en su cátedra', *Arte y Letras* (Barcelona), 2 (1901), 674-76.
On the character and personality of LA as a professor.

B360 Fabbiani Ruiz, José, 'Como gorgonas infernales', *El Universal* (Caracas) (15.1.57).
'El vivir fuera de la realidad, es algo determinante' in *LR*.

B361 ——, 'Pórtico de *La Regenta*', *El Universal* (Caracas) (22.1.57).
On the characters and the opening paragraph of *LR.*

B362 ——, 'Sola y rodeada de silencio', *El Universal* (Caracas) (5.2.57).
Discusses Ana Ozores' character and circumstances in *LR.*

B363 Feal Deibe, Carlos, "La anunciación a Bonis: análisis de *Su único hijo*", *BHS*, 51 (1974), 255-71.
An archetypal analysis of *SUH* and its obsession with *lo maternal.*

Fedón [pseud.] : See Altamira y Crevea, Rafael, B30.

B364 Fedorchek, Robert M., 'Clarín y Eça de Queirós', *NRFH*, 27 (1978), 336-45. Rpt. in *Archivum*, 29-30 (1979-80), 71-82.
Establishes parallels between *LR* and *O crime do padre Amaro* and *O primo Basílio.*

B365 ——, 'En torno a una imagen de *La Regenta*', *Horizontes* (Puerto Rico), 19 (1976), 71-75.
An interesting study on the use of ornithological images in *LR.*

B366 Fernández, Victoria, & Paco Abril, 'Leopoldo Alas, "Clarín" (1852-1901)', in their *Famosos personajes asturianos de todos los tiempos (biografías para niños)* (Salinas, Asturias: Ayalga, 1978), pp. 225-42.
Biographical sketch.

B367 Fernández Almagro, Melchor, *Cánovas, su vida y su política,* 2nd ed. (Madrid: Tebas, 1972), pp. 55, 302, 316, 318-20, 420, 422.
Extracts generous quotations from *Cánovas y su tiempo* as an example of a contemporary view of the statesman.

B368 ——, 'Crítica y sátira en "Clarín" ', *Archivum*, 2 (1952), 33-42. Rpt. in B723, pp. 147-53.
Author distinguishes between criticism and satire in LA's work.

B369 ——, '*Cuentos* de Leopoldo Alas', *ABC* (7.3.54), 57.
Favorable review of Ad28.

B370 ——, 'Crítica y noticias de libros. *Leopoldo Alas "Clarín"*, por Adolfo Posada', *ABC* (8.9.46), 41.

Posada's book (B973) reveals to us 'con detalles puntuales e inéditos, la intimidad de un hombre no bien conocido ...'

B371 ——, 'Leopoldo Alas "Clarín"', in his *Almanaque literario* (Madrid: Plutarco, 1935), pp. 188-91.

A general appreciation of LA's work.

B372 ——, 'Leopoldo Alas y Clarín', *Ínsula*, No. 31 (15.7.48), 1.

On the internal contradictions in LA's writings.

B373 ——, '*Obras selectas*, de Leopoldo Alas, "Clarín"', *ABC* (12.10.47), 22.

A review of Aa5.

B374 Fernández Bremón, José, 'Crónica general', *La Ilustración Española y Americana*, 23, No. 20 (30.5.79), 346.

A minor dispute with LA on the number of poets in Spain.

B375 ——, 'Crónica general', *La Ilustración Española y Americana*, 30, No. 8 (28.2.86), 130. Rpt. in B514, pp. 203-04.

Considers LA's discourse on Antonio Alcalá Galiano, given at the Ateneo, a fiasco.

B376 ——, 'D. Leopoldo Alas (Clarín)', *La Ilustración Española y Americana*, 45, No. 23 (22.6.01), 370.

An obituary.

B377 Fernández-Cordero y Azorín, Concepción, *La sociedad española del siglo XIX en la obra literaria de D. José María de Pereda* (Santander: Institución Cultural de Cantabria, 1970), pp. 108-09.

On Pereda's first meeting with LA.

B378 Fernández de la Mora, Gonzalo, 'Leopoldo Alas', in his *Pensamiento español, 1968. De Amor Ruibal a Zaragüeta* (Madrid: Rialp, 1969), pp. 277-84.

A review-article on B149. Author is generally favorable, although he criticizes a professed lack of objectivity on Beser's part.

B379 Fernández Flórez, Isidoro [pseud.: Fernanflor], 'Notas literarias. Del libro titulado *Solos de Clarín* y del autor del libro', *El Liberal* (25.9.81).

A severe, though not nasty, criticism of LA. Author believes LA's defects as a writer are the flaws and weaknesses of youth.

B380 Fernández Juncos, Manuel, *De Puerto-Rico a Madrid. Estudios de viaje* (Puerto Rico: Tip. de José González Font, 1886), pp. 162-65. 2nd ed., 1887: *De Puerto-Rico a Madrid por La Habana y Nueva-York. Estudios de viaje.*
Author meets LA in Oviedo, just after publication of *LR.*

B381 Fernández Luján, J., 'En burlas y en veras', *La Semana Cómica* (Barcelona), 6, No. 6 (12.2.92), 87, 90.
On the LA-Bobadilla dispute. It is a waste of time for Clarín to *critiquizar* (not *criticar*) people like Fray Candil.

B382 ――, 'Mi cuarto a espadas (Lo de Clarín)', *La Semana Cómica* (Barcelona), 6, No. 5 (5.2.92), 75, 78.
Admires LA, but 'Clarín, crítico de sana psicología, de profundo estudio, lleva en sí un enemigo implacable: su genio.' An example of LA's *genio* is his excessive harshness toward Pardo Bazán.

B383 ――, 'El último libro de Clarín. *Doña Berta*', *La Semana Cómica* (Barcelona), 6, No. 8 (25.2.92), 122-23.
A nice review, in which J.F.L. notes how the 'panteísmo poético a que trasciende la emoción estética, está exteriorizado; por dentro hay otra poesía no menos dulce.' And he adds, Clarín's novels 'hacen pensar.'

B384 Fernández-Miranda, Torcuato, 'Actitud ante Clarín', *La Nueva España* (Oviedo) (27-31.5.52). Rpt. in *CHA*, No. 37 (Jan. 1953), 33-48.
Martínez Cachero (B714, p. 97) notes that this piece was first given as a talk at the Univ. de Oviedo, 23.5.52. Author dislikes LA's anti-clericalism, though admitting that he is a great writer.

B385 Fernández Rodríguez-Avello, Manuel, *Algo sobre Clarín y sus paliques* (Oviedo: IDEA, 1963). 40 pp.
A monograph on LA's journalism. Of limited usefulness.
Review: .1. Kronik, John W. *Hispania* (U.S.A), 47 (1964), 870.

B386 ――, 'Carta inédita de Clarín a Juan Ochoa', *BIDEA*, 36, Nos 105-06 (Jan.-Aug. 1982), 319-24.
Discusses and rpts letter dated 15.9.96. See Af20.

B387 ――, 'El Centenario de la publicación de *La Regenta*', *Boletín de Información Municipal del Excmo Ayuntamiento*

de Oviedo, No. 3 (Mar. 1982), 8-10.
Discusses forthcoming international symposium on *LR*'s centennial
and reproduces letters from C. Richmond, G. Sobejano, N. Valis, and
M. Fernández Avello on the subject.

B388 *———, ' "Clarín", otra vez', *El Eco de Luarca*, No. 42 (14.12.52).

B389 ———, 'Clarín, Oviedo, Vetusta', *Argumentos* (Madrid), 8, Nos
63-64 (1984), 28-32.
Comments on how the Univ. de Oviedo in LA's time served as an
exemplar to the rest of Spain; and how 'Oviedo ya es Vetusta'.

B390 ———, 'El día que don Saturnino Bermúdez entrevistó a
Leopoldo Alas "Clarín" ', *Los Cuadernos del Norte* (Oviedo),
2, No. 7 (May-June 1981), 123-30.
An imaginary dialogue between Clarín and his own literary creation,
don Saturnino Bermúdez.

B391 ———, 'Oviedo, la muy noble y leal ciudad', *La Nueva España*
(Oviedo) (14.6.81). Rpt. in B183, pp. 11-12.
Contrasts the disappearance and destruction of the historical Oviedo
with the immortal Vetusta of fiction.

B392 ———, *Pérez de Ayala y la niebla* (Oviedo: IDEA, 1970), pp.
50-53.
On the presence of LA in some of Pérez de Ayala's stories about
animals, such as 'La Nación' and 'Don Paciano'.

B393 ———, 'Recuerdo de Clarín. Ayer se cumplió el LXXX
aniversario de su muerte', *La Nueva España* (Oviedo) (14.6.81).
Rpt. in B183, p. 8.
Contrasts his reputation then and now.

B394 ———, 'Recuerdo de Juan Ochoa Betancourt', *BIDEA*, 19, No.
54 (1965), 139-50.
Contains a previously unpublished letter to Ochoa, in which Clarín
asks his friend to write an article on *Teresa*. See Af19.

B395 ———, '*La Regenta*', *La Nueva España* (Oviedo) (23.3.72),
11.
On the difficulties involved in transferring *LR* to the screen.

B396 *———, '*La Regenta*, 1884-1984. Cien años', *La Nueva España*
(Oviedo) (20.2.83), 29.

B397   ——, '*La Regenta* y la niebla', *BIDEA*, 31 (1977), 17-27.
A suggestive article on the psychological, as well as decorative, use of mist, rain, and sun in *LR*. At times, though, author fails to penetrate beneath the surface in his analysis.

B398   ——, *Tomás Tuero (La leyenda de un periodista)* (Oviedo: IDEA, 1958), pp. 117-24, *et passim.*
Describes the friendship between LA and Tomás Tuero; and rpts LA's obituary of Tuero.

B399   ——, *Vida y obra literaria de Juan Ochoa Betancourt* (Oviedo: IDEA, 1955), pp. 171-76, 187-91, 199-203.
Contains correspondence from LA to Ochoa; correspondence from Menéndez y Pelayo and Galdós to LA; and excerpts from LA's writings on Ochoa (see also Af19, B386, 394, 865, 866).

Fernández Santos, Jesús: See Chacel, Rosa.

B400   [Fernández Shaw, Carlos], 'Veladas teatrales', *La Época* (21.3.95). Rpt. in Ae4, p. 173.
An unfavorable review of *Teresa.*

B401   Fernández Silvestre, Marta, '*La Regenta,* una novela de clave', *Argumentos* (Madrid), 8, Nos 63-64 (1984), 60-66.
An interview with J.M. Martínez Cachero, in which he talks about the initial reception of *LR*, LA's influence, his ideology and religious beliefs, the absence in *LR* of the Univ. de Oviedo, point of view in *LR*, LA's modernity and, above all, the 6-vol. *Obras completas* in press, completed by a five-member team of scholars.

B402   Fernández Villegas, Francisco [pseud.: Zeda], 'Leopoldo Alas (Clarín)', *Nuevo Mundo*, 8, No. 390 (26.6.01).
An appreciation of LA's work.

B403   ——, '*Su único hijo,* por Leopoldo Alas (Clarín)', *Revista de España*, 135 (1891), 498-510.
Author's judgment is summed up in this sentence: 'Siendo un libro menos que mediano, hay en él cuadros tan hermosos como el del bautizo, que casi hacen olvidar los defectos y monstruosidades en que abunda *Su único hijo*'.

B404   ——, 'Los teatros', *El Imparcial* (21.3.95). Rpt. in B731, pp. 459-60.
A very brief review of *Teresa,* in which author notes that perhaps the audience rejected the play for its gloomy subject matter.

Fernanflor [pseud.] : See Fernández Flórez, Isidoro.

B405 Ferrandiz Alborz, F., 'A los cincuenta años de la muerte de "Clarín" ', *El Día* (Montevideo) (9.12.51).
An anecdotal article.

B406 Ferrari, Emilio, 'A un enemigo', *El Imparcial* (11.3.95). Rpt. in his *Por mi camino. Poesías*, *O.C.*, I (Madrid: Imp. de la Revista de Archivos, 1908), pp. 111-14.
An anti-Clarín poem.

B407 Ferreira, Eduardo, 'De literatura y arte. Revistas rápidas', *La Alborada* (Montevideo), 5, No. 171 (23.6.01), n. pag.
A loving appreciation. LA's death is a great loss; and *LR* is 'una obra maestra todavía no muy bien comprendida'.

B408 ——, 'Revista literaria', *Revista Nacional de Literatura y Ciencias Sociales* (Montevideo), No. 10 (25.7.95), 148-49.
On B1205.

B409 Ferreras, Juan Ignacio, 'La prosa en el siglo XIX', in *Historia de la literatura española*, III, ed. J.M. Díez Borque (Madrid: Guadiana, 1974), pp. 116-18. Also: Madrid: Taurus, 1980, pp. 417-20.
Introductory material.

B410 ——, '*La Regenta* ante un nuevo método', *Les Langues Néo-Latines*, No. 169 (June-July 1964), 15-41. Rpt. in his *Introducción a una sociología de la novela española del siglo XIX* (Madrid: Edicusa, 1973), pp. 197-223.
The new method is the sociological approach to *LR*, which, in this study, is intended as a pedagogical tool for students.
Review: .1. Plinio. *Asturias Semanal*, No. 249 (9.3.74), 48-49.

B411 ——, '*La Regenta* cumple un siglo', *El País* (20.3.84), 26. Rpt. in *El País, Edición Internacional* (26.3.84), 20; and in *Spain: Boletín Cultural*, No. 30 (Apr. 1984), 30.
On *LR*'s former unpopularity and the present esteem it enjoys.

B412 Ferreres, Rafael, *Verlaine y los modernistas españoles* (Madrid: Gredos, 1975), pp. 47-51.
On LA's criticism of Paul Verlaine.

B413 Ferroni Clementi, Silvia, 'Rasgos biográficos y obra de Leopoldo Alas, "Clarín"', in *Dos cuentos: ¡Adiós, Cordera! Pipá* (see Ad33), pp. 5-12.

B414 Filippo, Luigi de, *Leopoldo Alas "Clarín" critico letterario* (Roma: [Aldo Chicca], 1964). 77 pp.
A rehash of LA's literary criticism.

B415 Fishtine, Edith, 'Clarín in his Early Writings', *RR*, 29 (1938), 325-42.
An early appreciation of LA's critical endeavors, which at that time were unjustly ignored. E.F. believes that the essential Clarín was 'the mystical idealist, the spiritual humorist', who was caught up in other currents of the era, though never completely. Also notes that, despite a new note here and there, LA's beliefs never really change very much throughout his literary career.

B416 Flagellus [pseud.], 'Galdós, Clarín, el teatro y la prensa política', *Nuevo Mundo*, 2, No. 54 (17.1.95), 7.
F. admires LA as a writer, but not as a drama critic, because he does not actually see the plays.

B417 Flor, Roger de, 'Respuesta a Clarín', *Heraldo de Madrid* (9.5.95).
A response to one of LA's *paliques* in the *Heraldo* (25.4.95), on the legitimacy of criticizing women writers.

B418 Flores García, Francisco, 'Cosas de antaño. El "Bilis-Club"', *La Ilustración Española y Americana*, 50, No. 17 (8.5.06), 286-87, 290.
An anecdotal article on the various exploits of the Bilis-Club, of which LA was one of the principal members.

B419 *Flórez, Adriano, 'Hay que humanizar a "Clarín"', *El Carbayón* (Oviedo) (7.5.31).

B420 F[raga Torrejón, Eduardo], 'Anotaciones marginales. "Clarín"', *La Nueva España* (Oviedo) (21.2.52).
How Spaniards of today will view LA.

B421 Francés, José, 'Clarín o la poligrafía apasionada', in his *De la condición del escritor: algunos ejemplos* (Madrid: Paez-Bolsa, 1930), pp. 153-59.
Sympathetic impressions of LA and his *opus*.

B422 ——, 'Tributo a Clarín', in his *Madre Asturias* (Madrid: Afrodisio Aguado, 1945), pp. 37-43.
LA as 'el arquetipo del novelista, del narrador por esencia y potencia'. Laments present ignorance of his work.

B423 *Francisco Rodríguez, José, 'Páginas asturianas: "Clarín"', *Norte* (Madrid) (Feb. 1932).

B424 Francos Rodríguez, José, *Contar vejeces. De las memorias de un gacetillero (1893-97)*(Madrid: Compañía Ibero-Americana de Publicaciones, 1928), pp. 154-56.
On the first night of *Teresa.*

B425 ——, *Cuando el rey era niño... De las memorias de un gacetillero (1890-92)* (Madrid: Imp. J. Morales, 1895), pp. 160-62, 191-92.
On the LA-Bobadilla duel; and the original publication of ' ¡Adiós, Cordera! ' in *El Liberal* (27.7.92).

B426 ——, 'Fotografías olvidadas. Bilis-Club', *Blanco y Negro*, No. 1449 (23.2.19), n. pag.
A nostalgic piece on the literary *tertulia*, Bilis-Club, and some of its members (LA, Palacio Valdés, Eduardo Bustillo, Marcos Zapata, etc.).

Fray Candil [pseud.] : See Bobadilla, Emilio.

Fray Mortero [pseud.] : See Miguel, Fray Juan de.

B427 Frézals, G[eorges?] de (F.-B. Navarro), '*La Regenta*. Roman de Léopold Alás (sic)', *Revue Britannique* (Paris), 62, No. 5 (1886), 139-51.
LR 'est écrit avec attention, conviction, sous l'inspiration d'une imagination puissante ranimant des faits et des histoires dont nul n'avait encore osé faire des récits si francs, si vrais.'

B428 Fuente, Carlos, '1984 es el año de *La Regenta* en la literatura española', *El País* (26.1.84).
On the 1984 facsimile ed. of *LR* (see Ac17), the one-hour television program on the novel, and other acts of commemoration.

B429 ——, 'Oviedo recibe con entusiasmo el estreno de *La Regenta*, en versión de Álvaro Custodio', *El País* (5.12.83), 33.
On Custodio's efforts to maintain a sense of continuity in the dramatic adaptation of *LR*. See Aj4.

B430 Fuente, Ricardo, '¿Clarín o Bonafoux?', *Revista Cómica*, 2, No. 58 (7.6.88), 6.
Bonafoux, says R.F., has attacked an institution.

B431 ——, 'Los paliques de Arimón', *El País* (26.4.95). Rpt. in his *De un periodista* (Madrid: Casa Editorial de Mariano Núñez Samper, 1897), pp. 79-84.
Defends LA against the scurrilous *ad hominem* attacks of J. Arimón (see B68, 69, 76, 77).

B432 ——, 'El socialismo en el teatro', in *De un periodista* (see B431), pp. 111-13.
Teresa is a failure as socialist propaganda.

B433 Fuentes, Víctor, 'Los límites del naturalismo de Clarín en *La Regenta*', *Arbor*, 111, No. 434 (1982), 173-80.
Using Lukács as a theoretical base, V.F. tries to show that in *LR* there is a 'falta de acción — de interacción socialmente conflictiva entre los personajes' and that characters and environment are not linked together. Not always convincing.

B434 Fuertes Acevedo, Máximo, *Bosquejo acerca del estado que alcanzó en todas épocas la literatura en Asturias, seguido de una extensa bibliografía de los escritores asturianos* (Badajoz: Tip. La Industria, a cargo de Felipe Mesía, 1885), pp. 123-24.
LA as an up-and-coming light of Asturias.

B435 G.R., '*Folletos literarios-IV. Mis plagios — Un discurso de Núñez de Arce*', *Revista Contemporánea*, No. 70 (30.4.88), 222.
A favorable review.

B436 El Gaitero [pseud.], 'A Martínez Ruiz en "Avisos de éste"', *El Progreso* (8.11.97).
Author believes that those who attack *Teresa* are envious and unnoteworthy individuals. Also mentions a Seville performance of the drama, put on by a troup of wandering players, 'unos pobres cómicos mal afeitados y unas pobres cómicas tan ajadas como sus trajes de raso'.

B437 Gallego Morell, Antonio, 'Clarín', in his *Poetas y algo más* (Sevilla: Univ., 1978), pp. 50-55.
On LA's early poetry and his poetic prose.

B438   Gamallo Fierros, Dionisio, 'La Academia, Galdós y Menéndez Pelayo – Una carta inédita de don Benito a "Clarín" ', *ABC* (10.12.70).
A letter on the politics of getting Galdós into the Spanish Royal Academy in 1888-89.

B439   *——, 'Aportaciones al estudio de Clarín', *La Nueva España* (Oviedo) (2.3.62).
Fernández Avello, in B385, notes this article, as well as some others published by G.F. in the same journal at the same time.

B440   ——, 'Aportaciones al estudio de Valle-Inclán', *RO*, 2a época, 15 (1966), 343-66.
Publishes and comments on correspondence between newcomer Valle-Inclán and maestro during the years 1895-97.

B441   ——, 'Campoamor, Zorrilla y Valera escriben a don Leopoldo Alas. Tres cartas inéditas del epistolario de "Clarín" ', *EstLit*, No. 2 (20.3.44), 3.
Campoamor (3.4.83) discusses literature; Zorrilla (1.1.93), his ill health, while wishing a happy new year to LA; and Valera (23.1.96), the reading public's attitudes toward writers and LA's apparent anti-academic stance in his review of Menéndez Pelayo's *Antología de poetas americanos.*

B442   *——, 'Un "Clarín" del XIX. Leopoldo Alas', *Imperio* (Zaragoza) (18.2.45).

B443   ——, 'En el centenario de un "Clarín" del siglo XIX. Tres nobles actitudes de Leopoldo Alas', *Pueblo* (25.4.52), 4.
Points out three moments in LA's life and work when the writer reveals his tender, sentimental side.

B444   *——, 'En el centenario de un malogrado gran escritor, Francisco Navarro Ledesma. Una carta que dirigió a "Clarín" ...', *Arriba* (Madrid) (5.9.69).

B445   *——, 'Evocación del Leopoldo Alas de 1882 – Los preparativos de su viaje de boda a Andalucía', *La Nueva España* (Oviedo) (27.9.62).

B446   ——, 'Páginas abandonadas de "Clarín". Sus 400 colaboraciones en *El Solfeo*', *Imperio* (Zaragoza) (7.1.49), 3.
G.F. discusses LA's early journalism in *El Solfeo*, noting the variety

of pseudonyms he employed at that time. Author also talks of publishing a volume of 1000 of LA's previously uncollected writings, a project which apparently did not get off the ground.

B447 ——, 'Primera etapa de la vida y obra de Pérez de Ayala (de los comienzos hasta 1905)', in *Pérez de Ayala, visto en su centenario 1880-1980* (Oviedo: IDEA, 1981), pp. 241-44, 258-65, 387-89, 408-12, 435-36.
Discusses the LA-Pérez de Ayala relationship; LA's friendship with Cejador y Frauca.

B448 ——, 'Las primeras reacciones de Galdós ante *La Regenta*', *La Voz de Asturias* (Oviedo) (30.7-10.12.78).
Issued in 12 parts. Part 9 (24.9) is titled 'Dos visiones galdosianas de *La Regenta*: 1885 y 1900'; parts 10-12 (8.10-10.12) are titled 'Dos enjuiciamientos galdosianos de *La Regenta*: 1885 y 1900'. An important series of previously unpublished letters from Galdós to LA, giving his frank, detailed and mostly admiring opinion on *LR*. Two defects, says Galdós, are the novel's dimensions and the excessive insistence on sex and lasciviousness. G.F. also contrasts G.'s first reaction to *LR* with his prologue of 1900.

B449 Gamoneda, Antonio, 'Elegía de Oviedo', *Asturias Gráfica* (Oviedo) (Sept. 1920), n. pag.
In a special no. dedicated to the city of Oviedo, this poem appears, urging that a monument to LA be erected.

B450 Gaos, Vicente, *La poética de Campoamor*, 2nd ed. rev. (Madrid: Gredos, 1969), pp. 140-61.
On the LA-Núñez de Arce polemic over the merits of prose versus poetry.

B451 Garagorri, Paulino, *Unamuno, Ortega, Zubiri en la filosofía española* (Madrid: Plenitud, 1968), pp. 229-44.
Discusses the philosophical tendencies in LA, which seem to anticipate the thought of Unamuno, Ortega, and Zubiri.

B452 García, Soledad Miranda, *Religión y clero en la gran novela española del siglo XIX* (Madrid: Pegaso, 1982), pp. 24-26, 51-55, 106-16, 164.
Goes over old ground on LA's religious beliefs and spiritual crisis.

B453 García Álvarez, María Teresa Cristina, 'Eça de Queiroz y Clarín (Cotejo entre *El primo Basilio* y *La Regenta*)', in

Estudios ofrecidos a Emilio Alarcos Llorach, IV (Oviedo: Univ., 1979), pp. 419-27.
Superficial parallels amongst the characters are pointed out.

Garazzola, Leda: See Schraibman, José.

B454 García Blanco, Manuel, ' "Clarín" y Unamuno', *Archivum*, 2 (1952), 113-40. Rpt. in his *En torno a Unamuno* (Madrid: Taurus, 1965), 183-214; and in B723, pp. 82-97.
Notes Unamuno's references to LA in his writings. Also includes an appendix: LA's criticism of Unamuno's *Tres ensayos*.

B455 *García de Castro, Ramón, 'Leopoldo Alas', *La Nueva España* (Oviedo) (23.9.80).
Part of series, 'Pérez de Ayala y sus maestros'.

B456 ——, 'Rubén Darío y Asturias', *PSA*, 46 (1967), 305-20.
Despite LA's official *anti-modernista* stance in his criticism, his personal library gives evidence he was on good terms with some of the leading *modernistas* of the day (pp. 318-19).

B457 García de J.M., Fray Emeterio, *Mística y novela* (Burgos: 'El Monte Carmelo', 1949), pp. 29-56.
Catalogues the references to Santa Teresa and San Juan de la Cruz in *LR*.

B458 García Domínguez, Elías, 'Los cuentos rurales de Clarín', *Archivum*, 19 (1969), 221-42.
In an analysis of several stories with rural settings, author delineates the most common situation found in them as the tension between individual consciousness and the external world.

B459 ——, 'Oviedo en la literatura', in *El libro de Oviedo* (Oviedo: Ediciones Naranco, 1974), pp. 210-25.
Notes how LA's Vetusta/Oviedo, treated as a 'compendio de todos los males, la cárcel de la Regenta y el Magistral, el símbolo de la castración de los impulsos vitales', turns into an ambiguous symbol of 'los valores positivos del pasado, que la ciudad, tercamente, se resiste a abandonar' in later novelists. Also discusses how Pérez de Ayala's Pilares points to a dual referent: the real city of Oviedo and the imaginary one of Vetusta. Concludes that 'Vetusta es la creación de un misántropo, con más fe en el hombre que en la sociedad; Pilares, la visión de un optimista radical.'

García Hortelano, Juan: See Chacel, Rosa.

B460　García Lorca, Laura de los Ríos de, *Los cuentos de Clarín.
Proyección de una vida* (Madrid: Revista de Occidente, 1965).
327 pp. A reworking of her Columbia Univ. diss., 'Los
cuentos de Clarín: proyección de una vida', 1958, 400 pp.,
which is abstracted in *DA*, 19 (1958-59), 1381.
Author tries to prove that 'el Clarín cuentista es una proyección vital
y necesaria del Alas hombre, que pone en sus seres de imaginación
todas sus desazones, decaimientos y desganos.' A somewhat superficial
analysis. Includes a long, error-prone bibliography.
Reviews: .1. Amorós, Andrés. *CHA*, No. 191 (Nov. 1965), 381-84.
　　　　　.2. B[eser], S[ergio]. *Índice Histórico Español*, 11 (1965),
　　　　　　　 282.
　　　　　.3. Cano, José Luis. *Ínsula*, No. 227 (Oct. 1965), 8-9.
　　　　　.4. García, José Ignacio. *BIDEA*, 22 (1968), 457-61.
　　　　　.5. M.D. *BA*, 41 (1967), 457.
　　　　　.6. Tejedor, Matilde I. *Revista de Literaturas Modernas*
　　　　　　　 (Mendoza, Argentina), No. 6 (1967), 139-40.
　　　　　.7. Thompson, Clifford R., Jr. *RF*, 79 (1967), 251-56.

B461　——, 'Leopoldo Alas y "Clarín" (1852-1901)', in *Cuentos
de Clarín* (see Ad30), pp. xi-xxiv.

B462　García Lorenzo, Luciano, 'De "Clarín" y Unamuno', *Prohemio*,
3 (1972), 467-72.
Author believes that 'Cambio de luz' contains the germ of two works
of Unamuno, *La venda* and *San Manuel Bueno, mártir*, since both
blindness and religious doubt constitute the fundamental motifs of
all three works.

B463　——, 'Leopoldo Alas, Clarín', in his *La novela del s. XIX*,
II. Literatura Española en Imágenes, 24 (Madrid: La Muralla,
1973), pp. 17-24.
Written to accompany a series of slides, this is an introductory text
on LA's life and fiction.

B464　García Mercadal, José, 'Críticas que fueron. Una pelea de
gallos', *EstLit*, Nos 402-04 (15.9.68), 92-93.
Recounts the feud between LA and the youthful Francisco Navarro
Ledesma and his circle of friends on the weekly paper, *Gedeón.*

B465　——, 'Prólogo', in Ramón Pérez de Ayala, *O.C.*, I (Madrid:
Aguilar, 1964), pp. xi-xxxiii.

Pérez de Ayala as a disciple of LA.

B466 ——, 'Prólogo', in Ramón Pérez de Ayala, *Tributo a Ingla-terra* (Madrid: Aguilar, 1963), pp. 9-14, 22-25.
Discusses Pérez de Ayala as LA's disciple; compares them as essay writers; and gives LA's opinion of academicians.

B467 *García Miñor, Antonio, 'Callejero de Oviedo: la calle de Leopoldo Alas', *La Voz de Asturias* (Oviedo) (27.4.80).

B468 García Pavón, Francisco, ' "Clarín" crítico en su obra narra-tiva', *Ínsula*, No. 76 (Apr. 1952), 5, 11.
LA uses his characters' speech patterns and defects to criticize faults of grammar and sloppy thinking. G.P. considers 'la intromisión de la crítica en la obra narrativa [de LA] como un lastre, que sí carac-teriza su estilo, pero que no está presente sino en lo menos puro de sus creaciones.'

B469 ——, 'Crítica literaria en la obra narrativa de "Clarín" ', *Archivum*, 2 (1952), 63-68.
LA's stories, says G.P., run the gamut from sarcastic 'cuentos-paliques' to pure narrations in which the critical judging element is absent. LA's critical insertions constitute a 'lapsus en el ritmo de sus narraciones'.

B470 ——, 'Un cuento de "Clarín" y una carta de Unamuno', *ABC* (18.3.56).
A good article. G.P. finds fault with the customary explanation of LA's religious sentiments, i.e., that he underwent a spiritual evolution from anticlerical to unorthodox believer (see B229, 1104). He notes that LA alternated throughout his life and work between the two extremes of belief and doubt. LA may also have taken the plot of his religious story, 'Viaje redondo', from a letter of Unamuno, dated 31 May 1895, which precedes by several months the story's publication.

B471 ——, 'Gentes humildes en la obra narrativa de "Clarín" ', *Arbor*, 22, No. 78 (June 1952), 186-92. Rpt. in B723, pp. 263-71.
The typology of one series of LA's characters, divided into three cate-gories: the picaresque; the amatory; and the intellectual.

B472 ——, 'Leopoldo Alas, "Clarín", como narrador', unpubl. diss., Univ. de Madrid, 1952. 154 pp. Abstracted in the *Revista de la Universidad de Madrid*, 1 (1952), 448-49.
An early attestation of the positive reevaluation and interest in

Clarín in Spain. Parts of this diss. later appeared as articles (B468-71, 473). With interesting bibliographical appendices.

B473 ——, 'El problema religioso en la obra narrativa de Clarín', *Archivum*, 5 (1955), 319-49.
As in B470, G.P. insists on the recurring periods of authentic belief and sarcastic anticlericalism in the life and work of LA.
Review: .1. M[ontserrat] Ll[orens], S[errano]. *Índice Histórico Español*, 3 (1957), 149.

——: See also Chacel, Rosa.

B474 García Rey, M., *Clarín y sus folletos* (Madrid: U. Montegrifo, Impresor, 1890). 60 pp.
A sarcastic look at LA the critic. Very unfavorable and polemical.

B475 G[arcía] Rosales, Carlos, 'A Clarín', *La Voz de Asturias* (3.5.31).
A poem in honor of the monument dedicated to LA in Oviedo.

B476 García Sánchiz, Federico, 'Leopoldo Alas', *El Imparcial* (5.12.12).
An appreciation of LA, on the eve of the appearance of vol. I of his *Obras completas.*

B477 García San Miguel, Luis, *De la sociedad aristocrática a la sociedad industrial en la España del siglo XIX* (Madrid: Edicusa, 1973), pp. 131-49, 195-96, 217-59.
Exploits *LR* in pseudodocumentary fashion to analyse the social classes and types prevalent in nineteenth-century Oviedo; also discusses LA's ideology in 'Un jornalero', in his prologue to Jhering's *La lucha por el derecho*, in his articles on the economic crisis in Andalusia (1882), and in other writings.
Review: .1. Plinio. *Asturias Semanal*, No. 249 (9.3.74), 48-49.

B478 ——, 'La sociedad asturiana en el siglo XIX', in *III, IV y V Ciclo de conferencias sobre Oviedo* (Oviedo: Gráficas Summa, 1972), pp. 63-76.
Uses 'Un jornalero' as an example of LA's political attitudes; and notes the dechristianization of the worker in *LR*.

B479 *García Santos, M., 'Cuando "Clarín", harto de predicar, quiso dar trigo. El violín de Ingres de Leopoldo Alas', *Proa* (León) (17.9.46), 3.

Cited by Martínez Cachero, B703, p. 415, who refers to it as a conversation with Salvador Canals on the opening of *Teresa*.

B480　García Sarriá, Francisco, *Clarín o la herejía amorosa* (Madrid: Gredos, 1975). 301 pp.

Uses *SUH* as the pivot around which author explains LA's personal difficulties with love and religion. The best part of this book is the publication of the LA-José Quevedo correspondence in the appendix (see Af28).

Reviews: .1. Bandera, Cesáreo. *HR*, 45 (1977), 462-64.
.2. Cerra, L. *Studium Ovetense* (Oviedo), 4 (1976), 559-60.
.3. Díaz, Janet W. *Hispano*, No. 66 (May 1979), 126-29.
.4. Díez Borque, José María. *EstLit*, No. 580 (15.1.76), 2338.
.5. Rutherford, John. *BHS*, 54 (1977), 254-56.

B481　——, 'Respuesta a una crítica de *Clarín o la herejía amorosa*', *HR*, 46 (1978), 513-15.

G.S. objects to Cesáreo Bandera's review (B480.1). See also B110.

B482　——, '*Su único hijo*: análisis de esta novela y de su importancia en la obra de Leopoldo Alas, "Clarín"', unpubl. diss., Univ. of Edinburgh, 1972-73. 334 pp.

See B480 for a revised version of this thesis.

B483　——, '*Su único hijo* en la obra de Clarín', in *Actas del Cuarto Congreso Internacional de Hispanistas*, I. (Salamanca: Consejo General de Castilla y León & Univ. de Salamanca, for Asociación Internacional de Hispanistas, 1982), pp. 599-609.

A preview of B480: the Congress was held at Salamanca in 1971, but the papers remained unpublished for eleven years.

B484　Garcíasol, Ramón de, 'Notas sobre el modernismo en España', *PSA*, 46 (1967), 197-226.

On LA's prose style as a precursor to *modernismo* (pp. 221-22).

B485　García Valero, Vicente, 'Romea y Clarín', in his *Dentro y fuera del teatro (Crónicas retrospectivas, historias, costumbres, anécdotas y cuentos)* (Madrid: Victoriano Suárez, 1913), pp. 21-33.

The actor Julián Romea is chagrined over LA's review of *El señor Joaquín*. Rpts LA's article on the *zarzuela* (*Madrid Cómico*, 3.9.98).

B486　*Gener, Pompeyo, 'Carta máxima a mi amigo Clarín', *La Publicidad* (?) (12.9.93).

B487 ——, *El caso Clarín. Monomanía maliciosa de forma impul-siva. (Estudio de psiquiatría)* (Madrid: Fernando Fe, 1894). 31 pp.
An unintentionally funny diatribe against LA for having criticized Gener's book, *Literaturas malsanas*. LA is, according to P.G., 'un caso de delirio malicioso de forma impulsiva'.
Review: .1. Anon. *Barcelona Cómica*, 7, No. 33 (11.8.94), 15.

B488 Gerrard, Lisa, 'The Romantic Woman in Nineteenth-Century Fiction: a Comparative Study of *Madame Bovary, La Regenta, The Mill on the Floss,* and *The Awakening*', unpubl. diss., Univ. of California–Berkeley, 1979. 157 pp. Abstracted in *DAI*, 41 (1980-81), 237-A.
On middle-class women characters and the conventional restrictions which turned them into dislocated romantics.

B489 Gil, Ildefonso-Manuel, 'Un verso de Garcilaso disimulado en la prosa de "Clarín"', *Ínsula*, No. 190 (Sept. 1962), 4.
Comments on the insertion of line 380 of Garcilaso's first eclogue in a passage of *SUH*.

B490 *Gil Cremades, J.F., 'Clarín, catedrático de Zaragoza', *El Heraldo de Aragón* (3.10.82).

B491 Gil Cremades, Juan José, *Krausistas y liberales* (Madrid: Seminarios y Ediciones, 1975), pp. 178-99.
A somewhat facile discussion of the Krausist *sabio* as a failure in several short stories of LA.

B492 ——, *El reformismo español. Krausismo, escuela histórica, neotomismo* (Barcelona: Ediciones Ariel, 1969), pp. 264-67.
LA is categorized as part of Spain's 'espiritualismo positivista'.

B493 Gil de Muro, Eduardo T., 'El anticlericalismo de "Clarín"', in *VI y VII Ciclo de conferencias sobre Oviedo* (Oviedo: Gráficas Summa, 1973), pp. 101-18.
Author concludes: 'Creo en el anticlericalismo de "Clarín". Pero a la distancia de ochenta y tantos años bendigo la osadía de un hombre que quiso ser anticlerical porque en el fondo se sentía profundamente cristiano.'

B494 ——, 'Clarín, un cristiano en la balanza', *Los Cuadernos del Norte* (Oviedo), 2, No. 7 (May-June 1981), 114-19.

On LA's open, almost ecumenical (and ultimately painful) position toward the Church and faith.

B495   Gilabert, Joan, *Narciso Oller. Estudio comparativo con la novela castellana del siglo XIX* (Barcelona: Ediciones Marte, 1977), pp. 32-33, 115-16.
On *LR*'s supposed flawed, sermonizing ending; and the fusing of its individual and collective levels.

B496   Gilman, Stephen, *Galdós and the Art of the European Novel: 1867-1887* (Princeton: Univ. Press, 1981), pp. 156-86.
An expansion of B497, in which he carries further the idea of inter-novel dialogue between Galdós and Clarín, detecting in them 'the tacit presence of Cervantes, Flaubert, Balzac, and, at one remove, Zola'.

B497   ——, 'La novela como diálogo: *La Regenta* y *Fortunata y Jacinta*', *NRFH*, 24 (1975), 438-48.
A suggestive article on the influence of *LR* on Galdós's *Fortunata y Jacinta*. S.G. sees Maxi Rubín and Fortunata herself as Galdosian responses to the Clarinian creation of Ana Ozores.

B498   Giner de los Ríos, Francisco, 'Tres cartas a Leopoldo Alas ("Clarín")', in his *Ensayos y cartas*. Ed. de homenaje en el cincuentenario de su muerte (Tezontle, México: Fondo de Cultura Económica, 1965), pp. 109-16. Originally printed in the *Boletín de la Institución Libre de Enseñanza*, 40 (18.2.16), 59-61; 50 (28.2.26), 57-59.
These letters were written in 1888, 1891, and 1896. On religion, the novel, *SUH*, and the death of LA's mother.

B499   Glendinning, Nigel, 'Some Versions of Carnival: Goya and Alas', in *Studies in Modern Spanish Literature and Art Presented to Helen Grant*, ed. Nigel Glendinning (London: Tamesis, 1972), pp. 65-78.
Focuses on the symbolic and emotional content of carnivalesque elements in Goya and in 'Pipá' and 'El entierro de la sardina'. A good, comparative analysis.
Review: .1. Munn, B.W. *Reflexión 2*, 2a época, 2, Nos 2-4 (1973), 165-67.

B500   Godoy Gallardo, Eduardo, 'El movimiento naturalista y la crítica española del siglo XIX', *Mapocho* (Santiago, Chile), No. 23 (Spring 1970), 55-70.
LA's position on naturalism (pp. 59-61).

B501 Gómez, Emilio, ' . . . . ', *Revista Popular* (Oviedo) (1.7.01), 16.
He says of LA: 'ante todo y sobre todo era bueno'. The title of the article is as given here.

B502 Gómez, Ulpiano, 'Recuerdo', *Revista Popular* (Oviedo) (1.7.01), 9-11. Rpt. in B514, pp. 200-02.
Recounts an anecdote which illustrates LA's emotional nature and obsession with the maternal.

B503 Gómez Baquero, Eduardo [pseud.: Andrenio] , 'Clarín y la crítica', *El Sol* (24.4.25), 1.
An appreciation of LA's contribution, as an exemplar, to criticism and to writing.

B504 ——, *'Cuentos morales*, por Leopoldo Alas (Clarín)', *Revista Crítica de Historia y Literatura Españolas, Portuguesas e Hispano-Americanas*, 1 (Mar. 1896), 129-31.
A favorable review, though author criticizes LA's ridicule and severity toward those who do not participate in the *fin de siglo* spiritual movement.

B505 ——, *El renacimiento de la novela española en el siglo XIX* (Madrid: Mundo Latino, 1924), pp. 92-93.
Emphasizes LA's fame as a critic, not as a novelist.

B506 Gómez Carrillo, Enrique, *Treinta años de mi vida. La miseria de Madrid*, III (Madrid: Sociedad de Librería, 1921), pp. 30-33, 104-12, 164-69. Rpt. in *O.C.*, XXVI (Madrid: Mundo Latino, 1923), pp. 33-36, 119-28, 191-92.
On Gómez Carrillo's friendship with LA; includes a letter from LA. See Af10.

B507 Gómez de la Serna, Ramón, 'El espaldarazo', in his *Azorín* (Madrid: Ediciones La Nave, 1930), pp. 71-77. A later ed.: *Azorín* (Buenos Aires: Losada, 1948), pp. 42-46.
One of LA's *paliques* in praise of Azorín provides the young Martínez Ruiz an entry into the literary world of late nineteenth-century Madrid.

B508 Gómez Galán, A., ' "Clarín" ', *Arbor*, 66, No. 253 (Jan. 1967), 95-96.
Comments on the general neglect of LA and welcomes the recent publishing of Clarín texts and criticism.

B509 Gómez Marín, J.A., ' "Clarín", crítico', in his *Aproximaciones al realismo español* (Madrid: Colección Básica, 1975), pp. 79-85.
Offers nothing new on LA as critic.

B510 Gómez Molleda, María Dolores, *Los reformadores de la España contemporánea* (Madrid: CSIC, 1966), pp. 314-16, 335-37, 347-54.
Notes how LA converted his *krausismo* into a form of eclecticism.

B511 Gómez-Santos, Marino, ' "Clarín" poeta (Dos composiciones en verso, inéditas, y una bibliografía)', *BIDEA*, 5 (1951), 396-401.
Prints two unpublished poems by LA and compiles a bibliography of LA's poetry (1876-81 and posthumous works). See also Ah51, B744.

B512 ———, ' "Clarín" y Leopoldo Alas', *Asturias* (Madrid), No. 13 (Apr. 1952), 8.
Contrasts the harshness of Clarín the critic with the softheartedness of LA the man.

B513 ———, 'Después del centenario de "Clarín" ', *Correo Literario*, 4, No. 68 (15.3.53), 11.
LA is 'un escritor de minorías, no de masas'. Also contains bibliographical material.

B514 ———, *Leopoldo Alas "Clarín": ensayo bio-bibliográfico*. Pról. de Gregorio Marañón (Oviedo: IDEA, 1952). 255 pp.
Though a superficial and sometimes disorganized biographical study, G.S.'s book is useful for the hard to find documents published in it. See Af13, 22, B375, 501, 520, 693, 906, 998, 1067, 1139, 1300, 1324, 1340, 1357.
Reviews: .1. Anon. *La Nueva España* (Oviedo) (29.3.53), 8.
.2. Cabal, C. *BIDEA*, 7 (1953), 148-50.
.3. Entrambasaguas, Joaquín de. *RL*, 4 (1953), 256-57.
.4. F[raga], [Eduardo de]. *La Nueva España* (Oviedo), (7.1.53), 8.
.5. G[ich], J[uan]. *Correo Literario*, No. 67 (1.3.53), 5.
.6. Révah, I.S. (?). *BEPIF*, 17 (1953), 273-74.

B515 ———, 'La religiosidad de Leopoldo Alas. Dos cartas del Clarín íntimo', *BIDEA*, 5 (1951), 240-44.
Cites two letters to the Bishop of Oviedo, Fray Ramón Martínez Vigil.

B516 *González, Etelvino, 'Asturias y los asturianos: Clarín y la cuestión social', *La Nueva España* (Oviedo) (4.11.79). Continued as *'Asturias y los asturianos: Clarín ante la cuestión social' (11.11.79).

B517 González Aurioles, Norberto, 'Teatro español. *Teresa*, drama en un acto y en prosa de D. Leopoldo Alas', *El Correo* (21.3.95), 2. Rpt. in B734, pp. 251-56.
Judges *Teresa* as an attempt to reform and modernize the Spanish theater.

B518 ——, 'Teatros. El drama de "Clarín" ', *El Correo* (2.5.95).
Believes public taste is not accustomed to the sober, simple plot of *Teresa* and that it is his duty as a critic to correct the public's misguided impressions.

B519 González Bardón, Francisco, ' "Clarín", el naturalismo y los escritores jóvenes', *El Español*, No. 176 (9.3.46), 7.
Seems like two different articles: one on LA's changing attitudes toward naturalism; and one on his fairly generous treatment of new writers.

B520 González-Blanco, Andrés, 'El aula de Clarín', *El III Centenario* [de la Univ. de Oviedo], No. 1 (Oviedo, Sept. 1908), p. 16. Rpt. in B514, p. 202; and in José María Martínez Cachero's *Andrés González Blanco: una vida para la literatura* (Oviedo: IDEA, 1963), p. 170.
A poem in honor of LA.

B521 ——, 'Clarín como crítico', *Nuestro Tiempo*, 23, No. 298 (Oct. 1923), 5-18.
An evaluation of LA's contribution to Spanish criticism.

B522 ——, *Escritores representativos de América* (Madrid: Editorial América, 1917), pp. 6-23, 26-29.
On LA as a critic and the difficulty of finding a writer of the same caliber after his death.

B523 ——, 'El espíritu de "Clarín" ', *Nuestro Tiempo*, 13, No. 169 (Jan. 1913), 67-74.
Comments on LA's personality and on the problems of getting the complete works published.

B524 ——, *Leopoldo Alas "Clarín". Juicio crítico de sus obras*,

La Novela Corta, 5, No. 250 (Madrid: Prensa Popular, 1920), n. pag. [47 pp.].
A general summary of LA's work. In his epilogue, G.-B. talks of LA's Asturianism, his idealism, and his role as a 'suscitador de ideas y de imágenes artísticas'.

B525 ——, 'La novela humorística', in his *Historia de la novela en España desde el romanticismo a nuestros días* (Madrid: Sáenz de Jubera, 1909), pp. 495-512.
Places LA within the category of Asturian humor, which the critic defines as a kind of 'humorismo espiritualista, mezclado con un lirismo elegíaco que se contiene'.

B526 González-Blanco, Pedro, 'Cómo conocí a "Clarín"', *Asturias* (Buenos Aires), No. 339 (Apr. 1952), 7-8.
An anecdote showing once more the strong personal influence LA exerted over many.

B527 *——, 'Los que gritamos " ¡Viva Clarín! " ', *Oviedo* (1952 ed.), n. pag. Cited by Martínez Cachero, B714, p. 100.

B528 González de Mesa, Amaro, 'Oviedo como personaje literario', in *III, IV y V Ciclo de conferencias sobre Oviedo* (Oviedo: Gráficas Summa, 1972), pp. 15-61.
Cites LA as well as Palacio Valdés, Pérez de Ayala, and Dolores Medio, as creators of a literary Oviedo.

B529 González López, Emilio, 'Entre el naturalismo y el espiritualismo: Clarín', in his *Historia de la literatura española. La Edad moderna (siglos XVIII y XIX)* (New York: Las Américas, 1965), pp. 501-12.
A nice introduction to the transitional nature of LA's work.

B530 González Ollé, Fernando, 'Del naturalismo al modernismo: los orígenes del poema en prosa y un desconocido artículo de Clarín', *RL*, 25, Nos 49-50 (1964), 49-67.
Rpts an article by LA, 'Pequeños poemas en prosa. Prólogo', which appeared in *La Revista del Antiguo Reino de Navarra* (15.5.88). G.O. sees in this article an anticipation of *modernismo*.

B531 ——, 'Prosa y verso en dos polémicas decimonónicas: Clarín contra Núñez de Arce y Campoamor contra Valera', *BBMP*, 39 (1963), 208-27.
LA's ideas on poetry and *lo poético*.

B532   González-Ruano, César, 'Releyendo a "Clarín"', *Arriba*, 2a
   época (3.12.47), 6.
   LA ought to be read today, since he is important in Spanish literary
   history.

B533   *G[onzález] Rubín, Pío, 'En el tren', *El Correo de Asturias*
   (Oviedo) (18.6.01), 2.
   An obituary, says Martínez Cachero, B703, p. 419.

B534   *——, 'Tres páginas de recuerdos', *El Correo de Asturias*
   (Oviedo) (8.4.06). Rpt. in *BIDEA*, 7 (1953), 360-63.
   Memories of LA, Palacio Valdés, and Tomás Tuero. LA, contrary
   to popular belief, was an authentic poet in verse and prose, declares
   G.R.

B535   González Serrano, U[rbano], 'La crítica en España', in his
   Estudios críticos (Madrid: Escuela Tipográfica del Hospicio,
   1892), pp. 123-32.
   LA, Menéndez Pelayo, and Palacio Valdés as representative of contemporary criticism.

B536   ——, 'Un día de luto', in his *La literatura del día (1900 a
   1903)* (Barcelona: Imp. de Henrich y Cía, 1903), pp. 141-
   47.
   On LA's death.

B537   ——, 'Leopoldo Alas', in his *Siluetas* (Madrid: B. Rodríguez
   Serra, 1899), pp. 47-50.
   A favorable portrait of LA as writer.

B538   ——, '*Museum*-Folletos literarios (VII) por Clarín (Leopoldo
   Alas)', in his *Estudios críticos* (see B535), pp. 149-55.
   Believes that LA's *Folletos literarios* will be 'en la historia interna de
   nuestra cultura lo que la *Comedia humana* de Balzac, en la sociedad
   que describe, una fotografía semoviente'.

B539   Goytisolo, José Agustín, 'Clarín en Italia', *Ínsula*, No. 173
   (Apr. 1961), 12.
   Notes the Italian translation of *LR* (see Ai24).

B540   Gracia Noriega, José Ignacio, 'Aspectos de Clarín', *La Nueva
   España* (Oviedo) (14.6.81).
   Rpt. in B183, pp. 9-11. Suggests one reason, *inter alia*, for *LR*'s relative
   obscurity (until recently): its 'irreductibilidad ... al bable' and

'patriotismo centraliego', which may have provoked the hostility of Asturian regionalists.

B541 Gramberg, Eduard Johannes, *Fondo y forma del humorismo de Leopoldo Alas, "Clarín"* (Oviedo: IDEA, 1958). 265 pp. Based on 'El humorismo de Leopoldo Alas, Clarín', diss., Univ. of California - Berkeley, 1957.

Establishes two major categories of humor in LA: 'el humorismo de piedad' and 'el humorismo de desprecio'. Also studies some of the stylistic devices used to comic effect. The last chapter, on *LR*, seems somewhat out of place and unconnected to the rest of the study.
Reviews: .1. Álvarez, Carlos Luis. *Punta Europa*, 5, Nos 55-56 (1960), 100-01.
.2. Beser, Sergio, *BHS*, 39 (1962), 53-55.
.3. Beser, Sergio. *Índice Histórico Español*, 6 (1960), 319.
.4. Borgers, Oscar. *Les Lettres Romanes*, 16 (1962), 309-11.
.5. García Lorca, Laura R. de. *RHM*, 26 (1960), 131-32.
.6. Hinterhäuser, Hans. *RF*, 73 (1961), 455-57.
.7. Martínez Cachero, José María. *BIDEA*, 13 (1959), 469-72.
.8. Martínez Cachero, José María. *RL*, 21 (1962), 208-09.
.9. Muñiz, Angelina. *NRFH*, 17 (1963-64), 407-08.
.10. Rand, Marguerite C. *Hispania* (U.S.A.), 43 (1960), 634-35.
.11. Sarmiento, Edward. *MLN*, 77 (1962), 202-03.

B542 ——, '*Su único hijo*, novela incomprendida de Leopoldo Alas', *Hispania* (U.S.A.), 45 (1962), 194-99. Rpt. in B723, pp. 204-11.

Author points out four literary problems inherent in *SUH*: 1) the vague contours of the setting; 2) the satiric view of pseudoromanticism; 3) the odd, euphemistic naturalist treatment of the characters; and 4) the principal theme of the work, especially in relation to the ending. E.G. does not, however, really explain why *SUH* is composed the way it is.

B543 ——, 'Tres tipos de ambientación en la novela del siglo diecinueve', *RHM*, 28 (1962), 315-26.

Studies three varieties of description in the realist novel: ambience as an independent value (Pereda); descriptive naturalism (Blasco Ibáñez and *LR*); and ambience as a manifestation of the characters' personalities ('¡Adiós, Cordera!').

B544 Granell, Manuel [pseud.: Manuel Cristóbal], ' "Clarín" y el ambiente literario de su tiempo', *Cultura Universitaria* (Caracas), 31 (1952), 73-88.

Describes the literary atmosphere of bickering mediocrities in which LA wrote; and gives three examples of LA's criticism (on Azorín, Gómez Carrillo, and Unamuno).

B545 ——, ' "Clarín" y la filosofía', *El Universal* (Caracas) (12.3.52), 4. Rpt. in *Asturias* (Buenos Aires), No. 339 (Apr. 1952), 16-17.
Regards LA as a philosophical precursor of Unamuno and Ortega; and, in particular, as one who anticipates the idea of the man of flesh and blood.

B546 ——, 'Clarín y Oviedo', *El Español*, No. 16 (13.2.43), 5.
Author senses LA's presence, his memory in the city of Oviedo, in the 'gama de grises con pincel nervioso y exacto'.

B547 ——, 'Un drama de Clarín', *Élite* (Caracas) (19.4.52), 40.
On *Teresa*, 'escrito con desmasiada emoción personal ... pero con escasa picardía técnica'.

B548 *——, 'Mi "Clarín" en el recuerdo', *El Nacional* (Caracas) (14.11.51). *Rpt. in *Asturias* (Buenos Aires), Nos. 334-35 (Nov.-Dec. 1951), 8-9.

B549 *——, 'La unidad de la cultura hispanoamericana', *El Universal* (Caracas) (13.6.52).

B550 Grau, Jacinto, 'Clarín', in his *Estampas* (Buenos Aires: Hachette, 1941), pp. 9-14.
An appreciation of LA, the man and artist, with a concluding paragraph on the injustice of the execution of his son during the Spanish Civil War.

B551 Green, Otis H., 'Blanco-Fombona, Pérez Galdós, and Leopoldo Alas', *HR*, 10 (1942), 47-52.
The Venezuelan writer drew upon *SUH* for his novel, *El hombre de hierro* (1905) and upon *LR* for *La mitra en la mano* (1925), though his adaptations are inferior to the Spanish originals.

B552 Griswold, Susan C., 'Rhetorical Strategies and Didacticism in Clarín's Short Fiction', *KRQ*, 29 (1982), 423-33.
On the use of a 'reliable, privileged, intrusive, and biased narrator' which engages the reader's complicity.

B553 Grossi, Rodrigo, 'Un episodio de *Tinieblas en las cumbres* a la luz de "Adiós, Cordera"', in *Nueva Conciencia*, Nos 20-21. Homenaje a Ramón Pérez de Ayala (Mieres del Camino, Asturias: Instituto Bernaldo de Quirós, 1980 [1982]), pp. 103-07.

On parallels between the Rosina episode and '¡Adiós, Cordera!' Cites use of symbolic names, *bable*, and similar intentions in both. Sketchy.

B554 Guastavino, Guillermo, 'Algo más sobre "Clarín" y *Teresa*', *BH*, 73 (1971), 133-59.

Cites letters from LA to the actress María Guerrero on the subject of *Teresa*'s opening. See Af11.

B555 Gubernatis, Angelo de, 'Alas, Leopoldo', in *Dictionnaire international des écrivains du jour* (Florence, 1890-91), p. 29.

A very brief note on LA.

B556 Guenoun, Pierre, 'À propos de l'entrée en scène d'Ana Ozores dans *La Regenta* de Clarín', in *Mélanges offerts à Charles Vincent Aubrun*, I, ed. Haïm Vidal Sephiha (Paris: Éditions Hispaniques, 1975), pp. 341-49.

Says that LA, like Cervantes, the Goncourts, Tolstoy, Colette, and others, little by little insinuates his main character into the text.

B557 Guerlin, Henri, *L'Espagne moderne vue par ses écrivains* (Paris: Librairie Académique & Perrin, 1924), pp. 270-73.

Sums up the plot of '¡Adiós, Cordera!'

B558 Gullón, Agnes, 'El esperpento romántico en manos de un realista: *Su único hijo*', *Río Piedras* (Puerto Rico), Nos 5-6 (Sept.-Mar. 1974-75), 103-12.

For A.G., 'la estructura de *Su único hijo* puede representarse gráficamente como la de un poliedro diamantino: forma y objeto sintetizan el sentido y el espíritu de la novela.'

B559 Gullón, Germán, ' "Clarín" o la complejidad narrativa', in his *El narrador en la novela del siglo XIX* (Madrid: Taurus, 1976), pp. 133-48.

G.G. describes the narrative voice of *SUH* as ironic, omniscient, and humoristic, a point of view which does not, however, exclude other perspectives. It is, nevertheless, the triangle of characters, who live and play act simultaneously, which constitutes the novelistic structure of *SUH*.

B560 ——, 'Invención y reflexividad discursiva en *La Regenta*, de Leopoldo Alas', in his *La novela como acto imaginativo (Alarcón–Bécquer–Galdós–"Clarín")* (Madrid: Taurus, 1983), pp. 123-47.

Discusses how the narrator's commentary on characters' words not only points to their inauthenticity but also turns the novel into a 'meta-text'.

B561 Gullón, Ricardo, 'Aspectos de "Clarín"', *Archivum*, 2 (1952), 217-26. Rpt. in *Ficción* (Buenos Aires), No. 31 (1961), 73-90.

Discusses a number of Clarinian aspects: LA's combativeness, patriotism, comradeship with ideological opposites, moral sense, tenderness, and provincialism.

B562 ——, 'Un centenario actual', *CHA*, No. 36 (Dec. 1952), 270-71.

On LA's modernity.

B563 ——, ' "Clarín", crítico literario', *Universidad. Revista de Cultura y Vida Universitaria* (Zaragoza), 26 (1949), 389-431. Rpt. in B723, pp. 115-46.

A sound article on the various elements of LA's criticism, which can be considered a forerunner to Beser (see B149) and other studies.

B564 ——, 'Las novelas cortas de Clarín', *Ínsula*, No. 76 (Apr. 1952), 3. Extracted in B1297, pp. 602-07.

A good analysis of LA's short stories ('Pipá', 'Doña Berta', 'Super-chería', etc.). In these linear narratives, which are centered on psychological truths, irony offsets incipient sentimentalism.

B565 ——, *Vida de Pereda* (Madrid: Nacional, 1944), pp. 172-73, 178-80.

On LA's and Pereda's meeting and friendship.

B566 Gutiérrez Abascal, José [pseud.: Kasabal], 'Leopoldo Alas (Clarín)', *La Ilustración Artística* (Barcelona), 19 (30.4.1900), 283.

A biographical sketch.

B567 ——, '*Teresa*', *La Ilustración Ibérica* (Barcelona), 13 (30.3.95), 194-95. Rpt. in Ae4, pp. 178-80.

The play did not please the public, even though it was well presented.

B568 Gutiérrez-Gamero, E., *Gota a gota el mar se agota (Memorias)* (Barcelona: Juventud, 1934), pp. 220-21.
On LA's death and his irascible temperament.

B569 Gutiérrez Llano, Francisco, *Clarín. Hombre de su tiempo* (Oviedo: Sindicato Español Universitario, 1952). 35 pp.
Generalizations and clichés.

Gutiérrez Marrone, Nila: See Marrone, Nila.

B570 H., 'Armando Palacio Valdés y Leopoldo Alas (Clarín) – *La literatura en 1881*', *Revista Contemporánea*, No. 39 (15.5.82), 105-07.
A favorable review.

B571 Hafter, Monroe Z., 'A Goncourt Clue to a Clarín Plot', *CLS*, 19 (1982), 319-34.
Sees the influence and continuing inspiration of *Charles Demailly* in 'Una medianía', 'Las dos cajas', 'Amor' è furbo', and *SUH.*

B572 ——, 'Heroism in Alas and Carlyle's *On Heroes*', *MLN*, 95 (1980), 312-34.
An interesting article on Carlyle's influence on *SUH* and later works of LA: 'Sincerity, simplicity, integrity, perceptivity, good will, these seem to be the hallmarks of heroism which Carlyle inspired in Clarín, a modest and moral conception of greatness which takes its strength from a searching view of human reality.'

B573 Hamblin, Ellen N., 'Adulterous Heroines in Nineteenth-Century Literature: a Comparative Literature Study', unpubl. diss., Florida State Univ., 1977. 198 pp. Abstracted in *DAI*, 38 (1977-78), 2761-A.
Contrasts *LR*, *Mme Bovary*, *Anna Karenina*, and *The Scarlet Letter.*

B574 Hampejs, Zdeněk, 'Cartas desconocidas de escritores españoles y catalanes dirigidas a Antonín Pikhart', *QIA*, 4, No. 26 (1961), 79-80.
Notes that one of the forty letters to Pikhart, the Czech Hispanist, is from LA. See also Af26.

B575 Haro Tecglen, Eduardo, 'La sombra de la provincia', *Los Cuadernos del Norte* (Oviedo), 5, No. 23 (Jan.-Feb. 1984), 34-36.
Interesting reminiscences of a Republican childhood, in which *LR* representado 'un fondo abismal de pasado continuo, de España que no cesa...'

B576 Hatzfeld, Helmut, 'La imitación estilística de *Madame Bovary* (1857), en *La Regenta* (1884)', *Thesaurus*, 32 (1977), 40-53.
H.H. details various stylistic techniques which LA creatively adapted from Flaubert: personification, certain comparisons, the tripartite rhythm, impressionism, indirect free discourse, insistent repetition, the use of italics, the deliberate abuse of rhetoric, and leitmotifs.

B577 ——, 'Two Stylizations of Clerical Tragedy: *O Crime do Padre Amaro* (1875) and *La Regenta* (1884)', in *The Two Hesperias. Literary Studies in Honor of Joseph G. Fucilla on the Occasion of his 80th Birthday* (Madrid: José Porrúa Turanzas, 1977), pp. 181-95.
Describes five stages in the moral decay of the priest protagonists: the setting of the stage, the growing temptations, the factor of jealousy, the explosion of scandal, and the turn to crime. A rather disappointing essay, touching mostly the surface of these novels.

B578 *Heras, Dionisio de las [pseud.: Plácido], 'Avisos del otro', *El País* (16.2.99). Rpt. in B158, pp. 49-51.
Attacks Azorín for duplicitous behaviour in publishing, he claims, an anonymous, abusive piece on LA in *Juan Rana.*

B579 ——, *El besugo Clarín: folleto crítico* (Madrid: Imp. 'La Propaganda', 1895). 55 pp.
Another scurrilous anti-Clarín attack (cf., for example, B487, 689, 700, 809). This one focuses principally on *Teresa*, a drama with no drama, says 'Plácido'.

B580 *——, 'Carne de "Clarín"', *Juan Rana* (10.6.97).
Cited by Romero, Ae4, p. 41.

B581 *——, ' "Clarín", previsor', *Juan Rana* (27.6.98).
Cited by Romero, Ae4, p. 41.

B582 *——, 'La cuestión "Clarín"- Navarro Ledesma. Historia de una entrevista', *Juan Rana* (1.4.97).
Cited by Romero, Ae4, p. 41.

B583 Heredero, Carlos F., 'Gonzalo Suárez frente a "Clarín": *La Regenta* en el cine', *Argumentos* (Madrid), 8, Nos 63-64 (1984), 54-55.
Although the film version of *LR* is seriously flawed, nevertheless, it possesses suggestive and unexpected images and details. See also Aj3.

B584 *Hermanz, Norberto, 'Leopoldo Alas "Clarín". 1852-1901',
Revista de Pedagogía (Barcelona), 17 (1938).
Cited by Laura de los Ríos, B460, p. 318.

B585 Hernández, Nicolás, Jr., 'Emma, Ana and Religion: a Comparative Study of *Madame Bovary* and *La Regenta*', *PVR*, 9, No.
1 (1981), 74-78.
Once again we are told that Emma and Ana confuse the carnal and the
spiritual. Awkwardly written.

B586 Hoar, Leo J., Jr., 'Galdós' Counter-Attack on his Critics: the
Lost Short Story, "El pórtico de la gloria" ', *Symposium*,
30 (1976), 277-307.
Discusses the possibility that the caricature Criptoas in G.'s satire, 'El
pórtico de la gloria', represents Clarín (pp. 295-96).

B587 Hodoušek, Eduard, 'Několik slov o autorovi a jeho hrdince'
['About the Author and his Heroine'], in Ai3, pp. 77-81.

B588 Horno Liria, Luis, 'Lo aragonés, en "Clarín" ', *Zaragoza*,
13 (1961), 107-29. Rpt. in his *Lo aragonés en algunos
escritores contemporáneos* (Zaragoza: Diputación Provincial,
Institución 'Fernando el Católico', 1978), pp. 93-119.
A superficial descriptive analysis of two Aragonese characters in *LR*:
D. Cayetano Ripamilán and Víctor Quintanar.

B589 Hortas Moragón, Carlos Rafael, 'The Moral Vision of Leopoldo Alas', unpubl. diss., Yale Univ., 1970. 307 pp. Abstracted in *DAI*, 31 (1970-71), 6611-A.
LA's moral sensibility is the chief element of his writings.

B590 *Huelga González, Vicente, 'En recordación del ilustre crítico,
novelista y jurisconsulto D. Leopoldo Alas García (sic),
"Clarín" ' (Mieres: Imp. Francisco Bárcena Sordo, 1952).
4 pp.
Cited by Martínez Cachero, B714, p. 102. A triptych of sonnets.

Huerta Calvo, Javier: See Aullón de Haro, Pedro.

B591 Humphrey, Laura Masotti, 'Krausismo and Leopoldo Alas's
La Regenta', unpubl. diss., Univ. of Rochester, 1981. 201
pp. Abstracted in *DAI*, 47 (1981-82), 2121-A.
Shows the conflict between the Krausist belief in the perfectability

of mankind and the inner and outer tensions and complexities govern-
ing *LR* which obstruct the Krausist ideal.

B592   Hurtado de Mendoza, Ambrosio [pseud.: Julio Jurenito],
'Una joya de la literatura nacional: *La Regenta*', *Cuaderno
Literario Azor*, No. 26 (June 1980), 26-30.
Comments on the popularity of the Alianza ed. (Ac7).

B593   Hurtado I Arias, E.G., 'Leopoldo Alas (Clarín)', *La Revista
Nueva* (Santiago, Chile), 4 (1901), 259-67.
An obituary. Latin-American youth, says this writer, looked upon
LA as a distant but influential leader.

B594   Ibargüengoitia, Jorge, 'Introducción', in *La Regenta* (see
Ac9), pp. ix-xix.

B595   Ibarra, Fernando, 'Las categorías estéticas en la crítica
literaria de Leopoldo Alas, Clarín', unpubl. diss., Univ. of
California - Los Angeles, 1968. 421 pp. Abstracted in *DA*,
29 (1968-69), 1898-A.
An analysis of LA's aesthetic ideas and judgements, including his
appraisals of the younger literary generation.

B596   ——, 'Clarín-Galdós: una amistad', *Archivum*, 21 (1971),
65-76.
Contributes nothing new to the subject.

B597   ——, 'Clarín y algunos escritores portugueses', *LBR*, 10
(1973), 52-67.
LA's criticism on Eça de Queiros, Antero de Quental, and Guilherme
de Azevedo.

B598   ——, 'Clarín y Azorín: el matrimonio y el papel de la mujer
española', *Hispania* (U.S.A.), 55 (1972), 45-54.
An interesting study on Azorín's reaction to *Teresa* and the roles of
woman and marriage in it.

B599   ——, 'Clarín y el teatro político', *RomN*, 13 (1971-72),
266-71.
On LA's notion of theater as a pedagogical tool.

B600   ——, 'Clarín y la liberación de la mujer', *Hispano*, No. 51
(May 1974), 27-33.

Comments on an early Clarín article, 'El amor y la economía' (*La Unión*, 14.7.79).

B601 ——, 'Clarín y Rubén Darío: historia de una incomprensión', *HR*, 41 (1973), 524-40.
Provides a detailed chronological analysis of their relationship.

B602 ——, 'El Dios de Clarín', in *Actas del Quinto Congreso Internacional de Hispanistas* [celebrado en Bordeaux del 2 al 8 de septiembre de 1974], II (Bordeaux: Instituto de Estudios Ibéricos e Iberoamericanos, Univ. de Bordeaux III, for Asociación Internacional de Hispanistas, 1977), pp. 467-79.
Presents the spiritual trajectory of LA and his lifelong need for a very real, personal God.

B603 Icaza, Francisco A. de, *Examen de críticos* (Madrid: Est. tip. Sucesores de Rivadeneyra, 1894), pp. 83-85.
LA as one of the major critics of the time.

B604 Ife, Barry W., 'Idealism and Materialism in Clarín's *La Regenta*: two Comparative Studies', *RLC*, 44 (1970), 273-95.
Compares *LR* to Eliot's *Mill on the Floss* in order to show that LA's position is both anti-idealist and anti-materialist and 'that all personality, the noble aspects as well as the ignoble, is social in origin.' A thoughtful article on the relationship between self and society.

B605 I[glesias] Eguren, Ricardo, 'D. Leopoldo Alas "Clarín". Los cuatro amores del maestro', *La Voz de Asturias* (Oviedo) (1.5.49).
On LA's love for his home, the Univ. de Oviedo, the Casino, and the Campo de San Francisco.

B606 *El Imparcial* (18.6.06).
Contains five articles, which appeared in *Los Lunes* section of the paper: B17, 142, 783, 940, 952.

B607 *Ínsula*, No. 76 (Apr. 1952).
Homage no. Contents: B114, 283, 468, 564, 1108, 1125.

B608 *Ínsula*, No. 451 (June 1984).
Contains articles written especially for the centenary of *LR*'s publication. See: B140, 269, 655, 739, 1041, 1168, 1271.

B609 Iriarte, Joaquín, 'La filosofía española y los casticismos del pre-'98'', *RyF*, 135 (1947), 403-04.
Ganivet's and Unamuno's ideas on mysticism are anticipated by LA's prologue to Posada's *Ideas pedagógicas modernas* (1892).

Itálico, Silvio [pseud.] : See Álvarez-Buylla, Benito.

B610 Izquierdo, Pascual, 'Apéndice' (see Ad38), pp. 233-53.

B611 J.A.C. [Juan Antonio Cabezas?] , 'Elisa Alas de la Llave, hija de "Clarín", nos habla de su padre', *Asturias* (Madrid), No. 13 (Apr. 1952), 11.
Memories of her father's affection and of his death.

B612 J.R., 'Los intelectuales españoles intentan impedir que *La Regenta* de "Clarín" se convierta en cine de consumo', *La Nueva España* (Oviedo) (18.4.72), 9.
A campaign is afoot to make sure *LR* is not exploited in its film version. See Aj3.

B613 Jackson, Robert M[anson] , ' "Cervantismo" in the Creative Process of Clarín's *La Regenta*', *MLN*, 84 (1969), 208-27.
An excellent article on the interpenetration of life and literature and the concept of multiple perspectives in *LR*.

B614 ——, '*La Regenta* and Contemporary History', *REH*, 11 (1977), 287-302.
A stimulating study on the historical allegory present in *LR*.

B615 ——, 'The Thematic Structure of Leopoldo Alas' *La Regenta*', unpubl. diss., Harvard Univ., 1968. 309 pp.
Studies *LR* as 'a successful compendium of the important themes found in the nineteenth century European novel', with history serving as 'the backbone of *La Regenta*', bound up inextricably in its fiction.

B616 Jeschke, Hans, *La generación de 1898*, 2nd ed. (Madrid: Nacional, 1954), pp. 53-55.
On LA's favorable attitude toward both liberal and conservative writers of the Restoration.

B617 *Jones, Julie, '*His Only Son*: a Translation of Leopoldo Alas' *Su único hijo*', unpubl. diss., Univ. of Virginia, 1970. xxv + 332 pp.

Abstracted in *DAI*, 32 (1970-71), 969-A. See Ai7.

B618 Jones, Margaret E.W., *Dolores Medio*, TWAS, 281 (New York: Twayne, 1974), pp. 53-55.
Discusses influence of *LR* on *Nosotros los Rivero* (1953).

B619 Jove y Bravo, Rogelio, 'Un siglo de prensa asturiana (1808-1916)', *BIDEA*, 3, No. 7 (May-Aug. 1949), 60, 67, 68, 70.
References to LA's collaboration in various Asturian journals and to the LA-Juan Menéndez Pidal dispute. See also B1324.

B620 *Junceda, Luis, 'Mi deuda con "Clarín"', *Umbral*, No. 8 (June 1952).

B621 Junceda Avello, E., 'Análisis sexológico de la novela de "Clarín": *Su único hijo*', *BIDEA*, 38, No. 111 (Jan.-Apr. 1984), 187-203.
On the sexual proclivities of the main character. A medical re-tread.

Jurenito, Julio [pseud.] : See Hurtado de Mendoza, Ambrosio.

B622 Juretschke, Hans, *España ante Francia* (Madrid: Nacional, 1940), pp. 90-109.
On LA's vision of France and the French; and his knowledge of French writers.

Kailing, Barbara Jean: See Rodríguez, Alfred.

Kasabal [pseud.] : See Gutiérrez Abascal, José.

B623 Krause, Anna, *Azorín, el pequeño filósofo* (Madrid: Espasa-Calpe, 1955), pp. 62-72, 98-99, 108-11, 223, 261-62.
Suggests Azorín's idea of a philosopher-educator in *La voluntad* was influenced by 'Cartas a Hamlet' and LA himself.

B624 Kronik, John W[illiam], 'Censo de personajes en los cuentos de "Clarín"', *Archivum*, 11 (1961), 323-406.
Intended as a guide to the reading of the short stories and to the great number of characters LA created.

B625 ——, 'Clarín and Verlaine', *RLC*, 37 (1963), 368-84.
Comments on and rpts 'Paul Verlaine (*Liturgias íntimas*)' (*La Ilustración Española y Americana*, 41, Nos 36-37, 1897).
Review: .1. Mombello, Gianni, *SFr*, No. 22 (1964), 182.

B626 ——, 'Clarín y la crítica destructiva', *Hispano*, No. 25 (Sept. 1965), 57-62.
A review-article on B221.

B627 ——, 'Un cuento olvidado de "Clarín"', *CHA*, No. 136 (Apr. 1961), 27-35.
On 'La guitarra', which is reprinted here.

B628 ——, 'The Function of Names in the Stories of Alas', *MLN*, 80 (1965), 260-65.
For LA, the choice of a name may be for humoristic or thematic reasons, or for character and personality portrayal. It is an ironic intellectual device, generally applied to types with whom he does not sympathize.

B629 ——, 'The Identification of "Clarín"', *RomN*, 2 (1960-61), 87-88.
Points out when the readers of *El Solfeo* became aware of LA's identity.

B630 ——, 'Leopoldo Alas, Krausism, and the Plight of the Humanities in Spain', *MLS*, 11, No. 3 (Fall 1981), 3-15.
How LA consistently defended the humanities in such texts as *Un discurso*, his prologue to Posada's *Ideas pedagógicas modernas*, 'Camus', the lead essay in *Crítica popular*, and the story 'Ordalías'.

B631 ——, 'La modernidad de Leopoldo Alas', *PSA*, 41 (1966), 121-34.
A fine article detailing LA's influence on, and relationship with, the Generation of 1898. J.K. points to LA's psychological and subjective depth and his existential anguish as signs of his affinity with the Generation of 1898.

B632 ——, 'La reseña de Clarín sobre *El amigo Manso*', *AGald*, 15 (1980), 63-71.
Comments on LA's literary perspicacity in his positive evaluation of G.'s main character; and rpts this uncollected review (from *El Día*, No. 752, 19.6.82).

B633 ——, 'Sesenta y ocho frente a noventa y ocho: la modernidad de Leopoldo Alas', in *Actas del Segundo Congreso Internacional de Hispanistas* (Nimega: Instituto Español de la Univ. de Nimega for Asociación Internacional de Hispanistas, 1967), pp. 371-76.
An abridged version of B631.

B634 ——, 'The Short Stories of Leopoldo Alas (Clarín): an Analysis and Census of the Characters', unpubl. diss., Univ. of Wisconsin, 1960. 396 pp. Abstracted in *DA*, 21 (1960-61), 1566.
On LA's creation of characters; the techniques and attitudes used to develop both types and individuals in the short stories.

B635 ——, 'Unamuno's *Abel Sánchez* and Alas's "Benedictino"': a Thematic Parallel', in *Spanish Thought and Letters in the Twentieth Century*, ed. Germán Bleiberg and E. Inman Fox (Nashville: Vanderbilt Univ. Press, 1966), pp. 287-97.
Comparative study which illustrates not only the omnipresence of envy, hatred and malevolence in the two stories, but the absence of love itself.

B636 Küpper, Werner, 'Leopoldo Alas, "Clarín", und der französische Naturalismus in Spanien', unpubl. diss., Univ. of Köln, 1958. 193 pp.
As noted by Gramberg, W.K.'s conclusion that LA is the only authentic representative of naturalism in Spain, is contradicted by the rest of the thesis, which details the ways in which he did not follow naturalistic tenets.
Review: .1. Gramberg, Eduard J. *Archivum*, 11 (1961), 447-52.

B637 L. [Eduardo de Lustonó], 'Un estudio biográfico', in *El libro del año*, ed. Ricardo Ruiz y Benítez de Lugo et al (Madrid: Est. Tipolitográfico Sucesores de Rivadeneyra, 1899), pp. 11-14.
Serves as an introduction to a Clarín piece, 'Filosofía y letras'.

B638 L.J.A., 'La Regenta de Gonzalo Suárez', *Asturias Semanal*, No. 272 (24.8.74), 32-35.
Director of film version of *LR* emphasizes that his adaptation is not LA's novel. See Aj3.

B639 Ladrón de Guevara, Pablo, *Novelistas buenos y malos*, 4th ed. rev. (Bilbao: El Mensajero del Corazón de Jesús, 1933), pp. 33-34.
LA is a bad writer, i.e., immoral, anticlerical, and generally scandalous.

B640 Laffitte, G., '*Madame Bovary* et *La Regenta*', *BH*, 45 (1943), 157-63.
Establishes parallels between the two novels in the delineation of character, ambience, and tone.

B641 Laporta, Francisco J., *Adolfo Posada: política y sociología en la crisis del liberalismo español* (Madrid: Edicusa, 1974), pp. 23-24, 26-28.
Discusses LA's decisive influence on Posada's political and philosophical beliefs.

B642 Lara y Pedraja, Antonio [pseud.: Orlando], 'Revista literaria. *La Regenta*, por D. Leopoldo Alas', *Revista de España*, 106 (10.9.85), 124-43.
One of the few critics of LA's time to appreciate warmly and fully the greatness of the book. Despite the article's long-windedness, it is quite worth reading. Rpt. in B1236, pp. 631-47.

B643 Laso Prieto, José María, 'La religión en *La Regenta*', *Argumentos* (Madrid), 8, Nos 63-64 (1984), 38-43.
Situates LA's religious trajectory within the historical and cultural contexts of Leo XIII and the Restoration.

B644 Lázaro, J[osé], 'Crónica general', *La España Moderna*, 1, No. 8 (Aug. 1889), 186-87.
On LA's feud with Manuel del Palacio; and *A 0,50 poeta.*

B645 ——, 'Revista general', *La España Moderna*, 1, No. 7 (July 1889), 211.
On *A 0,50 poeta* and LA's literary activity in 1889.

B646 Lázaro Carreter, F., & E. Correa Calderón, *Literatura española contemporánea*, 4th ed. rev. (Salamanca: Anaya, 1964), pp. 99-100. 1st ed., 1963.
Introductory. Criticizes LA's ideology.

B647 Lebredo, Gerardo Gregorio, 'Fermín de Pas y Ana Ozores en *La Regenta*', unpubl. diss., Florida State Univ., 1970. 169 pp. Abstracted in *DAI*, 32 (1971-72), 440-A.
A character study.

B648 LeCount, Virginia G., 'Leopoldo Alas, "Clarín": a Study of Nineteenth-Century Society in Spain as Depicted in his Novels and Short Stories', unpubl. M.A. thesis, Columbia Univ., 1940. 261 pp.
Describes the social, economic, political, and religious life of towns and individuals in LA's works.

B649 El Lector [pseud.] , 'Leyendo *Madrid Cómico*. "Clarín" y Benavente fueron directores', *EstLit*, No. 23 (15.3.45), 7.
Among other things, discusses the LA-Ricardo de la Vega exchange and the LA-Azorín relationship.

B650 ——, 'Leyendo *Madrid Cómico*. Tesis satírica. – Dirección "in absentia" de Clarín. – "Los desastres de la guerra", de Goya. – Benavente y el modernismo', *EstLit*, No. 24 (5.4.45), 18.
Cites from 'Palique' (No. 778, 15.1.98), in which one finds a 'profesión de fe moral satírica de *Madrid Cómico*'. Also discusses LA's period as editor of *Madrid Cómico*.

B651 Ledesma Miranda, [Ramón] , 'Clarín en edición de lujo', *Arriba*, 2a época (9.10.47).
Review of Aa5.

B652 León Sánchez, Manuel, & José Cascales Muñoz, *Antología de la Cuerda Granadina* (México: Imp. Manuel León Sánchez, 1928), pp. 138-41.
On the LA-Manuel del Palacio literary feud.

B653 Lillo, Juan de, ' "Clarín", evocado por su hija', *Alerta* (Santander) (17.11.66), 6.
Daughter Elisa recalls LA's moments of tenderness and bad humor. Anecdotal.

B654 ——, 'Profesor Martínez Cachero: "confiar *La Regenta* a gentes de segundo plano es incurrir en riesgo de mediocridad", *La Nueva España* (Oviedo) (27.4.72), 1-2.
Opposition to the makers of the film version of *LR* grows in Asturias and elsewhere. Martínez Cachero points out that it is a difficult novel to film for its psychological emphasis and its characters. See Aj3.

B655 Lissorgues, Yvan, 'La autenticidad religiosa de Leopoldo Alas', *Ínsula*, No. 451 (June 1984), 3.
On the anti-dogmatic and open character of LA's religious spirit.

B656 ——, 'Concepción de la historia en Leopoldo Alas (Clarín): una *historia artística* al servicio del progreso', *Los Cuadernos del Norte* (Oviedo), 2, No. 7 (May-June 1981), 50-55.
Describes LA's concept of history and the historian, which he himself sums up as 'una historia filosófica, artística, documentada y pintoresca,

sin el andamiaje de la erudición, pero no sin sus frutos, sin la falsedad
de la leyenda y de la novela, pero no sin sus atractivos y su verdad
sentimental y sintética.'

B657 ——, 'Enseñanza y educación', in *Clarín político* (see Ab31),
II, pp. 47-93.

B658 ——, 'España ante la guerra colonial de 1895 a 1898: Leopoldo
Alas (Clarín), periodista, y el problema cubano', in *Cuba: les
étapes d'une libération. Hommage à Juan Marinello et Noël
Salomon. Actes du Colloque International des 22, 23 et 24
Novembre 1978* (Toulouse: Univ. de Toulouse-Le Mirail,
Centre d'Études Cubaines, 1979), pp. 47-76.
A well-documented study tracing LA's ethical, Republican-flavored
attitude to the Cuban situation, his emphasis on cultural rather than
economic or administrative, unity between Spain and Cuba, and his
fervent desire for Spain's redemption after the 1898 war.

B659 ——, 'Idée et réalité dans *Su único hijo* de Leopoldo Alas,
"Clarín" ', *Les Langues Néo-latines*, No. 243 (1982), 47-64.
Studies how LA's idea of what reality should be like predominates
over what that reality is in *SUH*. It is this 'prédominance de l'idée'
which gives unity to the novel.

B660 ——, 'Introducción', in *Clarín político* (see Ab30), I, pp.
xvii-lxxxviii.

B661 ——, 'Literatura y sociedad', in *Clarín político* (see Ab31),
II, pp. 121-70.

B662 ——, *La Pensée philosophique et religieuse de Leopoldo
Alas (Clarín)–1875-1901* (Paris: Éditions du CNRS, 1983).
460 pp.
With chapters on LA's criticism of the Spanish Catholic Church, his
ideas on religion and society, reason versus spirit in his works, and
his search for authentic religious feeling. A solid investigation of LA's
thinking. Also includes an appendix on his collaboration with the
Ateneo's Escuela de Estudios Superiores; letters to Segismundo Moret
(see Af18) and José Victoriano de la Cuesta (see Af6); and articles
by Mínimo (see B815) and Azorín (see B762).

B663 ——, 'Periodismo y cultura', in *Clarín político* (see Ab31),
II, pp. 17-30.

B664 *——, 'La producción periodística de Leopoldo Alas (Clarín). Índices', unpubl. diss. [?] , Univ. de Toulouse-Le Mirail, 1981.

B665 Little, William Thomas, 'Don Juanism in Modern European Literature', unpubl. diss., Washington Univ., 1973. 440 pp. Abstracted in *DAI*, 34 (1973-74), 3401-A.
Ch. 4 of this diss. studies the degeneration of the Don Juan figure in *LR* and *SUH.*

B666 Little, William, & Joseph Schraibman, 'Notas sobre el motivo de la paternidad en *Su único hijo* de "Clarín" ', *BIDEA*, 32 (1978), 21-29.
Makes use of two Biblical passages as a literary source for *SUH* and as a means of re-evaluating the novel.

B667 Litvak, Lily, 'La idea de la decadencia en la crítica anti-modernista en España (1888-1910)', *HR*, 45 (1977), 397-412.
LA is one of the examples of antimodernist criticism in Spain.

B668 Llave Alas, Pedro de la, 'Leopoldo Alas, 1852-1901. En el centenario de "Clarín" ', *Arriba*, 2a época (25.4.52), 21.
A modest, well-intentioned article by a grandson.

B669 Lope, Juan M., & Huberto Batis, 'Introducción', in *La Regenta* (see Ac5), pp. vii-xxx.

B670 López Jiménez, Luis, 'Leopoldo Alas (Clarín) (1886, 1887, ¿1890?)', in his *El naturalismo y España (Valera frente a Zola)* (Madrid: Alhambra, 1977), pp. 296-303.
Discusses LA's comments on Valera's *Apuntes sobre el nuevo arte de escribir novelas* (1886-87).

B671 López Landeira, Ricardo, 'Pipá: maniqueísmo, ironía y tragedia', *Archivum*, 29-30 (1979-80), 83-106.
On the ironic use of dualism and contrast as an instrument of tragedy.

B672 López Sanz, Mariano, 'Puntualizaciones en torno al naturalismo literario español', *CA*, 37, No. 216 (Jan.-Feb. 1978), 210-12, 213, 218-20.
Uses Clarín's comments on naturalism as an example of *el naturalismo mitigado*, i.e., the Spanish expression of the literary movement.

B673 Lorda Alaiz, F.M., 'Descripción científica de la obra literaria, " ¡Adiós, Cordera! " de Leopoldo Alas', *BRAE*, 52 (1972),503-10.

A good deal of linguistic jargon is poured into this article to tell us that the theme of LA's story is the inhumanity of civilization, as illustrated in the tension between two different worlds, the Asturian countryside and the city.

B674 ——, 'Morphématique littéraire (sur le chapitre VIIIe de *La Regenta* de Leopoldo Alas)', in *Handelingen van het tweendertigste Nederlands Filologen Congres: Gehonden te Utrecht op woensdag 5, donderdag 6 en vrijdag 7 april 1972*, XXXII (Amsterdam: Holland Univ. Press, 1972), pp. 217-20.
Four pages of semantic diagrams and lists add up to no critical enlightenment at all.

B675 Lott, Robert E., 'El estilo indirecto libre en *La Regenta*', *RomN*, 15 (1973-74), 259-63.
Gives examples of the technique.

Los Lunes de El Imparcial: See *El Imparcial.*

Lustonó, Eduardo de: See L.

B676 Lutaybe [pseud.], 'D. Leopoldo Alas (Clarín)', *Barcelona Cómica*, 7, No. 46 (10.11.94), 10-11.
A graphological analysis of LA's character: LA is 'un hombre que tiene un infierno en la cabeza.' With an LA autograph addressed to Carlos Ossorio y Gallardo.

B677 McBride, Charles Alfred, 'Afinidades espirituales y estilísticas entre Unamuno y "Clarín"', *CCU*, 19 (1969), 5-15.
A reworking of the last chapter of author's thesis (see B680).

B678 ——, 'Alienation from Self in the Short Fiction of Leopoldo Alas, Clarín', in *Homenaje a Casalduero (Crítica y poesía)*, ed. Rizel Pincus Sigele and Gonzalo Sobejano (Madrid: Gredos, 1972), pp. 379-87.
Giving examples from 'El dúo de la tos', 'Zurita', and 'Superchería', author notes that LA's self-alienated characters are either lyrical representations or stand for a moral issue.

B679 ——, 'Literary Idealism in Clarín's Creation of Setting', *CH*, 2 (1980), 149-56.
Setting in LA is often conceived introspectively, 'for the inner world of memory'.

B680 ——, 'Narrative Modes in Three Works of Leopoldo Alas (Clarín)', unpubl. diss., Univ., of Texas - Austin, 1968. 218 pp. Abstracted in *DA*, 29 (1968-69), 609-A.
Analyses 'Doña Berta' as 'the heroism of sentiment', 'Cuervo' as 'the theme of death, through caricature and contrast', and 'Superchería' as *'angustia vital*, through retrospection and the dematerialization of reality'. Also contains a final chapter on the LA-Unamuno literary relationship.

B681 M., *'Doña Berta. – Cuervo. – Superchería'*, *Revista Contemporánea*, No. 85 (29.2.92), 440-41.
A favorable review.

B682 *Maceín, F., 'Chantage literario', *El Heraldo de París*, 32 (1.6.01), 2. Rpt. in B208, pp. 181-83.
An anti-Clarín attack, which is immediately followed by an acidic commentary penned by Luis Bonafoux.

B683 Maestre, Eloy, *'La Regenta*, adaptada al teatro', *Madrid*, No. 199 (Oct. 1983), 30.
Praises the adaptation (see Aj4).

B684 ——, *'La Regenta*, en el escenario de El Escorial', *La Nueva España* (Oviedo) (11.9.83), 28-29.
An enthusiastic review of the acting, direction, and adaptation (see Aj4).

B685 *Maeztu, Ramiro de, 'Apuntes para un manual sobre el vigente Katipunan literario', *Las Noticias* (Barcelona) (14.12.1900).
Cited by Paul Smith in his *Vicente Blasco Ibáñez: an Annotated Bibliography*, Research Bibliographies & Checklists, 14 (London: Grant and Cutler, 1976), p. 92.

B686 ——, 'Clarín, Madrid Cómico and C° Limited', *Revista Nueva*, 1 (15.10.99), 49-54.
An anti-Clarín attack by one of the 'gente nueva'. See B688.

B687 Mainer, José-Carlos, 'Algunas utopías españolas 1840-1868-1928-1944', *El Urogallo*, 3, No. 14 (1972), 81-88.
LA's view of the significance of the Revolution of 1868.

B688 ——, 'Introducción', in facs. ed. of *Revista Nueva 1899*, 1 (Barcelona: Puvill, 1979), pp. 18-19.
How LA was treated by contributors to the *Revista Nueva*. See B686.

B689 *Máinez, Ramón León [pseud.: Baltasar Gracián], 'Las sandeces de Clarín', *El Eco Montañés* (Cádiz) (1891-92).
See Martínez Cachero, B705, pp. 254-73, for a rpt of nos 3 and 4 of the six articles attacking LA, which were published as a literary supplement to *El Eco Montañés* (Imp. de J. Rodríguez). On 'Pipá', 'Amor' è furbo', 'Un documento', 'Avecilla', *LR*, and *SUH.*

B690 Manent, Albert, 'Las memorias literarias de Narcís Oller (Su epistolario con Galdós, Pereda, Pardo Bazán, Clarín, Valera...)', *Ínsula*, Nos 188-89 (July-Aug. 1962), 21.
Mentions LA in connection with his defense of writing in 'el verbo natural' (i.e., Catalan).

B691 Marañón, Gregorio, 'Menéndez y Pelayo y "Clarín". Reflexiones sobre un epistolario', *La Nación* (Buenos Aires) (21.9.43).
Same as B692.

B692 ——, 'Prólogo', in *Epistolario* (See B16), pp. 5-17. Rpt. as 'Dos vidas en el tiempo de la concordia', in his *Ensayos liberales* (Madrid: Espasa-Calpe, 1946), pp. 128-43.
Extracted in Ah8, pp. 606-07. On the exemplariness of LA's and Menéndez Pelayo's friendship; LA's critical importance during the Restoration; and his personality.

B693 ——, 'Prólogo', in *Leopoldo Alas "Clarín"* (see B514), pp. 7-12.
On the question of LA's religious sensibility.

B694 Maravall, José Antonio, 'La mascarilla de "Clarín"', *Arriba*, 2a época (27.12.41), 3.
Comments on the appearance of the correspondence from Unamuno, Palacio Valdés, and Menéndez Pelayo (B15): 'Esa mascarilla vaciada sobre la personalidad de "Clarín" es el molde ajustado a un alma'.

B695 Marías, Javier, '*La Regenta*, en inglés', *Los Cuadernos del Norte* (Oviedo), 5, No. 23 (Jan.-Feb. 1984), 38-39.
Contains interesting comments from John Rutherford on translating difficulties and hoped-for impact of *LR*'s English version. See Ai6.

B696 Marías, Julián, 'Clarín', in *Diccionario de literatura española* (Madrid: Revista de Occidente, 1949), pp. 133-34. 4th ed., 1972, pp. 194-95.
Introductory.

B697 Marqués, Bernardo, 'Introducción', in *Su único hijo* (see Ac32), pp. 7-14.

B698 Marrero, Vicente, *Historia de una amistad*, Colección Novelas y Cuentos, 94,(Madrid: Emesa, 1971), pp. 134-43, 152-59, 252-57.
Quotes a great deal from various *epistolarios* to illustrate the friendship among LA, Pereda, Galdós, Menéndez Pelayo, and Valera.

B699 Marrone, Nila, 'Hacia un análisis lingüístico comparativo del estilo de Clarín en *La Regenta*, Juan Rulfo en *Pedro Páramo*, y Gabriel García Márquez en *Cien años de soledad*', in *The Analysis of Hispanic Texts: Current Trends in Methodology*, ed. Mary Ann Beck, Lisa Davis, et al. First York Coll. Colloquium (New York: Bilingual Press, 1976), pp. 170-90. Rpt. slightly rev., in her *El estilo de Juan Rulfo: estudio lingüístico* (New York: Bilingual Press, 1978), pp. 10-28.
Uses transformational generative grammar in her stylistic analysis.

Martín Gaite, Carmen: See Chacel, Rosa.

B700 Martín Galí, Emilio (?) [pseud.: Martingalas de Martinete], *La autopsia de Clarín* (Madrid: Librería de Fe, 1895). 90 pp.
An anti-Clarín satire, composed mainly of *ad hominem* attacks and sprinkled throughout with snide remarks on the first night of *Teresa*.

B701 ——, 'Mirón ... y errarla', *Barcelona Cómica*, 1, No. 6 (18.7.89), 6-7, 10.
Replies to LA's 'Martingalicismos' (*Madrid Cómico*, No. 333, 6.8.89). On the question of author's publishing rights.

B702 Martínez, Renée Corty, 'La mujer en la obra de Leopoldo Alas', unpubl. diss., Univ. of Virginia, 1971. 212 pp. Abstracted in *DAI*, 32 (1971-72), 4620-A.
Studies the personalities of the chief female characters in *LR*, *SUH*, 'Doña Berta', and *Teresa*.

B703 Martínez Cachero, José María, 'Adiciones a una bibliografía sobre Leopoldo Alas, "Clarín"', *Archivum*, 2 (1952), 408-20.
Provides useful references to the Clarín bibliography.

B704 ——, 'Algunas referencias sobre el anti-modernismo español', *Archivum*, 3 (1953), 311-33.

LA is one of several examples cited of an *antimodernista* critic.

B705 ——, 'Un ataque a "Clarín". Seis artículos de Ramón León Máinez', *Revista de la Universidad de Oviedo*, 11 (1950), 247-73.
Rpts part of 'Las sandeces de Clarín', in which León Máinez attacks several of LA's stories, *LR*, and *SUH*. See also B689.

B706 ——, 'Bibliografía reciente sobre Clarín', *BIDEA*, 13 (1959), 469-72.
Discusses Blanquat (see B162) and Gramberg (see B541).
Review: .1. B[eser], S[ergio]. *Índice Histórico Español*, 6 (1960), 319.

B707 ——, 'Cien años después', *Ateneo*, No. 7 (26.4.52), 3.
Urges serenity and objectivity in judging LA's work today.

B708 ——, 'Clarín', in *Gran Enciclopedia Asturiana*, V (Gijón: Heraclio Fournier, [1970?]), pp. 17-19.
A good, informative article.

B709 ——, 'Clarín crítico de su amigo Palacio Valdés', *BIDEA*, 7 (1953), 401-12. Rpt. in B1429, pp. 161-71.
M.C. comments on the objectivity with which LA reviewed Palacio Valdés's novels and stories.

B710 ——, ' "Clarín", crítico de la literatura asturiana de su tiempo', in *Estudios y trabayos del Seminariu de Llingua Asturiana*, II (Oviedo: Univ., 1980), pp. 13-23. Rpt. in B1429, pp. 145-59.
Recounts some of LA's criticism on Asturian writers, emphasizing three in particular: Ceferino Suárez Bravo, Palacio Valdés, and Campoamor.

B711 ——, ' "Clarín", crítico desde Oviedo de la literatura española (1883-1901)', in *VIII y IX Ciclos de conferencias sobre Oviedo* (Oviedo: Gráficas Summa, 1976), pp. 163-67.
Attempts to focus on LA's interests and personality during the period !883-1901.

B712 ——, ' "Clarín" y "Azorín" ', *Archivum*, 3 (1953), 159-80. Rpt. in B1429, pp. 121-38.
LA as one of the chief influences on the young Martínez Ruiz; rpts three letters from M.R. (26.10.97, 19.4.98, 12.5.98), on LA and Dicenta; *Un discurso*; and LA's Ateneo lectures.

B713 ——, 'La Condesa de Pardo Bazán escribe a su tocayo, el poeta Ferrari (Ocho cartas inéditas de doña Emilia)', *Revista Bibliográfica y Documental* (Madrid), 1 (1947), 255-56.
Pardo Bazán's reaction to the death of LA (see also B514, p. 103).

B714 ——, 'Crónica y bibliografía del primer centenario de Leopoldo Alas, "Clarín": años 1951 y 1952', *Archivum*, 3 (1953), 79-112. Rpt. in B1429, pp. 53-86.
A useful annotated source of secondary material on LA.

B715 ——, 'Cuando José Martínez Ruiz empezaba ... "Clarín" le anunció en 1897, como una de las pocas esperanzas de la literatura "satírica" ', *ABC* (17.4.54), n. pag.
On the LA-Azorín friendship; also reproduces a photograph from Azorín, dedicated to LA.

B716 ——, 'Un dato para la fortuna de Grün en España', *Archivum*, 1 (1951), 157-58.
Rpts a Grün sonnet which LA translated for the *Revista de Asturias* (25.4.79).

B717 ——, 'Un dato para la fortuna de Víctor Hugo en España', *Archivum*, 2 (1952), 314-18.
Reproduces LA's article on Hugo's *Toda la lira (La Ilustración Ibérica*, 11, 1893).

B718 ——, 'Doña Berta de Rondaliejo en Madrid (Leopoldo Alas: "Doña Berta", VIII)', in *El comentario de textos*, 3 *La novela realista*, by Andrés Amorós et al (Madrid: Castalia, 1979), pp. 255-78. Rpt. in B1429, pp. 235-52.
A close textual analysis of the passage when Doña Berta steps out into the snow-laden streets of Madrid.

B719 ——, 'Dos fragmentos narrativos de Leopoldo Alas', *Archivum*, 12 (1962), 479-506.
Rpts LA's 'Un paraíso sin manzanas' (Ch. 6 of the collective novel, *Las vírgenes locas*) and 'Mosquín' (Ch. 1 of 'Palomares'). See also Ah27, Ah34, B1090.

B720 *——, 'Dos novelistas y una ciudad (antología incompleta)', *Revista Oviedo* (1948), 41 ff.

B721 ——, 'Introducción', in *Palique* (see Ab23), pp. 7-56. Extract in B1429, pp. 175-206.

B722 ——, 'Introducción', in *La Regenta* (see Ac6), pp. ix-xciii.
Extracts in B1429, pp. 19-32, 225-33.

B723 ——, ed., *Leopoldo Alas 'Clarín'*, El Escritor y la Crítica,
105 (Madrid: Taurus, 1978). 276 pp.
Contains previously published essays and a 'nota preliminar' by M.C.
Bibliography. One objection: the selection was limited to articles
written originally in Spanish, which excluded several fine studies
published in English and French and superior to some of the articles
chosen. See: B34, 41, 56, 111, 120, 126, 154, 281, 283, 368, 454,
471, 542, 563, 733, 744, 778, 821, 972, 1054.
Reviews: .1. Bonet, Laureano. *Ínsula*, Nos 392-93 (July-Aug. 1979), 10.
.2. Romera Castillo, José. *NE*, No. 11 (Oct. 1979), 94-95.
.3. Rutherford, John D. *HR*, 48 (1980), 506-07.

B724 ——, 'Leopoldo Alas "Clarín", desde hoy', *ABC* (13.6.81),
i-ii. Rpt. in B183, pp. 23-26; and in B1429, pp. 11-16.
Reviews LA's solid place in nineteenth-century Spanish literature, and
wonders if his harsh view of Restoration Spain was not skewed.

B725 ——, 'Leopoldo Alas, narrador (sus cuentos, sus novelas, *Su
único hijo)*', *EstLit*, Nos 402-04 (15.9.68), 21-24.
Some of the characteristics of the Clarinian narrative.

B726 ——, 'Luis Bonafoux y Quintero, "Aramís", contra "Clarín"
(Historia de una enemistad literaria)', *RL*, 3 (1953), 99-111.
Details the causes and chronology of the LA-Bonafoux quarrel.

B727 ——, 'Más referencias sobre el anti-modernismo español',
Archivum, 5 (1955), 131-35.
LA's opinion of Valle-Inclán's *Epitalamio*.

B728 ——, *Menéndez Pelayo y Asturias* (Oviedo: IDEA, 1956), pp.
74-79, 85-109, 112-13, 119-21, 131-42, 264-77, *et passim*.
Rpt, slightly modified, as 'Menéndez Pelayo y "Clarín"'.
(Historia de una amistad)', *BIDEA*, 10 (1956), 169-96.
Recounts the LA-Menéndez Pelayo friendship, their views of each
other's work, their correspondence.
Review: .1. N[adal] [Oller], J[orge]. *Índice Histórico Español*, 3
(1957), 153.

B729 ——, 'Necrologías sobre "Clarín"', *Los Cuadernos del Norte*
(Oviedo), 2, No. 7 (May-June 1981), 2-7. Rpt. in B1429, pp.
43-52.

Recounts some respectful and not so respectful obituaries, including those of *El Progreso de Asturias* (B990), Luis Bonafoux (B188), Emilio Bobadilla (B172), José Fernández Bremón (B376), Francisco Navarro Ledesma (B845), and Urbano González Serrano (B536).

B730 ——, 'Nota liminar', in *Cuentos* (see Ad28), pp. 5-8.

B731 ——, 'Noticia de más críticas periodísticas sobre el estreno de *Teresa*', *BIDEA*, 32 (1978), 459-81. Rpt. in B1429, pp. 293-317.
A continuation of B734. M.C. publishes reviews on *Teresa*, by Zeda (B404), Don Cualquiera (B331), Antonio Sánchez Pérez (B1118), Joaquín Arimón (B76), some of LA's responses to the criticism, and the Asturian reaction to the play.

B732 ——, 'Noticia de otras novelas largas del autor de *La Regenta*', *Los Cuadernos del Norte* (Oviedo), 5, No. 23 (Jan.-Feb. 1984), 87-92. Rpt. in B1429, pp. 253-66.
Reviews several uncompleted projects: 'Speraindeo', 'Las vírgenes locas', 'Palomares', 'Una medianía', 'Cuesta abajo', and 'Tambor y gaita.' Occasionally adds new information. See also B1090.

B733 ——, 'Noticia de tres folletos contra "Clarín"', *BIDEA*, 13 (1959), 225-44. Rpt. in B723, pp. 69-81.
A well-documented study on three anti-Clarín reactions: those of Fray Juan de Miguel, Dionisio de las Heras, and Martingalas de Martinete. See B579, 700, 742, 809.
Review: .1. B[eser], S[ergio]. *Índice Histórico Español*, 6 (1960), 319.

B734 ——, 'Noticia del estreno de *Teresa* ("Ensayo dramático en un acto y en prosa, original de Don Leopoldo Alas", 1895) y de algunas críticas periodísticas', *Archivum*, 19 (1969), 243-73. Rpt. in B1429, pp. 267-91.
Documents the external history of *Teresa*'s failure and rpts three reviews of the play, those of Norberto González Aurioles (B517), Salvador Canals (B241), and Eduardo Bustillo (B222). See also B731.

B735 ——, 'Una opinión sobre *El señor y lo demás son cuentos*, de Leopoldo Alas', *Archivum*, 2 (1952), 312-13.
Reproduces Alfredo Opisso's favorable review (*La Ilustración Ibérica*, 11, 1893). See B876.

B736 ——, 'Oviedo en dos novelas del siglo XIX', *BIDEA*, 15 (1961), 381-90. Rpt. in B1429, pp. 319-25.

Compares LA's treatment of the city of Oviedo in *LR* with Palacio
Valdés's in *El maestrante* (1893). Both writers present a negative
vision of the Asturian capital, though LA's is by far the superior.
Some interesting documentation in the notes.

B737 ——, 'Prólogo', in *Doña Berta y otros relatos* (see Ad35),
pp. 9-16.

B738 ——, '*La Regenta*', in *Gran Enciclopedia Asturiana*, XII
(Gijón: Heraclio Fournier, [1970?]), pp. 165-68.
A nice introduction.

B739 ——, '*La Regenta* y Clarín en sus días: noticia de una crítica
negativa', *Ínsula*, No. 451 (June 1984), 7.
Comments on León Máinez's negative evaluation of *LR* (see also B689,
705).

B740 ——, 'Salvador Rueda escribe a "Clarín" ', *Revista de la
Universidad de Oviedo*, 4, Nos 49-50 (1948), 137-40.
M.C. discusses and prints an unpublished letter in verse to LA, occa-
sioned by Clarín's promise to write a prologue for S.R.'s *Cantos de la
vendimia*. See also Ag23.

B741 ——, 'Silencio sobre "Clarín" ', *La Nueva España* (Oviedo)
(28.4.52), 12.
Complains of the neglect of LA's centenary in Spain.

B742 ——, 'El temido y odiado "Clarín". Noticia de tres raros
y curiosos folletos', *ABC* (6.12.59).
Essentially a shortened version of B733.

B743 ——, 'Trece cartas inéditas de Leopoldo Alas a Rafael Alta-
mira, y otros papeles', *Archivum*, 18 (1968), 145-76. Rpt. in
B1429, pp. 89-119.
M.C. prints thirteen letters from LA, as well as LA's prologue to A.'s
Mi primera campaña, and Altamira's ' "Clarín" y Palacio Valdés en Italia'
(see Af1, Ag1, B30).

B744 ——, 'Los versos de Leopoldo Alas', *Archivum*, 2 (1952), 89-
111. Rpt. in B723, pp. 105-11.
LA's poetry, though quite inferior to his prose, reveals two characteristics:
his profound religious feelings, despite his doubts, and his protest against
excessively rational and scientific attitudes. Includes examples of his verse:
'La ofrenda'; 'La voz de Dios'; 'Símbolo'; 'Pulso de liras y en las cuerdas

de oro'; 'La bayadera y el muní (Diálogo del Oriente)'. See also Ah51, B511, 1411.

———: See also Fernández Silvestre, Marta.

B745 Martínez Olmedilla, Augusto, 'Leopoldo Alas, "Clarín"', *ABC* (4.1.31).
LA should be remembered as a writer of stories and novels, rather than as a critic.

B746 ———. *Periódicos de Madrid: anecdotario* (Madrid: Aumarol, 1956), pp. 33-36, 52.
On LA's contribution to *El Solfeo* and *Madrid Cómico*.

B747 Martínez Montón, R., 'Los investigadores extranjeros, sorprendidos por el interés universitario hacia Clarín', *El País* (24.3.84), 26.
Summary of Mar. 1984 symposium in Barcelona.

B748 Martínez Ruiz, José [pseud.: Azorín], 'Asturias', in his *El paisaje de España visto por los españoles* [1917], *O.C.*, III (Madrid: Aguilar, 1947), pp. 1152-58.
One of Azorín's impressionistic essays on the character of LA.

B749 ———, 'Avisos de éste', *El Progreso*, 1 (7.11.97). Rpt. in his *Soledades* [1898], *O.C.*, I (Madrid: Aguilar, 1947), pp. 352-54.
On M.R.'s first meeting with LA. Gives a portrait of LA and also talks about his projected play, *La millonaria. Soledades* is dedicated to Clarín.

B750 ———, 'Avisos de éste', *El Progreso*, 1 (24.11.97).
On LA's religious eclecticism. Ramos-Gascón rpts this piece (B1013, p. 423).

B751 ———, 'Avisos de éste', *El Progreso*, 1 (5.12.97).
M.R. disagrees with LA's belief in an authentic religious revival in France.

B752 ———, 'Avisos de éste', *El Progreso*, 1 (8.12.97).
Discusses LA's lecture given at the Ateneo, on Verlaine and Baudelaire.

B753 ———, 'Avisos de éste', *El Progreso*, 2 (9.2.98).
On 'Cuervo'.

B754 ——, *Buscapiés (Sátiras y críticas)* [1894], *O.C.*, I (Madrid: Aguilar, 1947), pp. 65-67, 70.
Speaks of Alas as 'un obrero perseverante' of cultural and critical ideals, but then goes on to criticize him for no longer being a champion of the new.

B755 ——, *'La campana de Huesca', ABC* (25.1.51), [1].
On rereading the novel by Cánovas which was lambasted by LA, M.R. finds the book much better than LA did.

B756 ——, *Charivari* [1897], *O.C.*, I (Madrid: Aguilar, 1947), pp. 256, 267-71, 272-73.
Extracts of a letter from LA, published in *La Saeta* (Jan. 1897); literary sketch of him as 'el sabio maestro' struggling for the truth and for freedom of thought; criticism of his 'concepto errado' of Federico Balart.

B757 ——, 'Los ciegos', in his *Escritores* (Madrid: Biblioteca Nueva, 1956), pp. 69-70.
Uses LA's 'Cambio de luz' and its blind protagonist as an example of *los ciegos.*

B758 ——, 'Los cinco Cánovas', in *Escritores* (see B757), pp. 51-52.
Azorín appears to ignore the harshly satiric bent of LA in *Cánovas y su tiempo.*

B759 ——, ' "Clarín" ', *ABC* (13.6.06). Rpt. in *Escritores* (see B757), pp. 25-28.
On LA's spiritual evolution.

B760 ——, 'Clarín', *ABC* (11.10.47), [1].
A suggestive essay on the difficulties of understanding how LA came to be what he was. Rpt. in his *Varios hombres y una mujer* (Barcelona: Aedos, 1962), pp. 142-44.

B761 ——, 'Clarín', in his *Madrid*, [1941], *O.C.*, VI (Madrid: Aguilar, 1948), pp. 222-24.
LA was an admirable maestro who saw the multiple aspects of a problem.

B762 ——, ' "Clarín" en el Ateneo', *El Progreso*, 1 (17.11.97). Rpt. in his *Artículos olvidados de J. Martínez Ruiz (1894-1904)* (Madrid: Narcea, 1972), pp. 121-27; and in B662, pp. 422-26.
Sums up LA's discourse on religion, given at the Ateneo. The young Azorín, still in his anarchist phase, is somewhat critical of the talk.

B763   ——, 'Clarín y la inteligencia', in his *Andando y pensando*
[1929], *O.C.*, V (Madrid: Aguilar, 1948), pp. 191-94.
'La vida para Alas', says M.R., 'es todo inteligencia.'

B764   ——, 'Corresponsales en París', *ABC* (24.2.46).
On the LA-Bonafoux dispute over the originality of *LR*.

B765   ——, 'La crítica literaria', in his *Ultramarinos* (Barcelona:
Edhasa, 1966), pp. 33-38.
Dated 12 Oct. 1930. LA's juridical background sometimes makes his
criticism seem heavy and pedantic.

B766   ——, *La crítica literaria en España* [1893], *O.C.*, I
(Madrid: Aguilar, 1947), pp. 21-25.
Cautious praise for LA as a critic.

B767   ——, 'De la vida de "Clarín" ', in *Andando y pensando* (see
B763), pp. 195-99.
On the need for a definitive ed. of LA's work, and a thorough bio-
graphy of the novelist.

B768 *——, 'Echegaray, Clarín', *El Pueblo* (Valencia) (25.3.95).

B769   ——, 'El homenaje a "Clarín" ', *ABC* (8.9.25). Rpt. in
Escritores (see B757), pp. 29-34.
Homage to LA and also to Campoamor.

B770   ——, 'Una lección de estilo', in his *Ejercicios de castellano*
(Madrid: Biblioteca Nueva, 1960), pp. 133-35.
Azorín looks at first sentence of *SUH* and asks himself, 'por qué esas
siete palabras?'

B771   ——, 'Leopoldo Alas', in his *Clásicos y modernos* [1913],
O.C., II (Madrid: Aguilar, 1947), pp. 782-89.
M.R. discusses LA as a moralist in the seventeenth-century sense of
the word.

B772   ——, 'Leopoldo Alas', in *Superchería* (see Ad19), pp. 7-21.
Rpt. as 'Clarín' in Ad22, pp. 3-9.

B773   ——, 'Los maestros', in *Madrid* (see B761), pp. 259-60.
LA's intuitions about the potential of the Generation of 1898 (Valle-
Inclán, Azorín, Benavente).

B774   ——, 'El misticismo de Ureña (Boceto de un estudio)', in

Buscapiés (see B754), pp. 141-45.
A subjective portrait of LA and his spiritual attitudes.

B775 ——, 'Nicolás Serrano', *Blanco y Negro*, No. 786 (25.5.06), n. pag. Rpt. as 'Nicolás Serrano (1892)', in his *España* [1909], *O.C.*, II (Madrid: Aguilar, 1947), pp. 478-80.
On Nicolás Serrano, from 'Superchería'.

B776 ——, ' "Una novela" [*Su único hijo*] ', *ABC* (1.2.50), 3.
A provocative article on the difficulty of classifying *SUH*, both in its essential nature and its temporalness. M.R. also notes an influence from Luis Taboada in the novel ('un Taboada trascendental').

B777 ——, 'Una opinión autorizada', *La Libertad* (6.3.34).
Uses LA's words spoken at the Ateneo in 1886 on Spanish constitutionalism and the existence of secret societies in the early nineteenth century, to prove Azorín's point that secret societies are corruptive and responsible for the loss of liberty. Also emphasizes LA's liberalism.

B778 ——, 'Oviedo – En la biblioteca de "Clarín" ', in his *Los clásicos redivivos – Los clásicos futuros* [1945], *O.C.*, VIII (Madrid: Aguilar, 1948), pp. 98-105. Rpt. in B723, pp. 60-65.
A description of LA's study and library, including a notebook in which he jotted down facts and figures of his daily life.

B779 ——, 'Oviedo. I. Una ciudad espiritual', in his *Veraneo sentimental* [1944], *O.C.*, VII (Madrid: Aguilar, 1948), pp. 362-65.
On Oviedo and *LR*; and LA's influence on the Asturian city.

B780 ——, 'Prólogo', in *Páginas escogidas* (see Aa2), pp. 13-19. Rpt. in his *A voleo*, *O.C.*, IX (Madrid: Aguilar, 1954), pp. 1197-1204. 2nd ed., 1963.
M.R. in 1917 defines LA's intellectual position as one of 'espiritualismo laico'. (Articles in *A voleo* are dated 1905-53.)

B781 ——, 'Un recuerdo. Clarín', *España* (24.8.04). Rpt. in his *Tiempos y cosas* [1944], *O.C.*, VII (Madrid: Aguilar, 1948), pp. 187-91.
Reflections on 'Doña Berta' and 'Superchería'.

B782 ——, 'Revista literaria. Leopoldo Alas, "Clarín" ', in his *Literatura* [1896], *O.C.*, I (Madrid: Aguilar, 1947), pp. 229-33.

Comments on LA's creative assimilation of Flaubert and Renan in his work; and also on the Christian character of *Teresa.*

B783 ——, 'Sugestiones de Clarín', *El Imparcial* (18.6.06).
'Un escritor es grande, no tanto por lo que dice claramente, como por las cosas que nos sugiere', writes M.R.

B784 ——, '*Teresa*', *ABC* (17.1.48). Rpt. in *A voleo* (see B780), pp. 1204-06.
On the reasons for the play's failure.

B785 ——, 'La *Teresa* de Clarín', in his *La farándula* [1945], *O.C.*, VII (Madrid: Aguilar, 1948), pp. 1163-68.
One of the few positive evaluations of the play.

B786 ——, 'La vida literaria', *La Prensa* (Buenos Aires) (14.6.16), 6.
LA as 'una transición entre la literatura consagrada y el pensar rebelde.'

B787 Martínez Torrón, Diego, 'El naturalismo de *La Regenta*', *CHA*, No. 380 (Feb. 1982), 257-97. *Rpt. in his *Estudios literarios* (Madrid: Akal, 198?).
Takes an inordinate amount of time to reach the not very illuminating point that *LR* is, in many ways, a stricter application of naturalism's laws than Zola's own work.

Martingalas de Martinete [pseud.] : See Martín Galí, Emilio.

B788 *Masip Acevedo, Julio, 'Asturias y los asturianos: el Arzobispo Cos y Fermín de Pas: de lo vivo a lo pintado', *La Nueva España* (Oviedo) (16.9.79).

B789 Massano, Giulio, 'A Feminist Approach to the Study of Nineteenth-Century Spanish Novels', *Hispania* (U.S.A.), 60 (1977), 112-13.
G.M. describes a course given at Southeastern Massachusetts Univ., in which six novels, including *LR*, were analysed using the feminist approach. Students thought of the *regenta* as a 'beautiful object seen as the property of the whole town'.

B790 Matlack, Charles William, 'Leopoldo Alas and Naturalism in the Spanish Novel, 1881-1892', unpubl. diss., Univ. of New Mexico, 1954. 177 pp. Abstracted in *DA*, 15 (1954-55), 124.

Considers *LR*, *La desheredada*, *Lo prohibido*, and *La espuma* to be the most naturalistic of the novels studied in this diss.

B791 Mayoral, Marina, 'Clarín y Valera, críticos literarios', *RO*, 2a época, No. 83 (1970), 97-103.
A review-article on Beser (see B149) and Bermejo Marcos' *Don Juan Valera, crítico literario*. Author compares the two critics and their approaches.

B792 Mazzeo, Guido, 'The Banquet Scene in *La Regenta*, a Case of Sacrilege', *RomN*, 10 (1968-69), 68-72.
Interprets the banquet offered in honor of Don Pompeyo Guimarán in *LR* as a caricature of the Last Supper.

B793 ——, 'La voluntad ajena en *Los pazos de Ulloa* y *La Regenta*', *DHR*, 4 (1965), 153-61.
On the diminution of free will in *LR*.

B794 Medina, Jeremy T., *Spanish Realism: the Theory and Practice of a Concept in the Nineteenth Century* (Potomac, Maryland: José Porrúa Turanzas, Studia Humanitatis, 1979), pp. 189-221.
A somewhat disjointed effort to study the authorial perspective, description, language, characterization, and other elements found in *LR*. Relies excessively on past critical endeavors without coming to any startlingly new conclusions.

B795 Melón Fernández, Santiago, *Un capítulo en la historia de la Universidad de Oviedo (1883-1910)* (Oviedo: IDEA, 1963), pp. 29-32, 41-44.
On the Oviedo of LA's time and LA as educator at the University.

B796 ——, 'Los dos últimos siglos', in *El libro de Oviedo* (Oviedo: Ediciones Naranco, 1974), pp. 85-87.
Fermín Canella's *Libro de Oviedo* (1887) reflects the city 'por fuera', while *LR* sees it 'por dentro'. Thus, 'el *Libro de Oviedo* guarda ocultas afinidades con *La Regenta*.'

B797 ——, 'La Generación del Carbayón y la *Revista de Asturias*', *Los Cuadernos del Norte* (Oviedo), 2, No. 7 (May-June 1981), pp. 104-08.
Notes that LA - one of the Generación del Carbayón - during his ten years in Madrid served as an intermediary between the capital and his Asturian friends and also as a kind of often unfashionable moral mainstay.

B798 Melón Ruiz de Gordejuela, Santiago, ' "Clarín" y el bovarysmo', *Archivum*, 2 (1952), 69-87.
Contrasts three sets of characters in *LR* and *Mme Bovary*: Ana- Emma, the husbands, and the lovers.

B799 *Méndez Toca, Luis, 'Un gran literato: Leopoldo Alas', *Región* (Oviedo) (192?).

B800 Menéndez Arranz, Juan, ' "Clarín" y don Marcelino', *Cultura* (El Salvador), No. 9 (May-June 1956), 128-32. Rpt. in *Índice de Artes y Letras*, Nos 95-96 (Dec. 1956-Jan. 1957), 8-9.
On LA's admiration for Menéndez Pelayo.

B801 ——, 'Clarín y Valle-Inclán', *Índice de Artes y Letras*, 13, No. 127 (July 1959), 10, 20.
Discusses and rpts LA's *palique* on Valle-Inclán's *Epitalamio* (1897).

B802 ——, 'Una tarde con Unamuno', *Índice de Artes y Letras*, 11, No. 102 (July 1957), 4.
In conversation with M.A., Unamuno, despite earlier disappointment over Clarín's negative criticism of *Tres ensayos*, remembers and admires LA's skill as a writer.
Review: .1. B[eser], S[ergio]. *Índice Histórico Español*, 4 (1958), 494.

B803 ——, 'Unamuno juzgado por "Clarín" ', *Índice de Artes y Letras*, 11, Nos 105-06 (Sept.-Oct. 1957), 8-9.
On LA's criticism of Unamuno's *Tres ensayos*. Rpts the Clarín article, originally published in *El Imparcial* (7.5.1900).
Review: .1. B[eser], S[ergio]. *Índice Histórico Español*, 4 (1958), 494.

B804 ——, 'Unamuno responde y juzga a "Clarín" en una carta que es una confesión', *Índice de Artes y Letras*, 12, No. 108 (Jan. 1958), 3-5.
Reproduces the letter Unamuno wrote in response to the criticism of his *Tres ensayos*.
Review: .1. B[eser], S[ergio]. *Índice Histórico Español*, 4 (1958), 494.

B805 *Menéndez Mori, Paciente, *El Excelentísimo Señor Cardenal Sanz y Forés (obispo de Oviedo, 1868-1882): algunos datos biográficos* (Oviedo: 'La Cruz', 1928).
Correspondences between Sanz y Forés and *LR*'s Fortunato Camoirán.

B806 Meregalli, Franco, *Clarín e Unamuno* (Milano: La Goliardica, 1956). 152 pp.

Divided into four sections: 'L'uomo Clarín'; 'Clarín narratore'; 'Unamuno narratore'; and 'Clarín e Unamuno'. The last section is an early version of B807.

B807 ——, 'Da Clarín a Unamuno', *Annali di Ca'Foscari* (Milano), 4 (1965), 77-86; and in his *Parole nel tempo (Studi su scrittori spagnoli del novecento)* (Milano: U. Mursia, 1969), pp. 11-24. Trans. as 'Clarín and Unamuno: Parallels and Divergencies', in *Unamuno Creator and Creation*, ed. José Rubia Barcia and M.A. Zeitlin (Berkeley: Univ. of California Press, 1967), pp. 156-70.
A good comparative article on the affinities and divergences in LA's and Unamuno's personalities and works. 'The continuity', writes F.M., 'between them is so apparent that it sometimes makes us think of different periods in the development of the same person, rather than of two different ones.'

B808 Merrill, Jack Dow, 'The Role and Function of Fermín de Pas in *La Regenta* by Leopoldo Alas', unpubl. M.A. thesis, Univ. of Virginia, 1969. 45 pp.
Fermín as victim.

B809 Miguel, Fray Juan de [pseud.: Fray Mortero], *Cascotes y machaqueos. Pulverizaciones a Valbuena y Clarín* (Madrid: Hernando, [1892]). xxiv + 248 pp. 2nd ed., 1898.
Another polemical attack on Clarín. LA is 'un escritor parcialísimo, sin miaja de gusto literario y menos de gramática'.
Review: .1. [Álvarez Sereix, Rafael]. *Revista Contemporánea*, No. 88 (15.11.92), 333.

B810 ——, 'Coxalgias literarias', *Revista Contemporánea*, No. 89 (15.2.93), 301-05.
A response to the Pedreira article (B922). Fray Mortero complains P. did not understand his book on LA (B809).

B811 Milazzo, Elena, 'Modernità ed esemplarità di Clarín (Leopoldo Alas)', *Cenobio*, 4 (1955-56), 461-66.
On LA's eclecticism and impartiality as a critic. Author seems to be unaware of the LA-Pardo Bazán feud.

B812 Miller, Martha LaFollette, 'Oppositions and their Subversion in Clarín's "La rosa de oro" ', *MLS*, 12, No. 3 (Summer 1982), 99-109.

A good article on the perplexing ambiguities of this Krausist-influenced story. Analyses it as a subverted apocalyptic allegory.

B813   Miller, Michael Barry, 'A Study of Male Characterization in the Spanish Naturalistic Novel', unpubl. diss., George Washington Univ., 1974. 206 pp. Abstracted in *DAI*, 35 (1974-75), 2285-A.
Studies those male characters who are 'hopelessly base, corrupt or frustrated individuals', in *LR*, *Los pazos de Ulloa*, and *La barraca*.

B814   Miller, Stephen, 'Ortega, en la Casa Museo Pérez Galdós', *Canarias 7*, 1, No. 272 (3.7.83), 27.
Discusses how LA as a contemporary saw clearly Galdós's 'ecuación del arte', in contrast to the Ortegas' (José and Soledad) twentieth-century misunderstanding - or lack of proper perspective - of Galdós.

B815   *Mínimo [pseud.], 'Ateneo. Conferencias de D. Leopoldo Alas', *El Globo* (12, 19.11.97; 1, 8, 13, 15.12.97). Rpt. in B662, pp. 387-421.
Summaries, each one more incoherent than the last, of LA's lectures on 'teorías religiosas de la filosofía novísima'.

B816   Miquel y Badía, F., '*Teresa*. Ensayo dramático por D. Leopoldo Alas', *Diario de Barcelona* (18.6.95). Rpt. in Ae4, pp. 180-85.
An unfavorable review. *Teresa* offers only 'fragmentos de una novela puesta en diálogo.'

B817   Miralles, Andrés, 'La revista de "Clarín" ', in his *De mi cosecha (Colección de artículos)* (Madrid: Sáenz de Jubera, Hermanos, 1891), pp. 161-75.
On the Clarín-Pardo Bazán dispute in *La España Moderna*, and LA's opinion of P.B.'s novels.

B818   Miralles, Enrique, *La novela española de la Restauración (1875-1885): sus formas y enunciados narrativos* (Barcelona: Puvill, 1979). 331 pp.
Refers to LA throughout the book, since he uses *LR* as a prime example for a rather superficial, pseudostructuralist approach to the nineteenth-century Spanish novel. See pp. 325-27 for an example.

B819   Miranda, Sebastián, 'Lejanos recuerdos de mi juventud. Y otros más recientes', in *I y II Ciclo de conferencias sobre Oviedo* (Oviedo: Gráficas Summa, 1969), pp. 58-59.

An anecdote on LA's notorious temper; and a reference to two residents of Oviedo who served as models for Don Álvaro and Trabuco in *LR.*

B820 Mira Valles, Luis, 'El mundo asturiano de Clarín', *Asturias Semanal*, No. 331 (11-18.10.75), 20-21.
Talks about LA's summer retreat in Concejo de Carreño and its appearance in some of his fiction.

Montero Díaz, Santiago: See Anon., B1306.

B821 Montes Huidobro, Matías, 'Leopoldo Alas: el amor, unidad y pluralidad en el estilo', *Archivum*, 19 (1969), 207-20. Rpt. in B723, pp. 253-62.
A good study of the tripartite structure and themes found in ' ¡Adiós, Cordera! ' 'Es Leopoldo Alas', says M.H., 'quien nos ofrece otras dimensiones en el estilo y quien nos sumerge en un laberinto que partiendo de lo horizontal llega hacia lo profundo.'

B822 ——, 'Riqueza estilística de *La Regenta*', *REH*, 2 (1969), 43-59.
An excellent essay on the psychological and stylistic complexity of *LR.* It is Ana Ozores' inner labyrinth, representative at the same time, in microcosm, of the Hispanic universe, which justifies the complex style of the novel.

B823 ——, '*Su único hijo:* sinfónico avatar de Clarín', *Archivum*, 22 (1972), 149-209.
The first to recognize the importance of the musical element in *SUH.*

B824 Montesinos, José F., *Pedro Antonio de Alarcón*, 2nd ed. (Madrid: Castalia, 1977), pp. 281-88.
Discusses the question of Alarcón's literary idleness. J.F.M. uses and rpts two of LA's articles on Alarcón to explain why he stopped writing.

B825 Montseny y Carret, Juan [pseud.: Urales, Federico], 'Cuatro palabras a "Clarín" ', *La Revista Blanca*, 2, No. 35 (1.12.99), 304-06.
Attacks LA's religiosity and defends his own anti-Christian beliefs.

B826 *Morote, Luis, '*La Regenta*', *La Opinión* (Palma de Mallorca) (16.10.85). Rpt. in B144, pp. 303-09.
A sympathetic, contemporary review. Praises LA's powers of observation

and analysis. Thinks, though, that Ana should have become Fermín's lover, not Álvaro's.

B827 Moxhet, Albert, 'La Composition des personnages dans les contes de Leopoldo Alas (Clarín)', unpubl. diss., Univ. de Liège, 1963. 152 pp.
Author studies LA's personality, 'l'homme intérieur', as reflected in the short stories. Includes a bibliographical appendix of some of LA's collaboration in various journals and newspapers.

B828 Muiñós Sáenz, Fray Conrado, 'Polémica literaria. A la ilustre escritora doña Emilia Pardo Bazán', *CdD*, 26 (1891), 356-64, 424-34, 522-35.
Scattered attacks on LA's novels, his criticism, and his ideology.

B829 ——, 'Realismo galdosiano', *CdD*, 22 (1890), 524-26.
Author believes that LA makes use of the method of analysis for unfavorable reviews and synthesis for favorable ones, such as those on Galdós.

B830 Muñiz, María Elvira, *Historia de la literatura asturiana en castellano* (Salinas, Asturias: Ayalga, 1978), pp. 127-37.
A summary of LA's life and works.

B831 Muñiz Martín, Oscar, 'Contorno literario de Oviedo', in *III, IV y V Ciclo de conferencias sobre Oviedo* (Oviedo: Gráficas Summa, 1972), pp. 127-32.
Descriptive article on the various literary manifestations of the Asturian capital, including Vetusta in *LR*.

B832 *Muñoz de Diego, Alfonso, 'Actualidad asturiana: el discípulo que habló con el maestro', *Norte* (Madrid) (Mar. 1931).
Gómez-Santos (B514, p. 75) indicates that this article was rpt. in *La Aurora Social* (8.5.31).

B833 Munteanu, Dan, 'Clarín', in *Pasiunea Anei Ozores* (see Ai26), I, pp. v-xv.
A general introduction to the life and times of LA and to the Romanian translation of *LR*.

B834 Muruais, Jesús, 'Los plagios de Clarín', *Galicia Humorística*, 1 (30.4.88), 239-40.
Recounts the LA-Bonafoux quarrel and agrees with Bonafoux that LA has plagiarized from Flaubert, Fernanflor, and probably Zola.

B835   N.G., '*La Regenta*, en el Real Coliseo de Carlos III', *ABC*
(15.8.83), 49.
Report on the play version (see Aj4).

B836   Narbona, Rafael, 'Misión de la crítica. Evocación de "Clarín"',
La Tarde (4.9.48), 3.
Journalistic praise of LA the critic.

B837   Navarrete, Rosina D., 'Análisis algebraico de un retrato', *ETL*,
1, No. 2 (1973), 125-28.
A structuralist series of arrows and units on LA's portrait of the secondary character, Trabuco, in *LR*.

Navarro, F.-B.: See Frézals, G[eorges?] de.

B838   Navarro Ledesma, Francisco, 'Batir de alas', *Gedeón*, 3, No.
69 (4.3.97).
On the origins of the feud between LA and F.N.L.

B839   ——, 'Batir de Alas', *Gedeón*, 3, No. 70 (11.3.97).
Enumerates 'todas las tonterías dichas por Clarín en su última "Revista
literaria"', in particular, what LA has to say about the poet, Balart.

B840   ——, 'Batir de alas', *Gedeón*, 3, No. 72 (25.3.97).
Continues to berate LA and his article on Balart (B839).

B841   ——, 'Batir de alas', *Gedeón*, 3, No. 73 (1.4.97).
Ridicules ' ¡Adiós, Cordera! '

B842   ——, 'Batir de alas', *Gedeón*, 3, No. 76 (22.4.97).
F.N.L.'s final *ad hominem* attack.

B843 *——, 'Cartas abiertas, I. Al señor "Clarín" en Vetusta', *El
Globo* (1.2.89).

B844 *——, 'Cartas abiertas, II. Al señor "Clarín" en Vetusta',
El Globo (6.2.89).

B845   ——, 'Clarín (Apuntes para un estudio psicográfico)', *La
Lectura*, 2 (1901), 361-70.
A fascinating psychological portrait of LA, the man and writer. For
F.N.L., 'el *parecerle todo literatura a Clarín* le acarreó los mayores
disgustos de su vida y le concitó los más feroces odios que pueden
amargar existencia de hombre.'

B846 ——, 'De ojeo', *Gedeón*, 2, No. 50 (22.10.96).
'Casi todos los catedráticos de la Universidad de Oviedo escriben muy mal', says F.N.L.

B847 ——, 'De ojeo', *Gedeón*, 2, No. 52 (5.11.96).
LA, notes the author, has now come to the defense of Univ. de Oviedo professors, whom F.N.L. has been criticizing in this and the previous 'De ojeo'.

B848 ——, 'De ojeo', *Gedeón*, 2, No. 59 (24.12.96).
Author is critical of LA's attitude toward the death of Maceo, the Cuban guerrilla leader.

B849 ——, 'De ojeo', *Gedeón*, 3, No. 61 (7.1.97).
Attacks LA for not offering kind words of encouragement to young writers, the 'gente nueva'.

B850 ——, 'De ojeo', *Gedeón*, 3, No. 63 (21.1.97).
LA's offer to protect *Gedeón* is not needed, thank you sir, says F.N.L.

B851 ——, 'De ojeo', *Gedeón*, 3, No. 65 (4.2.97).
F.N.L. would like to end the literary quarrel with LA, but he does not at this time (see B842).

B852 Neira, J[esús], 'Clarín, símbolo de Oviedo y de Asturias', *La Nueva España* (Oviedo) (25.4.52).
On LA's love of the Asturian land.

B853 Neira Martínez, Jesús, 'La función del disparate lingüístico y del dialectalismo en *La Regenta*', *Los Cuadernos del Norte* (Oviedo), 5, No. 23 (Jan.-Feb. 1984), 60-63.
Reviews LA's use of language in order to characterize, including *galicismos, latinismos, bable, dialectalismos*, and linguistic errors of social origin. It is not clear whether this author is the same as that of B852.

B854 Nelson, Jeanne Pla, 'Développement du thème en fonction de la structure dans "El sustituto" de Leopoldo Alas (Clarín)', *RomN*, 13 (1971-72), 262-65.
On the theme of abnegation and its role in the narrative structure.

B855 Nicoletti Rossini, Flaviarosa, 'Introduzione', in *La Presidentessa* (see Ai24), I, pp. 5-28.
A general introduction to LA and *LR*.

B856 Nimetz, Michael, 'Eros and Ecclesia in Clarín's Vetusta', *MLN*, 86 (1971), 242-53.
An interesting study which explains how 'sex and religion occupy the same shrine and neutralize each other in the process.'

B857 Norwood, Carole Gene Knowles, 'Clarín's View of Society', unpubl. M.A. thesis, North Texas State Univ., 1975. 127 pp. Abstracted in *Masters Abstracts*, 14, No. 1 (Mar. 1976), 33.
A study of social criticism in LA's works.

B858 Noval Fernández, Francisco, 'Vetusta, Clarín, Frígilis (Aproximación a *La Regenta*)', *BIDEA*, 26 (1972), 743-63.
'Vetusta', states the critic, 'no ha sido superada por D. Fermín ni por la Regenta.' The looseness of the title is indicative of the article's lack of focus.

B859 Nueda, Luis, 'Alas (Leopoldo) ("Clarín")', in his *Mil libros (Recuerdos bibliográficos)*, I, 6th ed. Rev. by Antonio Espina (Madrid: Aguilar, 1972), pp. 50-51. First publ. 1940.
Sums up *LR* and *SUH*, noting that *LR* is visibly influenced by Zola, especially his *La Conquête de Plassans*, and *SUH* is written in an 'estilo irónico y zumbón'.

B860 Núñez de Villavicencio, Laura, 'La creatividad en el estilo de Leopoldo Alas, "Clarín"', unpubl. diss., Univ. of Maryland, 1972. 278 pp. Abstracted in *DAI*, 34 (1972-73), 743-A.
See B861 for a revised version of this diss.

B861 ——, *La creatividad en el estilo de Leopoldo Alas, "Clarín"* (Oviedo: IDEA, 1974). 285 pp. Extract in B1297, pp. 594-97.
I concur with G.G. Brown's review, in which he notes that the book 'is an odd mixture of the painstaking and the slapdash.' Author is too restricted by her chapter and section headings and her compilations of grammatical or syntactical structures, and the results are labored and obvious.
Reviews: .1. Brown, G.G. *BHS*, 54 (1977), 69-70.
.2. Díaz, Janet W. *Hispano*, No. 65 (Jan. 1979), 116-19.
.3. Quiroga Clerigo, Manuel. *CHA*, No. 324 (June 1977), 573-75.
.4. Rutherford, John. *MLR*, 71 (1976), 940-41.
.5. Ullman, Pierre L. *Hispania* (U.S.A.), 59 (1976), 375.

B862 ——, 'Reiteración y extremismo en el estilo creativo de Clarín', *Hispania* (U.S.A.), 54 (1971), 459-69. Rpt. in B144, pp. 273-92.
A good article on the various techniques of repetition and exaggeration found in LA's extremely suggestive and contradictory style.

B863 Obregón, Antonio de, 'Cada día: "Clarín"', *Madrid* (12.5.52), 3.
Another journalistic article in homage to LA's centenary.

B864 *Ochart, Luz Ivonne, 'La Restauración española a través de las lecturas de los personajes en *La Regenta*', unpubl. diss., SUNY-Stony Brook, 1981. 221 pp. Abstracted in *DAI*, 42 (1981-82). 4448-A.

B865 Ochoa Betancourt, Juan, 'Esquicios. Clarín', in B399, pp. 150-51.
An unpublished piece on LA's enemies.

B866 ——, 'Leopoldo Alas (Clarín). *La Regenta*', in B399, pp. 147-50.
An unpublished, unfinished review of *LR*.

B867 ——, '[*Teresa*]', *Revista Crítica de Historia y Literatura*, 1, No. 2 (Apr. 1895), 61-62.
Emphasizes LA's message in *Teresa*, rather than the technical defects.

B868 *O'Connor, Dolores J., 'Leopoldo Alas and the Spanish Realist Novel, 1876-1890', unpubl. diss., Univ. of California-Berkeley, 1982.

B869 ——, 'The Telescoping of Time in Clarín's *Su único hijo*', *RomN*, 23 (1982-83), 134-39.
LA's disconcertingly shifting chronology is used as an indicator of Bonifacio's changing spiritual biography, showing how 'Bonis reacts to and is to a great extent the product of ideas and modes of feeling which are rooted in a historical reality'. Suggestive.

B870 Oleza [Simó], Juan, 'Clarín: las contradicciones de un realismo límite', in his *La novela del XIX: del parto a la crisis de una ideología* (Valencia: Bello, 1976), pp. 141-213, 218-22.
An analysis of LA's dualism and of *LR* as the most concentrated vision of Restoration Spain, its complexities and contradictions, to be found in a single work: 'Lo que caracteriza al *espacio* humano y natural de

La Regenta es su enorme capacidad englobadora, la desmenuzada impresión de totalidad que ofrece.'

B871 ——, 'Introducción', in *La Regenta* (see Ac19), I, pp. 11-104.

B872 ——, 'Introducción', in *La Regenta* (see Ac19), II, pp. 11-45.

——: See also Taléns Carmona, Jenaro.

B873 Oller, Narcís, *Memòries literàries (Història dels meus llibres)* (Barcelona: Aedos, 1962), pp. 125-28.
Rpts one of LA's *paliques* on the question of literary separatism in order to demonstrate the divergence of opinion between LA and Oller.

B874 Ontañón de Lope, Paciencia, 'Las "Novelas de cura" de Zola en la literatura española', *Anuario de Letras* (México), 19 (1981), 299-303.
Parallels between *LR* and *La Conquête de Plassans*.

B875 ——, '*Nuestro Padre San Daniel, El obispo leproso* y *La Regenta*', in her *Estudios sobre Gabriel Miró* (México: UNAM, 1979), pp. 127-34.
A rather weak comparative article to show that Miró was familiar with *LR*.

B876 Opisso, Alfredo, '*El señor y lo demás son cuentos*, por Leopoldo Alas', *La Ilustración Ibérica* (Barcelona), 11 (2.9.93), 558.
A review. See also B735.

B877 Orejas, Francisco G., 'El asesinato de "Clarín"', in his *El asesinato de Clarín y otras ficciones* (Madrid: Ediciones Penthalón, 1981), pp. 37-49.
A humorous short story in which the nephew of Archbishop Benito Sanz y Forés, enraged by the presumed portrait of his uncle (as Fortunato Camoirán) in *LR*, tries to kill off Clarín. Mixes history and fiction. See also B245.
Review: .1. Méndez Riestra, Eduardo. *Los Cuadernos del Norte* (Oviedo), 2, No. 10 (Nov.-Dec. 1981), 87.

B878 *——, '*La Regenta*: prosa real y jerga oficial', *La Voz de Asturias* (Oviedo) (13.3.80).

B879 Oria, José A., ' "Cuesta abajo", obra inédita de "Clarín" ',
La Nación (Buenos Aires) (15.4.56).
Terms LA's story a kind of confessional literature and notes the
possible influence of Renan. See also Aa9, B164, 732, 880.

B880 ——, 'Vislumbres sobre la "Cuesta abajo" de "Clarín" ',
La Nación (Buenos Aires) (27.5.56).
Author believes this story was not finished or republished because
it seemed to depict the lives of actual residents of Oviedo, and LA
may not have wanted to hurt anybody's feelings. J.A.O. thinks the
story is worthwhile and should be printed again. An interesting
article. See also Aa9, B164, 732, 879.

Orlando [pseud.] : See Lara y Pedraja, Antonio.

B881 Orozco Díaz, Emilio, 'El concepto y la palabra *barroco* en
los novelistas españoles del siglo XIX (unas notas sueltas
centradas en Alarcón, Galdós y Clarín)', in *Homenaje a
Gonzalo Torrente Ballester* (Salamanca: Biblioteca de la
Caja de Ahorros y M. de P. de Salamanca, 1981), pp.
583-613.
See pp. 591-93 for commentary on LA's ironic use of the term in
Ch. 2 of *LR*.

B882 D'Ors, Eugenio, ' "Clarín" ', *Arriba*, 2a época (15.3.47), 3.
The more popular LA becomes, the less we seem to understand him.

B883 ——, 'Clarín', in his *El Valle de Josafat* (Buenos Aires:
Espasa-Calpe, 1944), pp. 121-22.
LA, as a man, was a figure to inspire pity.

B884 ——, 'Más, sobre "Clarín" ', *Arriba*, 2a época (16.3.47), 3.
Notes parallels between the personalities of LA and Zola.

B885 ——, *Novísimo glosario*, I (Madrid: Aguilar, 1946).
See 'Índice onomástico' for references to LA.

B886 ——, *Nuevo glosario*, I-III (Madrid: Aguilar, 1947-49).
See 'Índice onomástico' for references to LA.

B887 Ortega, José, 'Don Fermín de Pas: un estudio "de Superbia
et Concupiscentia Catholicis" (*La Regenta*, de Clarín)', *REH*,
9 (1975), 323-42. Rpt. in *La figura del sacerdote en la moderna narrativa española*, by J.O. and Francisco Carenas

(Caracas: Casuz Editores S.R.L., 1975), pp. 25-47.
A psychological study of Fermín de Pas, LA's most successful character creation, says J.O. Although the author alludes to Fermín as a type, his analysis of the character seems to confirm the priest's individuality, rather than his archetypicality. One might also question whether, in truth, 'la figura de Ana carece de la complejidad del tortuoso Fermín y su conducta obedece a unas pautas emocionales claras y definidas.'

B888 Ortega Munilla, José, *'Doña Berta*, por Leopoldo Alas', *El Imparcial* (29.2.92).
A review of *Doña Berta, Cuervo, Superchería*, though O.M. only discusses 'Superchería'.

B889 ——, 'Leopoldo Alas', *El Imparcial* (11.6.01).
A moving eulogy by one of LA's friends.

Ortiz, Lourdes: See Chacel, Rosa.

B890 Ortiz Aponte, Sally, *Las mujeres de "Clarín" (Esperpentos y camafeos)* ([Río Piedras] : Edit. Universitaria, Univ. de Puerto Rico, 1971). 200 pp.
Appears to be a reworking of her diss., *'La mujer en la obra de Leopoldo Alas', Univ. de Puerto Rico. Contains a prologue by Juan Antonio Cabezas, pp. vii-x. A very simplistic view of LA's feminine characters, full of dubious judgements which refer, for example, to the simplicity of Ana Ozores' soul and the pathological uniqueness of Emma Valcárcel. With bibliography.

B891 Ortiz Armengol, Pedro, 'Introducción', in Benito Pérez Galdós, *Fortunata y Jacinta*, I (Madrid: Hernando, 1979), pp. 9-53.
Pp. 11-12: on the 'misteriosa "hermandad"' of *LR* and *F y J*; and LA's reaction to Galdós's novel.

B892 Ossorio y Bernard, Manuel, *Ensayo de un catálogo de periodistas españoles del siglo XIX* (Madrid: Imp. y Litografía de J. Palacios, 1904), p. 154.
Brief notice of LA's career as a journalist.

B893 Ossorio y Gallardo, Carlos, 'Vida moderna', *Blanco y Negro*, No. 21 (27.9.91), 323-24.
A quick review of the 4th ed. of *Solos*.

B894 Otálora Otálora, Gaspar, 'Lo grotesco en la narrativa española de medio siglo (1884-1936)', *Reflexión 2*, 2a época, 3-4 (1974-75), 206-42.

Uses *LR* as an example, noting that the element of the grotesque in the Spanish nineteenth-century novel is employed only as an isolated detail.

B895 Ots, José María, 'Leopoldo Alas', *Madrid: Cuadernos de la Casa de la Cultura* (Valencia), No. 2 (May 1937), 87-88. This journal was rpt. by Kraus (1974).
An appreciation of LA's son, who was executed during the Spanish Civil War.

B896 P., 'Los estrenos. *Teresa*, ensayo dramático en un acto y en prosa de Leopoldo Alas (Clarín)', *El País* (21.3.95). Rpt. in Ae4, p. 174.
A bad play, this reviewer regretfully notes.

B897 Pabst, Walter, 'Clarín. Naturalismus und irrationales Weltbild', *Die Neueren Sprachen*, 41 (1933), 202-11.
On the significance and persistence of naturalism and illusion in LA's work, and the gradual, though not extreme, change from a basically naturalist outlook to a more idealistic one, in which illusion and the irrational predominate. *SUH*, for W.P., is the best example of this change and has influenced later generations of Spanish writers.

B898 Padrós de Palacios, Esteban, 'Introducción', in *La Regenta* (see Ac8), pp. iii-xv.

B899 Palacio, Eduardo de, 'Carta a Clarín', *Madrid Cómico*, No. 572 (3.2.94), 59.
Praises LA for honoring writers while they are still alive (Galdós, Campoamor, etc.).

B900 Palacio, Manuel del, 'A Clarín. Para su corona poética', *Madrid Cómico*, No. 341 (31.8.89), 2-3.
An anti-Clarín poem.

B901 ——, 'A Clarín. Para su corona poética', *Madrid Cómico*, No. 342 (7.9.89), 2-3.
Another anti-Clarín poem.

B902 ——, *Clarín entre dos platos (Letras a la vista)* (Madrid: Librería de Fernando Fe, 1889). 42 pp.
The author's response to LA's opinion that there are only two and a half good poets in Spain today.

B903 ——, 'Contestación al señor don Leopoldo Alas', *Madrid Cómico*, No. 343 (14.9.89), 3.
'Ha puesto usted [LA] tan sucia el agua, que por más que hago no alcanzo a ver en ella ni al crítico, ni al caballero, ni al hombre', says M.P.

B904 Palacios, Leopoldo, 'El filósofo', *Revista Popular* (Oviedo) (1.7.01), 21-23.
Labels LA a Krausist, but believes it is difficult to pinpoint the originality of his philosophy, given the heterogeneous elements of his personality and writings.

B905 Palacio Valdés, Armando, 'El Ateneo', in his *La novela de un novelista*, *O.C.*, II, 2nd ed. (Madrid: Aguilar, 1948), pp. 813-17.
Recalls his friendship with LA who, in a singular omission, is described only as an eminent critic and ignored as a novelist and short story writer.

B906 ——, 'Crónica', *Revista de Asturias*, 2a época, 2 (15.1.87), 39. Rpt. in B514, pp. 204-05. On *Alcalá Galiano*, Ab8.

B907 ——, 'Del epistolario de Palacio Valdés', *BIDEA*, 7, No. 19 (1953), 342.
Letter dated 6.7.1901 to Fermín Canella on the subject of publishing LA's works.

B908 ——, 'La familia y los amigos', in his *Testamento literario*, *O.C.*, II, 2nd ed. (Madrid: Aguilar, 1948), pp. 1318-26.
A character analysis of LA's predominantly intellectual nature.

B909 Palau, Melchor de, 'Acontecimientos literarios (1889). 0,50 de poeta. Muerte de Vicente Wenceslao Querol', *Revista Contemporánea*, No. 76 (30.11.89), 426-36.
Refers to LA-Manuel del Palacio feud; and also wonders why Clarín failed to mention Querol in his list of noteworthy poets.

B910 Palls, Byron P., 'El naturalismo de *La Regenta*', *NRFH*, 21 (1972), 23-39.
The unsurprising conclusion to this study is that *LR* is naturalistic, 'pero no desde el punto de vista filosófico... sino por su técnica estética, que sobrepasa la practicada por los escritores realistas del siglo XIX'.

Palmerín de Oliva [pseud.] : See Ruiz Contreras, Luis, B1089.

B911 Panebianco, Candido, 'Aspetti narrativi di *La Regenta*', *SGym*, n.s., 24 (1971), 206-17.
LR is a novel built on memory and symbol and, in this way, approaches the form of the modern novel.

B912 ——, 'Personaggi e problematica ne *La Regenta*', *SGym*, n.s., 23 (1970), 158-74.
A suggestive psychological analysis of the open-endedness and dialectical elements found in the characters of *LR*. Author sees LA's novel as a study of the crises and decadence of the Spanish bourgeoisie; in this sense, *LR* plays a pivotal role in the transition from the realist to the decadentist novel.

B913 Paniagua, Domingo, *Revistas culturales contemporáneas*, I *(De Germinal a Prometeo) (1897-1912)* (Madrid: Punta Europa, 1964), pp. 75-77.
On Maeztu's anti-Clarín article (B686).

B914 Pardo Bazán, Emilia, '*Mezclilla*, por Clarín (Leopoldo Alas)', *La España Moderna*, 1 (Feb. 1889), 185-90.
A generally favorable review, in which P.B. takes note of several characteristics in LA's criticism.

B915 París, Luis, *Gente nueva (Crítica inductiva)* (Madrid: Imp. Popular, n.d.), pp. 68-70.
Compares the critical temperament of LA and Luis Bonafoux.

B916 ——, '*Su único hijo*', *El Cascabel*, 21, No. 1138 (3.12.91), 4; No. 1139 (10.12.91), 4, 9.
The piece found in No. 1138 is a continuation of one published in *No. 1137; the conclusion is in *No. 1140. I have been unable to locate either of these two parts. L.P. contrasts Clarín the critic and Clarín the novelist, and ultimately finds both wanting.

B917 Parra, Antonio, 'Gonzalo Sobejano, profesor de español de la Universidad de Filadelfia, ha preparado una edición refundida de *La Regenta*', *La Nueva España* (Oviedo) (14.6.81). Rpt. in B183, pp. 12-14.
On the resurgence of literary and cultural activity devoted to LA (a ceremony in Oviedo; the homage vol. of *Los Cuadernos del Norte* (B296); new editions; etc.).

B918 Patac y Pérez, Ignacio, 'El ensayo de "Clarín" (Conato de estudio)', *El Carbayón* (Oviedo) (26.4.95).
A very favorable review of *Teresa.*

B919 Pattison, Walter T., *El naturalismo español* (Madrid: Gredos, 1969), *passim.*
See 'Índice de nombres propios'.

B920 Pecchia, Teresa, 'Renan en España: contribución al estudio de la expresión religiosa en la literatura española de 1870 a 1915', unpubl. diss., Univ. of Pennsylvania, 1972. 425 pp. Abstracted in *DAI*, 33 (1972-73), 1692-A.
Studies the influence of Renan on LA, Galdós, Unamuno, and Valle-Inclán.

B921 Pedraza Jiménez, Felipe B., & Milagros Rodríguez Cáceres, 'Leopoldo Alas, "Clarín"', in their *Manual de literatura española*, VII. *Época del realismo* (Tafalla, Navarra: Cénlit Ediciones, 1983), pp. 784-849, *et passim.*
A synthesis, relying heavily on other critics.

B922 Pedreira, Leopoldo, 'La crítica menuda', *Revista Contemporánea*, No. 89 (30.1.93), 166-78.
LA is an example of 'crítica menuda', i.e., criticism which only touches the surface of things. See also B810.

B923 Pedro, Valentín de, '"Clarín" y Rodó', *Asturias* (Buenos Aires), No. 339 (Apr. 1952), 8-9.
With LA and Rodó, we are transported to that 'región del espíritu donde no caben fanatismos, ni religiosos, ni anti-religiosos, ni políticos.'

B924 Pelegrín, Benito, 'Doña Ana en la cama, La Regenta en el diván', *Cahiers d'Études Romanes* (Aix-en-Provence), No. 5 (1979), 139-66.
A rather unilluminating *explication de texte* of a passage from the *regenta*'s private confession in her bedroom. B.P. criticizes the scene for its supposed repetitiveness.

B925 Peña, Vidal, 'Algunas retóricas de *La Regenta*', *Los Cuadernos del Norte* (Oviedo), 2, No. 7 (May-June 1981), 36-42.
Makes note of LA's ideologically neutral, hence ambiguous, position in *LR* as illustrated in certain techniques, such as aligning an apparently respectable thesis with an obvious piece of stupidity and presenting

characters' imbecilic remarks as a *donnée* alrea·ly known. Ultimately however, only 'la posición superior del que ironiza sobre todas las opiniones' prevails. See also B926 for an earlier analysis of the same theme.

B926　——, 'Crítica ideológica en *La Regenta'*, *Asturias Semanal*, No. 32 (27.12.69), 52-55.
A condensed but suggestive article on the ideological stance implicit in LA's ironic, distanced point of view. See also B925.

B927　Pence, Ruby Amelia, 'Religion in Some of the Nineteenth-Century Spanish Novels', unpubl. M.A. thesis, Univ. of Southern California, 1932. 114 pp.
Ch. 4, pp. 82-109, deals with *LR* and religion, mostly giving plot summaries.

B928　Penzol, Pedro, 'Parentescos', *Archivum*, 2 (1952), 421-26. Rpt. in his *Escritos*, II (Oviedo: IDEA, 1974), pp. 205-10.
Notes the parallels in the isolated stance of the priest figure in the nineteenth-century novel (*LR*, *Notre-Dame de Paris*, *La Faute de l'abbé Mouret*).

B929　Percival, Anthony, 'Sexual Irony and Power in *Su único hijo'*, in *La Chispa '83: Selected Proceedings*, ed. Gilbert Paolini (New Orleans: Tulane Univ., 1983), pp. 221-29.
SUH as 'a grotesque inversion of middle-class values'.

B930　Pereda, Rosa María, 'Carolyn Richmond y la vocación crítica e hispanista', *El País* (7.8.83), 8.
Interview. C.R. on her critical approach to LA.

B931　Pérez de Ayala, Ramón, 'A "Azorín"', in his *O.C.*, II, ed. J. García Mercadal (Madrid: Aguilar, 1963), pp. 148-51.
An epistolary poem set in 'mi amada Vetusta', in the 'hora asoleada y lenta / con que principia nuestro gran libro, *La Regenta*'.

B932　——, 'Alarcón, "Clarín", Pereda, Galdós', in his *Pequeños ensayos* (Madrid: Biblioteca Nueva, 1963), pp. 302-05. Originally printed in *El Liberal* (17.6.28).
On the inclusion of a Clarín selection in Jean Sarrailh's anthology (see Ah42); and LA's opinion of Galdós's style.

B933　——, 'Clarín, Valera y Menéndez Pelayo', *ABC* (12.9.57). Rpt. in his *Amistades y recuerdos* (Barcelona: Aedos, 1961), pp. 9-11.

On the three writers as critics.

B934 ——, ' "Clarín" y don Leopoldo Alas', in *Doña Berta, Cuervo, Superchería* (see Ad5), pp. 7-26. Rpt. in *Archivum*, 2 (1952), 5-21; in *Amistades y recuerdos* (see B933), pp. 11-30; and in *Superchería, Cuervo, Doña Berta* (see Ad6), pp. 9-30.

B935 ——, 'Ensayo-Prólogo', in *Paisajes de Reconquista (Un maravilloso rincón de España)*, by Juan Díaz-Caneja (Madrid: Calpe, 1926), pp. 39-40. Rpt. as 'La Universidad de Oviedo', in P. de A.'s *O.C.*, I (Madrid: Aguilar, 1964), p. 1153.
On LA's inherent mystical qualities.

B936 ——, 'La iglesia y el siglo', in his *Tributo a Inglaterra* (Madrid: Aguilar, 1963), pp. 275-80.
An amusing account of yet another polemic, this time between LA and a canon named Ángel X, or Angelón, in Oviedo: 'Era, pues, a modo de una guerra de las investiduras, entre el *sermo vulgaris* teológico y el *sermo eruditus* universitario.'

B937 ——, 'El maestro', *El Imparcial* (11.4.04). Rpt. in his *O.C.*, I (Madrid: Aguilar, 1964), pp. xvii-xx; and in *Tributo a Inglaterra* (see B936), pp. 11-14.
A disciple's fond memory of the *maestro*.

B938 ——, 'La novela y la nivola', in his *Divagaciones literarias, O.C.*, IV (Madrid: Aguilar, 1963), pp. 909-14.
Anecdotes on LA's penchant for billiards and chess.

B939 ——, 'Los novelistas españoles y "Clarín" ', *ABC* (3.6.52). Rpt. in *Amistades y recuerdos* (see B933), pp. 30-34.
LA was one of the few Spaniards of the nineteenth century who wrote for a living.

B940 ——, 'El paisaje en Clarín', *El Imparcial* (18.6.06). Rpt. in *O.C.*, I (Madrid: Aguilar, 1964), pp. 1113-17.
LA's style represented a crystallization of the Asturian landscape.

B941 Pérez de Castro, José Luis, ' "Clarín", crítico e introductor de Rodó', *El Día* (Montevideo) (24.7.60).
LA's favorable reaction to *Ariel* provided the Uruguayan writer an entrée to the Hispanic literary world.

B942 ——, *Huella y presencia de Asturias en el Uruguay*

(Montevideo: Centro Asturiano de Montevideo, 1961), pp. 33-37.
On LA's influence on José Enrique Rodó and Víctor Pérez Petit.

B943 *——, 'Leopoldo Alas, "Clarín", y José Enrique Rodó', *Cuatro Vientos* (México), No. 189 (1963), 145-47.

B944 ——, 'El magisterio de "Clarín" en la juventud americana', *El Día* (Montevideo) (3.7.60).
Discusses LA's influence on, and reaction to, *La Revista Nacional de Literatura y Ciencias Sociales* of Montevideo.

B945 ——, 'El magisterio de "Clarín" en la literatura uruguaya', *Archivum*, 13 (1963), 234-76.
A detailed account of LA's influence on turn of the century Montevideo (Rodó, Pérez Petit, *La Revista Nacional*).

B946 Pérez de la Dehesa, Rafael, 'Clarín, Azorín y *El Socialista*', in his *El Grupo Germinal: una clave del 98* (Madrid: Taurus, 1970), pp. 65-73, 75-77.
On LA's flirtation with socialism and his relationship with the radical Germinal group.

B947 ——, 'Zola y la literatura española finisecular', *HR*, 39 (1971), 49-60.
On LA's translation of *Travail* (pp. 56-57).

B948 Pérez Embid, Florentino, 'La participación de Menéndez Pelayo en la política activa', in *Estudios sobre Menéndez Pelayo* (Madrid: Nacional, 1956), pp. 404-06.
Refers to LA's support of Menéndez Pelayo's attempt to represent the Univ. de Oviedo in the Senate.

B949 Pérez Ferrero, Miguel, *Ramón Pérez de Ayala* (Madrid: Publicaciones de la Fundación Juan March, 1973), pp. 67-76, 83-85.
Tells a delightful story of Pérez de Ayala's shenanigans in LA's classroom; repeats story of LA's lack of skill in billiards and chess, his addiction to games of chance; details on Don José Sierra, presumed model for Álvaro Mesía.

B950 Pérez Galdós, Benito, 'Clarín, novelista', *Revista Popular* (Oviedo) (1.7.01), 11.
P.G. begs for more time and more rest in order to respond to the question of LA's worth as a novelist.

B951 ——, 'Las Letras', in his *Arte y crítica, Obras inéditas*, II,
ed. Alberto Ghiraldo (Madrid: Renacimiento, 1923), pp.
47-48.
'Es un verdadero Quevedo', says G. in this piece dated 30.3.86.

B952 ——, 'Prólogo', in *La Regenta* (Ac3), I, pp. v-xix. Also
appeared in *El Imparcial* (27.5.01), and in *Las Efemérides*
(Las Palmas de Gran Canaria) (5,7.6.01). Extracted in *Revista Popular* (Oviedo) (1.7.01), 23-24; in *El Imparcial*
(18.6.06), in *La Mañana* (Las Palmas de Gran Canaria)
(3.7.06); and in B144, pp. 310-17. Rpt. as 'Leopoldo Alas
(Clarín)', in *Memoranda* (Madrid: Perlado, Páez y Cía, 1906),
pp. 119-36; in *Ensayos de crítica literaria*, ed. Laureano
Bonet (Barcelona: Península, 1972), pp. 211-22; and in *O. C.*,
III (Madrid: Aguilar, 1975), pp. 1221-27.

B953 Pérez Gutiérrez, Francisco, 'Leopoldo Alas "Clarín" ', in his
*El problema religioso en la generación de 1868 ("La leyenda
de Dios")* (Madrid: Taurus, 1975), pp. 269-338.
A well-balanced, documented discussion of the religious question in
LA's life and work.

B954 Pérez López, Manuel María, 'Clarín: ¿maestro?', in his *Azorín
y la literatura española*. Acta Salmanticensia, 83 (Salamanca:
Univ., 1974), pp. 198-202.
Reviews Azorín's opinions on LA.

B955 Pérez Minik, Domingo, 'Revisión de Leopoldo Alas, "Clarín" ',
in his *Novelistas españoles de los siglos XIX y XX* (Madrid:
Guadarrama, 1957), pp. 131-55.
An appreciative evaluation of the then neglected LA as the first writer
of the period to possess a precise understanding of psychological
realism. See also Ac10.

B956 Pérez Petit, Víctor, 'A propósito de los "paliques" de Clarín',
Revista Nacional de Literatura y Ciencias Sociales (Montevideo),
No. 50 (25.6.97), 17-19; No. 51 (10.7.97), 34-45. Rpt. in his
Lecturas, O.C., IV (Montevideo: Edición Nacional, Claudio
García y Cía, 1942), pp. 107-43.
A somewhat verbose description of LA's criticism.

B957 Petriconi, H[ellmuth], *Die spanische Literatur der Gegenwart
seit 1870* (Wiesbaden: Dioskuren Verlag, 1926), pp. 64-65.

LA as a representative of Spanish realism.

B958 Phillips, Allen W., 'Nueva luz sobre Clarín y Gómez Carrillo', *RABM*, 81 (1978), 757-79.
Documents LA's opinions of G.C.'s work and the cordiality of their literary relationship.

B959 Picón, Jacinto Octavio, 'Libros', *El Correo* (6.5.88).
A favorable review of *Mis plagios*.

B960 ——, 'Prólogo', in Enrique Gómez Carrillo's *Literatura extranjera. Estudios cosmopolitas* (Paris: Librería de Garnier Hermanos, 1895), pp. iii-iv.
P. praises LA as a critic especially for his ability to persuade. Book is dedicated to LA.

B961 ——, '*La Regenta*. Novela de Leopoldo Alas (Clarín)', *El Correo* (15.3.85). Rpt. in B47, pp. 17-20; and in B1236, pp. 648-52.
One of the few pieces of criticism which J.O.P. wrote on the Spanish novel. He notes the indisputable originality of *LR* and its admirable æsthetic unity.

B962 Piscolavis [pseud.], 'A Clarín', *La Jeringa*, 1, No. 2 (14.8.87), 3, 6.
A satirical attack on LA's habit of ridiculing mistakes of grammar in inferior writers and, in this case, in Cánovas del Castillo.

Plácido [pseud.] : See Heras, Dionisio de las.

B963 *Plesencier, Casto, 'Asturias estética', *El Nalón* (Oviedo, n.d.).
Cited by Laura de los Ríos, B460, p. 321.

B964 Polo de Bernabé, José Manuel, 'Mito y símbolo en la estructuración narrativa de *La Regenta*', *PSA*, 68 (1973), 121-40.
An intelligent study of the narrative use of myth and symbol in *LR*. Both elements serve to reveal the inner mysteries of character and at the same time to structure the ironic vision of the novel in its totality.

B965 Posada, Adolfo, 'Alas y la "idea divina" ', *Revista Popular* (Oviedo) (1.7.01), 7-8.
On the ineffable quality of LA's religious sensibility.

B966 ——, 'Al hijo de Clarín, catedrático en Vetusta', *España*, 6, No. 282 (25.9.20), 15. Rpt. in *Boletín de la Institución Libre de Enseñanza*, 44 (31.10.20), 314-15.

Infused with remembrances of LA, Posada's best friend. Clarín, he says, believed that life 'para quien se siente humano, es un incesante examen de conciencia; un problema abierto siempre ...' Letter is dated 16.9.20.

B967 ——, 'Apreciación', in *Cuentos* (see Ad16), pp. 3-8. Originally published in **Hispania* (London) (Aug. 1913).

B968 *——, 'Clarín y Vetusta', *La Nación* (Buenos Aires) (12.6.27).

B969 ——, 'De Alas adentro', in his *Autores y libros* (Valencia: F. Sempere y Cía, 1909), pp. 235-38.

On LA's religious and philosophical qualities.

B970 ——, 'Escritos inéditos de Clarín [Papeles y recuerdos] ', *La Lectura*, 3 (1906), 211-16. Rpt. in *Autores y libros* (see B969), pp. 168-76.

A.P. takes inventory of the various fragments of novels and plays LA left at his death.

B971 ——, *Fragmentos de mis memorias* (Oviedo: Univ. 1983), pp. 59-63, 103-04, 117, 161, 180-81, 189-91, 203-04, 207-08, 213-19, 224-25, 258-59, 264-65, 284, *et passim*.

On LA's influence as friend and teacher; his personality quirks; his death; the creation of *LR*; the 'real' Pipá; *Trabajo*.

B972 ——, 'Leopoldo Alas', in his *España en crisis* (Madrid: Caro Raggio, 1923), pp. 185-99. Rpt. in B723, pp. 34-42.

LA as a thinker and educator in his life and works.

B973 ——, *Leopoldo Alas (Clarín)* (Oviedo: Imp. La Cruz, 1946). 232 pp.

An old friend reminisces, in loose biographical fashion, on the exemplarity of LA, man and writer. Also includes fragments of the LA-José Quevedo correspondence (published in its entirety in B480), a 1925 article on LA, and a bibliographical essay on LA's contributions to *La Revista de Asturias*. See also B54.

Reviews: .1. Fernández Almagro, Melchor. *ABC* (8.9.46), 41.
.2. R.G. [Ricardo Gullón?]. *BBMP*, 22 (1946), 190-91.
.3. Valdeavellano, Luis G. de. *Ínsula*, No. 12 (Dec. 1946), 2.

B974 ——, 'Leopoldo Alas "Clarín". Fragmentos biográficos', *El Heraldo de Madrid* (30-31.10.25). Rpt. in B973, pp. 207-24..

LA, remarks A.P., has not been well understood in his time or afterward. To appreciate Clarín, 'hace falta, ante todo, una disposición amorosa y cordial'.

B975 ——, ' "Mi Alas." "Mi Clarín" ', *Asturias* (Madrid), No. 13 (Apr. 1952), 7.
Extract from Ch. 3 of B973.

B976 ——, 'Los "peripatéticos" de Vetusta', *La Esfera* (13.9.30).
Anecdotes and comments on the friendship, walks, and discussions of LA, Tomás Tuero, Palacio Valdés, and Pío Rubín. A.P. fondly remembers his conversations and walks with LA through the streets of Oviedo.

B977 ——, 'El "Quijote" y "Clarín" (Un recuerdo)', *El Heraldo de Madrid* (6.5.05). Rpt. in *Autores y libros* (see B969), pp. 164-67.
On LA's lifelong enthusiasm for *Don Quijote*. 'Cervantes', LA is quoted here, 'empezó escribiendo el *Quijote*, y estoy por decir que acabó escribiendo el *Sancho*.'

B978 ——, 'La Revolución de 1868, vista por Leopoldo Alas "Clarín" ', in his *La llama íntima* (Valencia: Prometeo, n.d. [1925]), pp. 198-204.
Comments on LA's support of the Revolution of 1868, citing generously from Clarín's youthful journalistic effort, *Juan Ruiz*. References to LA also occur on pp. 6, 8-10, 22-23, 211-12.

B979 Prat de la Riba, Enric, 'Polèmica amb Clarín', in his *Per la llengua catalana* (Barcelona: Publicaciones de 'La Revista', 1918), pp. 9-46.
Originally published in *La Renaixença* (19.2.96, 1.4.96). Author debates LA on the question of the Catalan language as a proper and adequate literary instrument.

B980 Proaño [-Naveda], Franklin, 'Ascesis y misticismo en Ana Ozores', *BIDEA*, 26 (1972), 765-82.
On the traditional body-soul conflict in LA's heroine.

B981 ——, 'Cambios de identidad en Ana Ozores', *NRFH*, 23 (1974), 115-21.
F.P. distinguishes between the idealizing inner metamorphoses of personality in Ana Ozores and her degrading external changes of identity effected by others in the novel.

B982 *——, 'Contradicción vital en el magistral de *La Regenta* – Don Álvaro Mesía', *Revista de la Universidad del Zulia* (Maracaibo), No. 55 (1975), 71-73.

B983 ——, 'Dicotomías en los personajes de Leopoldo Alas', *BIDEA*, 29 (1975), 65-75.
On the relationship between the 'I' and the 'Other' in *SUH* and *LR*.

B984 ——, 'Leopoldo Alas, "Clarín", síntesis de tradición y evolución', *Revista de la Universidad del Zulia* (Maracaibo), No. 57 (Jan.-Dec. 1977), 160-67. Rpt. as 'Religious and Secular Aspects of Leopoldo Alas, "Clarín"', *UDR*, 13, No. 3 (Spring 1979), 27-31.
On LA's eclecticism and skepticism.

B985 ——, 'Posibilidades pluralísticas del yo en los personajes literarios de Leopoldo Alas, Clarín', unpubl. diss., Ohio State Univ., 1971. 318 pp. Abstracted in *DAI*, 32 (1971-72), 4017-A.
Explores LA's philosophical, spiritual, and human interpretation of the self in his fiction.

B986 ——, 'Presencia y problemática del yo en los personajes de "Clarín"', *BIDEA*, 27 (1973), 549-75.
Discusses the ambiguities and contradictions of the *yo* in *LR* and *SUH*.

B987 ——, *La problemática del yo en "Clarín"* (Quito: Imprenta del Colegio Técnico 'Don Bosco', 1977). 137 pp.
A shortened version of B985. B981, 983, 986, 988-89 appear in this book.

B988 ——, 'Tricotomías del yo en los personajes de Clarín', *BIDEA*, 28 (1974), 313-21.
On psychological conflict in 'Doña Berta', *LR*, and *SUH*.

B989 ——, 'El Yo y su doble en los personajes de Leopoldo Alas', *BIDEA*, 35, No. 104 (Sept.-Dec. 1981), 723-31.
'El yo y el otro', he writes, 'aparecen y desaparecen como centros de unidad, de proyección y reduplicación.'

B990 *El Progreso de Asturias* (Oviedo), 1, No. 65 (16.6.01).
A homage issue to LA. A summary of the contents is given in B1372.

B991 Pyper, Stanton [W.J.], 'Notes on a Spanish Writer. "Clarín"

(Leopoldo Alas)', *DM*, o.s., 2, No. 1 (Aug. 1924), 44-49.
A little-known Irish appreciation. The article rather charmingly wanders from subject to subject.

B992 *Quelen, Naik, 'La Peinture de la société et de la vie provinciales dans *La Regenta*, de Clarín', Diplôme, ref. 21-p-43, Biblioteca del Instituto Hispánico (Paris, n.d.).
Cited by Ferreras, B410, p. 219.

B993 Quesada, Luis, 'La programación navideña en Madrid', *EstLit*, No. 556 (15.1.75), 38.
A generally favorable review of the film version of *LR*. See Aj3.

B994 Quesnel, Léo, 'La Littérature contemporaine en Espagne', *La Nouvelle Revue*, 72 (1891), 557-60.
An extremely favorable review of *SUH*: 'un grand roman psychologique'.

B995 ——, 'Revue des publications espagnoles', *La Nouvelle Revue*, 45 (1887), 752-53.
Singles out the priest figure in *LR*, calling Fermín 'un prêtre de la décadence'.

B996 Quevedo, José, 'Leopoldo Alas. El hombre', *Revista Popular* (Oviedo) (1.7.01), 13-15.
J.Q.'s friendship with LA.

B997 *——, 'Un recuerdo', *La Ilustración Asturiana* (San Esteban de Pravia) (June 1904).
A poem, says Gómez-Santos, B514, p. 232.

B998 *——, 'Triste recuerdo', *El Progreso de Asturias* (Oviedo), 1, No. 65 (16.6.01). Rpt. in B514, pp. 207-09.
Movingly describes the generous, emotional side of LA's nature.

B999 Quintilius [pseud.], 'El Diccionario de la lengua castellana por la Academia Española. A Clarín', *El Liberal* (3.1.87).
A response to LA's criticism of the Dictionary. Points of grammar are discussed.

B1000 R., 'Folletos literarios – V. – *A 0,50 poeta*', *Revista Contemporánea*, No. 75 (15.8.89), 335.
A review.

B1001 ——, '*Nueva campaña*', *Revista Contemporánea*, No. 66 (30.6.87), 670.

LA, says this reviewer, sometimes exaggerates and becomes impassioned, but he writes with grace and wit.

B1002 ——, '*El Señor y los demás son cuentos*', *Revista Contemporánea*, No. 91 (15.8.93), 335.
A brief review.

B1003 R. [Salvador Rueda?], 'Los Maestros. Leopoldo Alas (Clarín)', *La Gran Vía* (Madrid), 3, No. 81 (13.1.95), 1.
Clarín, he says, 'es un excepcional poeta que escribe en prosa'.

B1004 R.A., '*Apolo en Pafos*', *Revista Contemporánea*, No. 78 (15.10.87), 111.
A review.

B1005 ——, '*Mezclilla*', *Revista Contemporánea*, No. 83 (30.1.89), 187.
A favorable review, in which LA's studies on Baudelaire and Bourget are singled out as especially praiseworthy.

B1006 R.T., 'El Coliseo de El Escorial abre la temporada de teatro con una versión de *La Regenta*', *El País* (20.11.83), 45.
More details on this dramatic condensation of *LR* (see Aj4).

B1007 Rabassa, Gregory, 'Padrões de frustação e impotência em *La Regenta*', *TB*, No. 7 (Oct. 1965), 107-18.
Points out how those characters endowed with powerful personalities are frustrated and those whose position permits them to act are incapable of doing so.

B1008 Ramos, Domingo de, 'Pisto literario. Proemio – Clarín y *La Correspondencia de España* – Un crítico incipiente', *Madrid Petit*, 1, No. 2 (11.3.91), 10-11.
Snipes at LA's criticism of Pardo Bazán in *La Correspondencia de España.*

B1009 Ramos-Gascón, Antonio, 'Clarín y el primer Unamuno', *DHR*, 10 (1971), 129-38. Rpt. in *CHA*, Nos. 263-64 (May-June 1972), 489-95.
Concludes that Unamuno's personal adherence to LA must be carefully scrutinized since his letters and other writings reveal a good number of contradictions in his attitude toward LA.

B1010 ——, 'Clarín y la gente nueva', unpubl. diss., Univ. of

California - San Diego, 1970. 242 pp. Abstracted in *DAI*, 31 (1970-71), 6627-A.
An analysis of the polemical relationship between LA and the *gente nueva* (Generation of 1898 and *modernistas*).

B1011 ——, 'Introducción', in *Obra olvidada* (see Ab29), pp. 11-33.

B1012 ——, 'Introducción', in *Pipá* (see Ad2), pp. 15-97.

B1013 ——, 'Relaciones Clarín-Martínez Ruiz: 1897-1900', *HR*, 42 (1974), 413-26.
Gives a good outline of the changes in attitude and ideology which Azorín experienced in his relationship with LA.

B1014 Randolph, Donald Allen, *Don Manuel Cañete, cronista literario del romanticismo y del posromanticismo en España*, UNCSRLL, 115 (Chapel Hill: Univ. of North Carolina Press, 1972), pp. 136-37, 234, 238-40, 249.
On a literary dispute involving LA, Cañete, and J.O. Picón; Cañete's opinion of *LR*; LA's and Cañete's view of the 1884 play, *La Pasionaria.*

B1015 Reiss, Katharine, 'Der Dichter Clarín', in Ai23, p. 7.

B1016 ——, 'Las narraciones breves de "Clarín" ', unpubl. diss., Univ. Heidelberg, 1954. 295 pp. + bibliography.
Analyses and classifies LA's short stories. See also B1017.

B1017 ——, 'Valoración artística de las narraciones breves de Leopoldo Alas, "Clarín", desde los puntos de vista estético, técnico y tématico', *Archivum*, 5 (1955), 77-126, 256-303.
A useful description of the techniques and themes found in LA's short stories. A revised chapter of her diss. (B1016).

B1018 *Revista Popular* (Oviedo) (1.7.01). 24 pp.
A special no. dedicated to LA. Contents: B5, 35, 39, 51, 257, 324, 325, 501, 502, 904, 950, 952, 965, 996, 1137, 1199, 1270. Also rpts: 'La idea de la muerte en Clarín. Trozos escogidos de sus *Ensayos y revistas*', by LA.

B1019 Reyes Nevares, Salvador, 'Prólogo', in *Leopoldo Alas (Clarín)* (see Aa7), pp. 9-22.
A biographical-literary sketch of LA.

B1020   Ribbans, Geoffrey, 'Riqueza inagotada de las revistas literarias modernas', *RL*, 13, Nos 25-26 (1958), 30-37.
On LA's role in *Madrid Cómico* and his attitude toward *la gente nueva.*

B1021   Ricart, Mayte, '*La Regenta* cumple cien años', *Comunidad Escolar*, 2, No. 24 (1-15.5.84), 34.
Discusses the process of critical re-evaluation LA's work has undergone.

B1022   Rice, Miriam Wagner, 'The Meaning of Metaphor in *La Regenta*', *REH*, 11 (1977), 141-51.
Points out LA's Darwinized universe in *LR* through the use of such implicit and explicit metaphors as those of hunting, hunters, and the hunted.

B1023   ——, 'Metaphorical Foreshadowing in *La Regenta*', *Hispano*, No. 71 (Jan. 1981), 41-52.
A good article on the use of setting and action as implicit metaphors, as, for example, in the animal trap in which Ana is caught (Ch. X, Part I), representing her 'trapped existence, her attempt to escape from it, and the destruction wrought around her in the process.'

B1024   ——, 'Vetusta invertebrada: el particularismo en un contexto asturiano', *SAB*, 42, No. 2 (May 1977), 67-75.
Author presents an interesting point of view, using Ortega's notion of *el particularismo español (España invertebrada)* as a point of departure for analysing *LR*'s universe. Sometimes, however, the terms 'masses' and 'superior being' are not altogether clear within the context of LA's novel.

B1025   Richmond, Carolyn, ' "Clarín" ante el decadentismo', *Ínsula*, No. 418 (Sept. 1981), 5, 7.
Review-article on Valis (B1235), and LA's *decadentismo.*

B1026   ——, 'Clarín y el teatro: el cuento de un crítico', *Los Cuadernos del Norte* (Oviedo), 2, No. 7 (May-June 1981), 56-67.
Offers a detailed analysis of 'La Ronca', which, according to C.R., stands as a mirror to LA's own personality with its dualities of innocence versus wisdom, heart versus intellect, and so on.

B1027   ——, 'Clarín's *Su único hijo*: a Novel of Ambiguity and Crisis', unpubl. diss., Univ. of Wisconsin, 1975. 386 pp.

Abstracted in *DAI*, 36 (1975-76), 8100-A.

SUH, in expressing a sense of confusion and ambiguity, 'reflects three crises: the æsthetic crisis through which the Spanish novel was passing in the late 1880's, the ideological crisis of these years, and Clarín's own personal crisis.' A good diss.

B1028 ——, ' "Un documento" (vivo, literario y crítico): análisis de un cuento de Clarín', *BIDEA*, 36, Nos 105-06 (Jan.-Aug. 1982), 367-84.

Studies the contrasts and parallelisms in the story's structure, such as the pairing of the protagonists Cristina and Fernando, the thematic conflict between reality and fiction, and the mirroring of points of view through the device of sight (*los ojos*).

B1029 ——, 'Un eco de Maupassant en Clarín. El desenlace de *Su único hijo*', *Los Cuadernos del Norte* (Oviedo), 3, No. 16 (Nov.-Dec. 1982), 28-33.

Sees three points of contact between *Monsieur Parent* (1886) and the ending of *SUH*: the henpecked middle-aged husband; the exaltation of fatherly love; and the doubtful paternity of the son.

B1030 ——, 'El escritor', in *Treinta relatos* (see Ad39), pp. 27-35.

B1031 ——, 'Una espléndida edición de *La Regenta*', *Ínsula*, Nos 392-93 (July-Aug. 1979), 10.

A glowing review-article on the Sobejano ed., Ac11.

B1032 ——, 'Gérmenes de *La Regenta* en tres cuentos de Clarín', *Argumentos* (Madrid), 8, Nos 63-64 (1984), 16-21.

Studies the process of *el desdoblamiento* as characters and situations in stories like 'El diablo en Semana Santa', 'El doctor Pértinax', and 'Mi entierro' are transferred to the longer, more complex genre.

B1033 ——, 'El heroísmo irónico de Vetusta', *Los Cuadernos del Norte* (Oviedo), 5, No. 23 (Jan.-Feb. 1984), 82-86.

Sees in *LR* a progressive degeneration in the concept of *lo heroico*.

B1034 ——, 'Introducción', in *Su único hijo* (see Ac33), pp. xi-lxiii. Extracted in B1297, pp. 598-601.

B1035 ——, 'La muerte', in *Treinta relatos* (see Ad39), pp. 335-44.

B1036 ——, 'Un nuevo epistolario de Clarín: la elaboración de

Su único hijo', *Ínsula*, No. 423 (Feb. 1982), 5, 12.
C.R. uses LA's correspondence with F. Fe and M. Fernández Lasanta
in order to suggest the opposite of Beser's thesis (see B151) about
the origins of 'Una medianía'; i.e., she thinks the fragment was first
intended as the beginning of 'Una medianía' and only later as the
introduction to *SUH*. Also suggests the fragment may have been
the 'impulso creador' to write *SUH*.

B1037   ——, 'La ópera como enlace entre dos obras de "Clarín":
          "Amor' è furbo" y *Su único hijo'*, *Ínsula*, No. 377 (Apr.
          1978), 3.
          Indicates parallels in plot, characters, and milieu, and concludes
          that the short story serves as an antecedent to the novel.

B1038   ——, ' "Peristyle" Without a Roof: Clarín's *Su único hijo*
          and its Unfinished Trilogy', in *Studies in Honor of Ruth
          Lee Kennedy*, ed. Vern G. Williamsen and A.F. Michael
          Atlee (Chapel Hill, N.C.: Estudios de Hispanófila, 1977),
          pp. 85-102. Rpt. as 'Un "peristilo" sin techo: *Su único
          hijo* de Clarín y su triología inacabada', *Torre*, 27, Nos
          103-06 (Jan.-Dec. 1979), pp. 113-40.
          C.R. discusses *SUH* within the context of the projected triptych of
          'Una medianía', 'Esperaindeo', and 'Juanito Reseco', and offers a
          solid explanation of why these novels were never finished.

B1039   ——, 'La polémica Clarín-Bonafoux y Flaubert', *Ínsula*,
          No. 365 (Apr. 1977), 1, 12.
          After reviewing the details of the LA-Bonafoux polemic, C.R.
          attempts to establish that in *SUH* Bonifacio represents, in a cryptic
          and subtle fashion, a caricature of LA's literary enemy, Bonafoux.
          The thesis, though suggestive, may be a little stretched: the preoccu-
          pation with Bonafoux is not so evident in *SUH* as is LA's interest
          in Flaubert.

B1040   ——, 'Prólogo', in *Treinta relatos* (see Ad39), pp. 9-15.

B1041   ——, *'La Regenta*, mirada y vista', *Ínsula*, No. 451 (June
          1984), 4.
          Interesting observations on the network of diagonal and horizontal
          miradas in *LR*, as a form of communication in some situations and
          of alienation and loneliness in other cases.

B1042   ——, 'Las relaciones interpersonales', in *Treinta relatos*
          (see Ad39), pp. 101-16.

B1043 ——, 'Relatos para casi todos los gustos', *El País* (13.6.81), 31. Rpt. in B183, p. 23.
Notes the profound stylistic and thematic unity of LA's stories.

B1044 ——, 'La religiosidad', in *Treinta relatos* (see Ad39), pp. 251-60.

B1045 Rico, Eduardo G., 'Medio siglo ha precisado Clarín para valorarse', *La Nueva España* (Oviedo) (27.9.53), 8.
Favorably reviews Martínez Cachero's ed. of *Cuentos* (Ad28) and establishes parallels between LA and Palacio Valdés.

B1046 Río, Ángel del, *Historia de la literatura española*, II (New York: Dryden Press, 1948), pp. 149-50. 2nd ed. (New York: Rinehart and Winston, 1963), pp. 214-17.
Notes influences on *LR* (Zola, Stendhal, Flaubert, and Galdós) and categorizes LA as a precursor of the Generation of 1898.

B1047 Río, Germán del, 'Hace un siglo … y *La Regenta*', *Ateneo*, No. 7 (26.4.52), 3.
Author slights *LR*'s literary significance by stressing only its historical importance and by criticizing the novel's presumed lack of objectivity.

B1048 Rioja, Eugenio de, 'Centenario de "Clarín"', *Ateneo*, No. 3 (1.3.52), 16.
What Asturias is doing to celebrate LA's centennial.

B1049 ——, 'Polémica y manzanilla en torno a "Clarín"', *Ateneo*, No. 10 (7.6.52), 15.
On the general neglect and official silence toward LA at the time of his centenary.

B1050 Riopérez y Milá, Santiago, *Azorín íntegro* (Madrid: Biblioteca Nueva, 1979), pp. 113-17, 155-60, 306, *et passim.*
On the early correspondence and friendship between LA and Azorín. Copious citations from letters and Azorín's work.

Ríos, Laura de los: See García Lorca, Laura de los Ríos de.

B1051 Rivas Santiago, Natalio, 'Manuel del Palacio y Leopoldo Alas, "Clarín"', in his *Retazos de historia (Páginas de mi archivo y apuntes para mis memorias)* (Madrid: Nacional, 1952), pp. 205-08.

Adds nothing new to the history of the LA-Manuel del Palacio literary dispute.

B1052 Rivkin, Laura Madelaine, 'Eclectic Naturalism in the Novels of Leopoldo Alas, "Clarín"', unpubl. diss., Univ. of California-Berkeley, 1980. 450 pp. Abstracted in *DAI*, 42 (1981-82), 241-A.
Studies the elusive, often contradictory stance LA took in his naturalist æsthetic and the conflicting vision of artifice and verisimilitude evidenced in his fiction.

B1053 ——, 'Extranatural Art in Clarín's *Su único hijo*', *MLN*, 97 (1982), 311-28.
An excellent article on the analogies of 'creative heroism' between LA's struggle with a new kind of narrative harmonizing feminine *poesía* and masculine *prosa*, and Bonifacio's 'extranatural' androgynous fusion as a *padre-madre* to bring forth a son.

B1054 Roberts, Gemma, 'Notas sobre el realismo psicológico de *La Regenta*', *Archivum*, 18 (1968), 189-202. Rpt. in B723, pp. 194-203.
Makes good use of Georg Lukács' theory of the novel in her analysis of LA's critical realism and Ana Ozores' personal and social conflicts.

B1055 Robin, Claire-Nicolle, 'Galdós et le naturalisme: la critique de Clarín', in her *Le Naturalisme dans "La desheredada" de Pérez Galdós* (Paris: Univ. de Besançon, 1976), pp. 18-22.
Runs through LA's 1881 analysis of *La desheredada*. See also Ai20.

B1056 Robles, Alfredo, ' "Clarín", el español universal', *La Nueva España* (Oviedo) (8.2.52), 3.
A.R. sees a need to judge LA 'sin pasión adversa ni superlativa en la línea de aquella Falange con sentido aristocrático y de pasión nacional.'

Roca Franquesa, José María: See Díez-Echarri, Emiliano.

——: See also Anon., B1309.

B1057 Rocamora, José, 'Leopoldo Alas', *El Español*, 4 (14.6.01).
An obituary.

B1058 ——, 'Un pensador menos. Leopoldo Alas', *Nuestro Tiempo*, 1 (July 1901), 48-56.

An appreciation of the man and his work: 'Ha muerto un hombre bueno, enamorado de la belleza y de la verdad.'

B1059   Ródenas, Miguel A., 'El modernismo', *El Nuevo Mercurio*, 1 (1907), 650.
Notes the significance of LA's 1887 essay on Baudelaire.

B1060   Rodó, José Enrique, 'Correspondencia – Con Leopoldo Alas', in his *O.C.*, ed. Emir Rodríguez Monegal (Madrid: Aguilar, 1957), pp. 1260-63.
R.M. rpts and comments on the epistolary friendship between LA and Rodó, noting their points of agreement and disagreement, especially over the issue of *decadentismo*. See also Af29.

B1061   ——, 'Correspondencia de José Enrique Rodó', *Fuentes* (Montevideo), 1 (1961), 67-69, 96-98.
Letter (5.9.97) to LA deals with the need to establish more harmonious ties between Spain and Latin America and efforts to do so by LA, Valera, Castelar, and others. See also Af30.

B1062   ——, 'La crítica de "Clarín" ', *Revista Nacional de Literatura y Ciencias Sociales* (Montevideo), No. 4 (20.4.95), 57; No. 5 (5.5.95), 75-76. Rpt. in *El que vendrá* (Barcelona: Cervantes, 1920), pp. 30-45; in *Los escritos de 'La Revista Nacional de Literatura y Ciencias Sociales': poesías dispersas* (Montevideo: Casa A. Barreiro y Ramos, 1945), pp. 31-44; in *O.C.*, ed. Alberto José Vaccaro (Buenos Aires: Antonio Zamora, 1948), pp. 53-60; and in *O.C.*, ed. Emir Rodríguez Monegal (Madrid: Aguilar, 1957), pp. 752-58.
Characterizes LA's criticism, emphasizing, *inter alia*, his tolerance, moral tone, and reformist tendencies. In *Los escritos de La Revista Nacional...*, p. 274, there is also an extract of LA's comment on Rodó and the *Revista Nacional*.

B1063   Rodríguez, Alfred, & Barbara Jean Kailing, '¿Hay ya intención irónico-burlesca en el título mismo de *Su único hijo*?', *RomN*, 24 (1983-84), 226-28.
Points out the possible comic allusion to the lottery term, *su único hijo (el número uno)*.

B1064   Rodríguez, Carlos, & José María Tosal, 'Emma Penella será "La Regenta" ', *La Nueva España* (Oviedo) (21.3.72), 11.
'La Regenta la veo como un símbolo, un prototipo', says the actress.

Also notes difficulties with LA's heirs, who thought it practically impossible to do justice to *LR* as a film. See Aj3.

B1065 Rodríguez Alcalde, José María G., *Leopoldo G. Alas y Ureña "Clarín"; "Clarín" y Menéndez y Pelayo* (Santander: "Revista de Santander" [Librería Moderna], 1932). 47 pp.
An appreciation of LA's literary achievements; and a glossing, using generous quotations from LA, of Clarín's critical fairness toward Menéndez Pelayo.

B1066 *Rodríguez Alonso, Ángel, 'Incidencias', *La Cruz de la Victoria* (1.2.90).
Gómez-Santos also notes that R.A. wrote a series of 'Incidencias' against LA (B514, pp. 136-37). See also B1067.

B1067 *——, 'Incidencias', *La Cruz de la Victoria* (8.1.95). Rpt., in part, in B514, pp. 213-14.
Attacks LA's obituary of Guillermo Estrada (*La Cruz de la Victoria*, 7.1.95).

B1068 Rodríguez Avecilla, C., 'Comentarios', *Madrid Cómico*, 5a época, No. 22 (14.10.05), 3, 6.
LA's aggressive criticism provided an antidote against mediocrity and inauthenticity.

Rodríguez Cáceres, Milagros: See Pedraza Jiménez, Felipe B.

B1069 Rodríguez Díez, Bonifacio, 'Un modelo de análisis crítico para los cuentos de "Clarín"', in *Homenaje a Don Emilio Hurtado Llamas: estudios humanísticos y jurídicos*, Unidad de Investigación, Pubs 3 (León: Colegio Univ. de León, 1977), pp. 337-53.
Uses Vladimir Propp's analysis of the fairy tale to study '¡Adiós, Cordera!' and concludes it is really a prose poem.

B1070 Rodríguez Marín, Rafael, *La novela en el siglo XIX* (Madrid: Playor, 1982), pp. 30-31, 46-48, 68-69, 73-75, 93-96, 107-12, *et passim*.
Comments on language and structure of *LR*; theme of country vs city life; and analysis of two landscape descriptions in *LR*.

B1071 Rodríguez Monegal, Emir, 'La agonía de don Miguel de Unamuno', *Marcha* (Montevideo) (8.2.57), 22-23.
Extracts letters of Unamuno to LA, in which he writes of his religious crisis.

B1072   Rodríguez-Moñino, Antonio, ' "Clarín" y Lázaro. Un pleito entre escritor y editor (1889-1896)', *Bibliofilia* (Valencia), 5 (1951), 47-70. Separately-paginated and retitled offprint, *Clarín y Lázaro; noticias de unas relaciones literarias, 1889-1896* (Valencia: Castalia, 1951). 30 pp.
Explains why LA ceased to be a contributor to *La España Moderna*. Reproduces José Lázaro Galdiano's correspondence with LA. Review: .1. C[harles]V. A[ubrun]. *BH*, 53 (1951), 448-49.

Rodríguez Puértolas, Julio: See Blanco Aguinaga, Carlos.

B1073   Rogerio Sánchez, José, *Autores españoles e hispanoamericanos (Estudio crítico de sus obras principales)* (Madrid: Perlado, Páez y Cía, 1911), pp. 39-40.
Introductory; believes Father Blanco García's judgement is too harsh (B161).

B1074   Rogers, Douglass, 'Don Juan, *Donjuanismo*, and Death in Clarín', *Symposium*, 30 (1976), 325-42.
The Don Juan figure in 'El caballero de la mesa redonda' (D. Mamerto Anchoriz) and his final, agonizing retribution represent LA's need for further elaboration of the Don Álvaro type in *LR*.

B1075   Rogers, Edith, 'Surrogates, Parallels, and Paraphrasings in *La Regenta*', *REH*, 18 (1984), 87-101.
How many of the subplots anticipate as preliminary sketches the novel's main action.

B1076   *Romero, Leonardo T., 'El año académico y literario de Clarín en Zaragoza (1882-83)', *El Heraldo de Aragón* (20.3.83).

B1077   ——, ' "Clarín", catedrático de la Universidad de Zaragoza (El naturalismo y la mano negra)', in *Cinco estudios humanísticos para la Universidad de Zaragoza en su centenario IV* (Zaragoza: Caja de Ahorros de la Inmaculada, 1983), pp. 119-72.
More details on LA's activities in 1882-83. Good documentation. Rpts as appendices the entire series of 'El hambre en Andalucía' (see Ah60) and a poem, 'A Menéndez Pelayo', by LA. See also B1100.

B1078   ——, 'Introducción biográfica y crítica', in *Teresa. Avecilla. El hombre de los estrenos* (see Ae4), pp. 7-57.

B1079   *Roque [pseud.], 'Un recuerdo a Clarín', *La Ilustración Asturiana* (San Esteban de Pravia), 1, No. 1 (Jan. 1904), 7.

B1080   Rosselli, Ferdinando, *Una polemica letteraria in Spagna: il romanzo naturalista*, Collana di Studi, 5 (Pisa: Istituto di Letteratura Spagnola e Ispano-Americana dell' Univ., 1963), pp. 44-54.
Reviews LA's ideas on naturalism.

B1081   Round, Nicholas G., 'The Fictional Integrity of Leopoldo Alas' "Supercheria"', *BHS*, 47 (1970), 97-111.
An intelligent essay on the principal theme of 'Supercheria': Nicolás Serrano's 'recovery of personal wholeness'.

B1082   Rovira y Pita, Prudencio, ... *Cartas son cartas (Varias fichas del archivo de Maura)* (Madrid: Espasa-Calpe, 1949), pp. 17-23.
Explains the background and consequences of a letter LA wrote to Antonio Maura (see also Af14).

B1083   ——, *'Trabajo', Nuestro Tiempo*, 1 (1901), 813-17.
Praises LA's translation of Zola's *Travail*. See Ag25.

B1084   Rubín, Antonio [pseud.: Tararí], ' "Clarín", el crítico y Palacio Valdés, el novelista', *Región* (Oviedo) (15, 18, 20, 21 & 23.9.51), 3, 6, 3, 4, 3, respectively.
Citing from correspondence and texts, author comments on the LA-Palacio Valdés friendship.

B1085   Rubio Jiménez, Jesús, *Ideología y teatro en España: 1890-1900* (Zaragoza: Univ., 1982), pp. 29-33, 38-40, 53-54, 102-04, 158-61, *et passim*.
On LA's defense of naturalism in the theater; and on his failed play.

B1086   [Ruiz Contreras, Luis], 'Clarindustrial', *Revista Nueva*, 2 (25.10.99), 120-21.
An anti-Clarín piece on the *paliques* and the remuneration LA receives for them.

B1087   ——, 'Los funerales de Clarín', *Revista Nueva*, 1 (25.2.99), 69-75. Rpt. in his *Memorias de un desmemoriado*, II (Madrid: Sociedad General Española de Librería, Diarios, Revistas y Publicaciones, [1917]), pp. 191-97.

'De todo lo que decía "Clarín", apenas quedará memoria. El nombre de "Clarín" va ligado a todo lo pasajero', writes L.R.C.

B1088   ——, *Memorias de un desmemoriado* (see B1087), II, pp. 42-52, 187-97.
L.R.C., after attacking A. González Blanco's favorable view of LA's criticism, declares that Clarín aggravated 'nuestra miseria intelectual en vez de remediarla en lo posible con su esfuerzo'.

B1089   —— [pseud.: Palmerín de Oliva], 'Palabras y plumas. — Teatros, etcétera', *Revista Contemporánea*, No. 76 (30. 12.89), 647-50.
A biting attack on *Rafael Calvo y el Teatro Español.*

B1090   Ruiz de la Peña, Álvaro, 'Una broma literaria de Clarín: "Las vírgenes locas" ', *Argumentos* (Madrid), 8, Nos. 63-64 (1984), 56-59.
Reaffirms Martínez Cachero's contention (see B732) that LA, using the name of 'Flügel', wrote Ch. 5 as well as Ch. 6 of the collective 'Las vírgenes locas'. See also Ah27, Ah34, B719.

B1091   Ruiz de la Peña, Juan Ignacio, 'Respuesta documentada a un insultante artículo sobre "Clarín" ', *Asturias Semanal*, No. 235 (1.12.73), 46-48.
Demolishes the error-ridden, undocumented, and badly composed article by Francisco de Cossío (B293).

B1092   Ruiz González, David, *El movimiento obrero en Asturias: de la industrialización a la segunda República* (Oviedo: Amigos de Asturias, S.A., 1968), pp. 103-08, 120-23.
On LA's role in the Extensión Universitaria of the Univ. de Oviedo and in the Gijón strike of 1901.

B1093   Ruiz Silva, J.C., 'Clarín y el amor como imposibilidad (En torno a "Superchería")', *Ínsula*, No. 365 (Apr. 1977), 1, 12.
Sees in 'Superchería' a perfect balance between two kinds of love: platonic love for a woman and affection for a child. Death and marriage frustrate both loves. Also notes parallels between LA's story and Mann's *Death in Venice.*

B1094   Rutherford, John D., 'Introduction', in *La Regenta* (see Ai6), pp. 7-17. Rpt. as 'Introducción a *La Regenta*', *Los Cuadernos del Norte* (Oviedo), 5, No. 23 (Jan.-Feb. 1984), 40-47.

B1095 ——, *Leopoldo Alas: La Regenta* (Critical Guides to Spanish Texts, 9) (London: Grant and Cutler, 1974). 79 pp.
An excellent, concise account of characterization within the context of the major themes, narrative techniques, and setting in *LR*. Especially illuminating are the pages on narrative discourse (pp. 58-64), although I find the abbreviations used in this section a little tedious. Reviews: .1. Beser, Sergio. *BHS*, 54 (1977), 70-71.
.2. Brown, G.G. *MLR*, 70 (1975), 675-76.

B1096 ——, 'The Novel in the 1880's (III) Alas', in *The Age of Realism*, ed. F.W.J. Hemmings (Harmondsworth: Penguin Books, 1974), pp. 302-06. Rpt. Hassocks: Harvester Press; Atlantic Highlands, N.J.: Humanities Press, 1978), pp. 302-06.
A well-written summary of the literary significance of *LR*.

B1097 Ruymal, Julio, 'Esto queda de la Vetusta de "Clarín"', *La Nueva España* (Oviedo) (26.3.72) [Sunday suppl.].
Notes how Clarín anticipates cinematic techniques in many scenes of *LR*; and how, for the film version, 'ya queda muy poco de Vetusta'.

B1098 S.S., 'Vida y obras de Leopoldo Alas (Clarín)', in *¡Adiós, Cordera! y otros cuentos* (see Ad25), pp. 5-9.

B1099 Saavedra, Luis, 'El pensamiento filosófico de Clarín', *BIDEA*, 35, No. 102 (1981), 75-110.
Traces the evolution of LA's philosophical position; and tries to show that he absorbed more of *krausista* thought than he was perhaps aware of, despite an apparent break with *krausismo* in the 1880s.

B1100 Saillard, Simone, 'Le Dossier universitaire de Clarín à Saragosse', *Les Langues Néo-Latines*, No. 164 (Mar. 1963), 37-61.
Discusses and rpts, in chronological order, the forty-two documents which constitute LA's dossier at the Univ. de Zaragoza, and which illuminate three events in his life during the years 1882-83: his nomination to the teaching post at the Univ. de Zaragoza, his trip to Andalusia, and his transfer to Oviedo. See also B1076, 1077.

B1101 *——, 'Leopoldo Alas (Clarín), collaborateur du journal *El Día*: du journalisme au roman (1881-1885)', unpubl. diss., Univ. de Toulouse, 1974.

B1102   Sáinz de Robles, Federico Carlos, 'Alas y Ureña, Leopoldo S. ("Clarín")', in his *Ensayo de un diccionario de la literatura*, II (1949; Madrid: Aguilar, 1973), pp. 33-34.
One of the few critics to judge *SUH* 'acaso más perfecta que *La Regenta* en la armonía de conjunto'.

B1103   ——, 'Introducción', in *Selección de ensayos* (see Aa8), pp. 7-19.

B1104   Sáinz Rodríguez, Pedro, *Discurso leído en la solemne apertura del curso académico de 1921-1922. Tema — La obra de Clarín* (Madrid: Gráfica Ambos Mundos, 1921). 94 pp. Rpt., in abridged form, as ' "Clarín" y su obra', *Revista de las Españas*, 2 (1927), 305-11, 441-44, 536-38, 604-13; and in *Clarín y su obra* (Madrid: La Unión Ibero-Americana, 1927). Rpt. unabridged, as 'La obra de Clarín', in his *Evolución de las ideas sobre la decadencia española y otros estudios de crítica literaria* (Madrid: Rialp, 1962), pp. 334-429.
A general study of LA as critic, teacher, writer, in which three phases in the evolution of his thought are noted: the religious-Krausist, the skeptical-naturalist, and the spiritual-idealist periods. Includes useful appendices and bibliography.
Review: .1. Ortega, R.G. de. *RFE*, 8 (1921), 417-18.

B1105   ——, 'Nostalgia de Oviedo y de "Clarín" ', *Los Cuadernos del Norte* (Oviedo), 2, No. 7 (May-June 1981), 94-97.
P.S.R. tells how he came to write his 1921 *discurso* on LA (B1104) and also talks about its influence on him and other critics.

B1106   ——. *Testimonio y recuerdos* (Barcelona: Planeta, 1978), p. 58.
Talks about B1104.

——: See also Artigas Ferrando, Miguel.

B1107   Salamero, C.R., 'Galdós y "Clarín" ', *Nuevo Mundo*, 27, No. 1389 (27.8.20).
On LA's attempts to squeeze biographical data out of the taciturn Galdós.

B1108   Salcedo, Emilio, ' "Clarín", Menéndez Pelayo y Unamuno', *Ínsula*, No. 76 (Apr. 1952), 5.

On Unamuno's admiration for LA, and LA's for Menéndez Pelayo.

B1109   Sánchez, Elizabeth [Doremus] , 'La dinámica del espacio en *La Regenta* de Clarín', *Los Cuadernos del Norte* (Oviedo), 2, No. 7 (May-June 1981), 28-35.
A suggestive article on how space in *LR* — both symbolically and concretely — demonstrates the 'sutil interdependencia de las cosas', with its dialectic of opposites: active/passive, organic/inorganic, matter/spirit. Also notes that despite the setting of conflict and exploitation and a few signs of uncorrupted energy (Frígilis, Camoirán, etc.), Vetusta and its inhabitants ultimately tend toward a form of entropy and inertia.

B1110   ——, '*Madame Bovary* and *La Regenta*: a Comparative Study', unpubl. diss., Purdue Univ., 1980. 290 pp. Abstracted in *DAI*, 41 (1980-81), 2593-A.
'While in *Madame Bovary* space seems passive though hostile in relation to the heroine, in *La Regenta* space is presented metaphorically as an organism actively engaged in engulfing its prey.' Sees in *LR* a more 'open-ended system' than in *Mme Bovary*.

B1111   Sánchez, Roberto, 'Clarín y el romanticismo teatral: examen de una afición', *HR*, 31 (1963), 216-28.
For comments on this and the next two items, see B1114.
Review: .1. Simon, Suzanne. *Les Lettres Romanes*, 19 (1965), 293-94.

B1112   ——, 'The Presence of the Theater and "the Consciousness of Theater" in Clarín's *La Regenta*', *HR*, 37 (1969), 491-509.

B1113   ——, 'Teatro e intimidad en *Su único hijo*: un aspecto de la modernidad de Clarín', *Ínsula*, No. 311 (Oct. 1972), 3, 12.

B1114   ——, *El teatro en la novela: Galdós y Clarín* (Madrid: Ínsula, 1974). 207 pp.
The last three chapters (pp. 151-207; previously published as B1111, 1112, and 1113) focus on Clarín. R.S. points out LA's dualistic romantic-realist nature in his relationship with theater. He also notes the social significance of theater in *LR* in comparison to the more intimate, personal sense of theater reflected in *SUH*.
Reviews: .1. Gullón, Germán. *HR*, 45 (1977), 460-61.
.2. Gullón, Ricardo. *Ínsula*, No. 341 (Apr. 1975), 10.

.3. Menéndez Onrubia, Carmen. *Segismundo*, 15 (1981), 294-97.

B1115 *Sánchez Calvo, Estanislao, 'A propósito del libro de D. Leopoldo Alas, *Solos de Clarín*', *Revista de Asturias*, 4 (1881), 316-18, 324-26.

B1116 Sánchez Pérez, Antonio, 'Acontecimientos teatrales: el fracaso de "Clarín"', *Nuevo Mundo*, 2, No. 64 (28.3.95), 5-6.
Despite *Teresa*'s failure, writes LA's friend, the play reveals a talented dramatist in the making.

B1117 ——, 'Alegato', *El Liberal* (17.3.89).
Comments on a dispute between LA and Antonio Peña y Goñi over a point of grammar.

B1118 ——, 'Noticias teatrales: Español', *Pro Patria*, 2a época, 2 (Mar. 1895), 230-31. Rpt. in B731, p. 463.
In this piece, S.P. tries to remain neutral toward *Teresa*.

B1119 ——, '*Su único hijo*', *Madrid Cómico*, No. 444 (22.8.91), 6-7. Also appended to *Un discurso* (Ab19).
A favorable review of *SUH*.

B1120 Sandoval, Manuel de, 'Palacio y "Clarín"', in *Homenaje a Manuel del Palacio* (Madrid: Imp. Torrent, 1932), pp. 110-14. First published in *La Época* (2.1.32).
Yet another piece on the Palacio-LA dispute.

B1121 San Juan, Mario, 'Don Leopoldo Alas (Clarín)', *La Ilustración Gallega y Asturiana*, 3 (8.9.81), 297-98.
Biographical details.

B1122 ——, 'D. Leopoldo Alas y Ureña (Clarín)', *Asturias* (Madrid), 3a época, 16 (Nov. 1899), 2-3; (Dec. 1899), 2.
A sympathetic biographical sketch.

B1123 Sans, Jaume, 'El personaje del intelectual en los cuentos de L. Alas "Clarín"', *Archivum*, 27-28 (1977-78), 71-100.
A superficial treatment of the theme; consists mainly of descriptive categorizing.

B1124 *Santullano, Luis, ' "Clarín": sus amigos, sus enemigos', *La Nación* (Buenos Aires) (5.8.50).

B1125 ——, 'En el centenario de "Clarín". Alabanzas y vejámenes ultramarinos', *Ínsula*, No. 76 (Apr. 1952), 4.
A review-article on Bull (B218) and Brent (B211). L.S. criticizes Bull's quantitative method in judging LA's knowledge of foreign writers, and finds fault with Brent's focus and some of the suppositions on the autobiographical elements in *LR*.

B1126 ——, 'En el centenario de "Clarín". *La Regenta* y su autor en la picota', *Asomante*, 8, No. 3 (1952), 5-13.
Refutes Brent's thesis (B211) that LA was a frustrated personality.

B1127 *——, 'Una lectura de Clarín en la Universidad de Oviedo', *El Nacional* (México) (9.5.48).

B1128 ——, 'Leopoldo Alas "Clarín". Cincuenta años después', *CA*, 10 (1951), 267-80.
Mostly anecdotal.

B1129 ——, 'Recuerdos y nostalgias, "Clarín" en Cimadevilla', *España Peregrina* (México), 1 (1940), 172-74.
Anecdotal reflections on LA's life in Oviedo.

B1130 Sanz Villanueva, Santos, 'Ediciones desconocidas de *La Regenta*', *CHA*, No. 370 (Apr. 1981), 173-77.
Interesting speculations on the existence of other editions, or more probably new impressions, between 1884-85 and 1900-01. S.V. has come across presumably early editions with some surprising modifications in them.

B1131 *Saugniex, Joel, 'Le Bovarysme dans l'œuvre narrative de Clarín', Diplôme, ref. 21-p-44, Biblioteca del Instituto Hispánico (Paris, n.d.). 223 pp.
Cited by Ferreras, B410, p. 219.

B1132 Savaiano, Eugene, *An Historical Justification of the Anticlericalism of Galdós and Alas*, Wichita State Univ. Studies, 24 (Wichita, Kansas, 1952). 14 pp.
Gives historical reasons for the harsh treatment of the priestly figure in the works of Galdós and LA.

B1133 Schraibman, José, 'Galdós y Clarín: del realismo al simbolismo', in *Actas del Congreso Internacional de la Asociación Europea de Profesores de Español*, ed. Mátyás Horányi (Budapest: Akadémiai Kiadó, 1980), pp. 23-37.

Despite the title, most of this deals with Galdós. Notes LA's greater
spiritual concerns and ambiguity in his later works.

B1134 ——, & Leda Garazzola, 'Hacia una interpretación de la ironía
en *La Regenta*', in *Studies in Honor of José Rubia Barcia*, ed.
Roberta Johnson and Paul C. Smith (Lincoln, Nebraska: Society
of Spanish and Spanish-American Studies, 1982), pp. 175-86.
Discusses different types of irony in *LR*: classical, romantic, historical,
and aesthetic; and gives examples of linguistic and situational irony.
Sometimes a diffuse essay, with misleading title (there is more categorizing description than interpretation).

——: See also Little, William.

B1135 Schreieck, Gertrud, 'Leopoldo Alas (Clarín) im Spiegel seines
Romans *La Regenta*', unpubl. diss., Univ. Erlangen-Nürnberg,
1951. 138 pp.
An analysis of LA's literary personality and of *LR*.

Schwartz, Kessel: See Chandler, Richard E.

B1136 Schyfter, Sara E., ' "La loca, la tonta, la literata": Woman's
Destiny in Clarín's *La Regenta*', in *Theory and Practice of Feminist Literary Criticism*, ed. Gabriela Mora and Karen S. Van
Hooft (Ypsilanti, Mich.: Bilingual Press, 1982), pp. 229-41.
A feminist reading to show how Ana Ozores' 'life ... conforms to the
classic female pattern of powerlessness, self-rejection, and failed
attempts to escape her plight.'

B1137 Sela, Aniceto, 'Alientos', *Revista Popular* (Oviedo) (1.7.01),
15.
LA as an exemplar for youth.

B1138 ——, 'La Extensión Universitaria en Oviedo', *Boletín de
la Institución Libre de Enseñanza*, 25 (31.8.01), 228-34.
Contains an obituary of LA (later published in B1139).

B1139 ——, *Universidad de Oviedo. Extensión Universitaria.
Memorias correspondientes a los cursos de 1898 a 1909
(Once años de Extensión Universitaria en Oviedo)* (Madrid:
Librería General de Victoriano Suárez, 1910), pp. 21-22,
37, 43-45, 48, 193, 199, 201, 203-04, 233-34. First pub-
lished in various vols of the *Anales de la Universidad de*

Oviedo (see, in particular, 1-2 (1901-03), 265-327, 225-38). Gómez-Santos rpts pp. 21-22, 37 in B514, pp. 205-07.
On LA's contribution to the Extensión Universitaria.

B1140   Semprún Donahue, Moraima de, 'La doble seducción de *La Regenta*', *PSA*, 71 (1973), 209-28. Rpt. in *Archivum*, 23 (1973), 117-33; and in *ETL*, 2 (1973-74), 241-49.
Discusses the close relationship between the double seduction of the sensual and the spiritual in *LR*.

B1141   *Señas Encinas, F., 'La casa del maestrante y el caserón de la Regenta', *Boletín de la Sociedad Ovetense de Festejos*, No. 4 (May 1953), 2, 3.

B1142   Sequeros, Antonio, 'Leopoldo Alas, "Clarín" (Adelantado) (1852-1901)', in his *Con el 98 y su proyección literaria* (Almoradí: Talleres Edijar, 1972), pp. 87-91.
LA as a precursor of the Generation of 1898.

B1143   Serrano, Eugenia, 'Fantasmas en el Ateneo', *Correo Literario*, No. 48 (15.5.52), 3.
LA's vision of Spain is not so very different from that of José Antonio's, writes E.S., who sees in LA what it suits her to see.

B1144   ——, 'Ideales estéticos de uno del sesenta y ocho', *RIE*, 10 (1952), 303-12.
A rather weak article which expounds on a traditional Catholic LA.

B1145   *Serrano Anguita, Francisco, 'Cuando "Clarín" no tenía tiempo para ser reo. Curioso proceso por la publicación de un "palique" agresivo', *Región* (Oviedo) (24.3.49).

B1146   Serrano Poncela, Segundo, 'Un estudio de *La Regenta*', *PSA*, 44 (1967), 19-50; and *CA*, 26, No. 152 (1967), 223-41. Rpt. in B144, pp. 139-61.
On 'el realismo irritado' of LA's novel. 'En *La Regenta* se respira continuamente una sutil atmósfera despectiva, degradatoria, por hombres y cosas; por creencias y acciones. Es una novela *desvalorizadora*.'

B1147   ——, *Prosa moderna en lengua española (Antología)* (Río Piedras: Univ. de Puerto Rico, Ed. de La Torre, 1955), pp. 139-41.

Comments on LA's almost prophetic modernity. Bibliography (pp. 157-58). See also Ah30, Ah45.

B1148 Shaw, Donald L., *A Literary History of Spain: the Nineteenth Century* (London: Ernest Benn; New York: Barnes and Noble, 1972), pp. 145-50. Trans. as *Historia de la literatura española:* V. *El siglo XIX* (Barcelona: Ariel, 1973), pp. 212-19.
A nice introduction to LA, though author fails to see the irony at work in *SUH*.

B1149 Siboni, Luis, '*La duda*', *Barcelona Cómica*, 11, No. 9 (26.2.98), 206-07.
Thinks D. Braulio in Echegaray's *La duda* is a portrait of LA.

B1150 ——, 'Letra menuda', *Barcelona Cómica*, 11, No. 7 (12. 2.98), 158-59.
LA's critical powers are going downhill, he says. Comments acidly on LA's efforts to drum up support for *La millonaria.*

B1151 ——, 'Letra menuda', *Barcelona Cómica*, 11, No. 8 (19.2. 98), 183.
Talks about how he excoriates LA in his forthcoming book, *Pan de compadres* (see B1155).

B1152 ——, 'Letra menuda', *Barcelona Cómica*, 11, No. 10 (5.3. 98), 226-27.
On the LA-Pardo Bazán dispute. 'Clarín no es un crítico', he says, 'sino uno de tantos seres enajenados de pasiones...'

B1153 ——, 'Letra menuda', *Barcelona Cómica*, 11, No. 11 (12.3. 98), 252.
Criticizes LA's editorship of *Madrid Cómico.*

B1154 ——, 'Letra menuda', *Barcelona Cómica*, 11, No. 12 (19.3. 98), 270.
Claims LA plays dirty as a critic.

B1155 ——, *Pan de compadres para Valbuena y Clarín* (Madrid: Est. tip. de Pedro Ortega, 1898). 213 pp.
An anti-Clarín tract, in which L.S. tears apart LA's grammatical and literary abilities in all his work (pp. 57-195).

B1156 Sieburth, Stephanie, 'James Joyce and Leopoldo Alas:

Patterns of Influence', *RCEH*, 7 (1982-83), 401-06.
On the Odyssey connection between *SUH* and *Ulysses*. The patterns are there, but is the influence? Did Joyce know Spanish?

B1157   Sobejano, Gonzalo, 'Clarín y el sentimiento de la Virgen', in *Aufstieg und Krise der Vernunft: komparatistische Studien zur Literatur der Aufklärung und des Fin-de-siècle*, ed. Michael Rössner and Birgit Wagner (Wien: Hermann Böhlaus, 1984), pp. 157-72.
Contrasts LA's vision of the Virgin as the Mother of God ('Theotokos'), with Zola's ('Eros virginal') and Antero de Quental's ('Thanatos hipnótico').

B1158   ——, 'Clarín y la crisis de la crítica satírica', *RHM*, 31 (1965), 399-417. Rpt. in his *Forma literaria y sensibilidad social* (Madrid: Gredos, 1967), pp. 139-77.
A useful study of LA's criticism and the times in which he wrote. Notes, in particular, the negative, limiting influence of *la literatura festiva* on LA's work.

B1159   ——, 'Commentary', in *Readings in Spanish Literature*, ed. Anthony Zahareas and Barbara Kaminar de Mujica (New York: Oxford Univ. Press, 1975), pp. 201-05.
General introduction to LA and a commentary on two stories included in this anthology, 'Protesto' and 'Un jornalero'. See also Ah32, 35.

B1160   ——, 'De Flaubert a Clarín', *Quimera* (Barcelona), No. 5 (Mar. 1981), 25-29.
On LA's literary affinities with Flaubert; and Flaubertian echoes in *LR*, *SUH*, 'Doña Berta', 'El Torso', and LA's criticism, as well as in Galdós, Unamuno, Azorín, Pérez de Ayala, etc.

B1161   ——, 'La inadaptada (Leopoldo Alas: *La Regenta*, capítulo XVI)', in *El comentario de textos*, by Emilio Alarcos, et al. (Madrid: Castalia, 1973), pp. 126-66. Rpt. (slightly cut), in B144, pp. 187-224. Extracted in B1297, pp. 584-89.
A detailed, textual analysis of specific passages of Ch. XVI.

B1162   ——, 'Introducción', in *La Regenta* (see Ac12), I, pp. 7-58.

B1163   ——, '*Madame Bovary* en *La Regenta*', *Los Cuadernos del Norte* (Oviedo), 2, No. 7 (May-June 1981), 22-27.

After detailing particulars which the novels share, G.S. goes on to point out the essential difference: '... consiste en que aquélla [*MB*] es una novela antirromántica sobre el alma romántica deteriorada, y *La Regenta* una novela romántica contra el mundo antirromántico y en homenaje al alma bella y buena, derrotada pero inadaptable.'

B1164 ——, *Nietzsche en España* (Madrid: Gredos, 1967), pp. 64-65, 83-84, 175-78.
Of all the writers of the Generation of 1868, LA best understood Nietzsche's work and especially appreciated his moral and metaphysical aspects.

B1165 ——, 'Ochenta años de la muerte de Leopoldo Alas, "Clarín"'. La vigencia de un novelista clásico', *El País* (13.6.81), 30. Rpt. in B183, pp. 20-21.
LR as the first Spanish model of the Lukácsian 'romanticism of disillusionment'.

B1166 ——, 'Prólogo (Leopoldo Alas, la novela naturalista y la imaginación moral de *La Regenta*' (see Ac11), pp. 11-58.

B1167 ——, 'Semblantes de la servidumbre en *La Regenta*', in *Serta Philologica F. Lázaro Carreter* (Madrid: Cátedra, 1983), pp. 519-29.
Discusses how class conflicts operate disguised as various passions, especially vengeance, in the servants. Also notes further parallels with Cervantes' *El curioso impertinente* and Eça de Queiros' *O primo Basilio*.

B1168 ——, 'Sentimientos sin nombre en *La Regenta*', *Ínsula*, No. 451 (June 1984), 1, 6.
On love as an unnameable yearning for the absolute and the infinite, in Ana Ozores and Fermín de Pas.

B1169 [Sola, A. de], 'Novedades teatrales. Español. Beneficio de María Guerrero', *El Día* (21.3.95).
A mixed review of *Teresa*.

B1170 *Soler y Miquel, José, 'Clarín', *La Publicidad* (Barcelona) (15.6.95).

B1171 ——, 'Los cuentos de Clarín', *La Vanguardia* (Barcelona) (14.2.95). Rpt. in his *Escritos* (Barcelona: Tip. 'L'Avenç' de Massó, Casas y Elías, 1898), pp. 43-52.

A very favorable, warm review-article on *El Señor... y lo demás son cuentos.*

B1172   ——, *'Cuentos morales'*, *La Vanguardia* (Barcelona) (19. 2.96). Rpt. in his *Escritos* (see B1171), pp. 53-65.
A favorable, perceptive review.

B1173   Solís, Jesús-Andrés, *Vida y obra de "Clarín"* (Gijón: Gráficas Guinea, [1975]). 135 pp.
Quoting generously from previous biographers, this is a very superficial account of LA's life and work. Mostly gives summaries of plots and contents.

B1174   Somovilla, Miguel, 'La conmemoración del centenario de *La Regenta* comenzó ayer con la representación teatral de la novela', *La Nueva España* (Oviedo) (4.12.83).
Details of forthcoming celebration. See also Aj4.

B1175   ——, 'Exponen en Oviedo las primeras ediciones y otros documentos sobre *La Regenta*, de Leopoldo Alas', *El País* (17.6.84). Rpt. in *El País, Edición Internacional* (25.6.84), 20.
Details of the continuing celebration of *LR*'s centenary.

B1176   Sotillo, Antonio, 'Clarín (Semblanza literaria)', in *Crítica popular* (see Ab24), pp. v-xvi.

B1177   Soto Duggan, Lilvia, 'La degradación del mundo en *La Regenta*', *PH*, No. 23 (1977), 25-33.
On the multiple uses of irony and its metaphysical significance to depict a degrading and degraded universe. Of interest is an analysis devoted to the technique of the parodistic echo in *LR*.

B1178   Sousa, Paco, ' "Clarín" en América', *Asturias* (Madrid), No. 13 (Apr. 1952), 6.
How Asturian émigrés in a Tampa tobacco factory reacted to *LR* read aloud.

B1179   *——, ' "Clarín" y los americanos', *Oviedo* (1952 ed.), n. pag.
Cited by Martínez Cachero, B714, p. 108.

B1180   Souto Alabarce, Arturo, 'Alas ("Clarín"): *La Regenta*', in his *Grandes textos creativos de la literatura española* (México: Pormaca, 1967), pp. 115-22.

The usual introductory material.

B1181   Suárez, Constantino [pseud.: Españolito], *Escritores y artistas asturianos (Índice biobibliográfico)*, I (Madrid: Sáez Hermanos, 1936), pp. 108-33.
Useful biobibliographical details.

B1182   *——, 'Revisiones: Leopoldo Alas, Clarín', *Solar Norteño* (Oviedo), No. 3 (1934).

B1183   ——, 'Semblanza', in his *Cuentistas asturianos (Antología y semblanzas)* (Madrid: Compañía Ibero-Americana de Publicaciones, 1930), pp. 93-97.
A summary of LA's life and work. See also Ah17, B1181.

B1184   Suárez Piñera, Rosario, 'Algunos recursos e ideas que se desprenden de una lectura crítica de *Su único hijo* de Clarín', *Archivum*, 29-30 (1979-80), 59-67.
On the conflict of interests between the individual and the historical reality. Somewhat disorganized.

B1185   Taboada, Luis, *Intimidades y recuerdos (Páginas de la vida de un escritor)* (Madrid: Administración de 'El Imparcial', 1900), pp. 127-29.
On LA's role in the newspaper, *El Solfeo.*

B1186   Taléns Carmona, Jenaro, Juan Oleza Simó et al, 'Leopoldo Alas "Clarín"', in *Historia de la literatura*, II, Unidad didáctica 5 (Madrid: Univ. Nacional de Educación a Distancia, 1976), pp. 21-24.
A general introduction to LA's writings.

Tararí [pseud.] : See Rubín, Antonio.

B1187   Taylor, Alan Carey, *Carlyle et la pensée latine* (Paris: Boivin, 1937), pp. 319-23.
Summarizes LA's introduction to the Spanish translation of Carlyle's *Heroes*, an 'introduction assez fouillée et remarquable'.

B1188   Thomas, Richard Loyce, 'Sensation and Feeling in Clarín's *La Regenta*', unpubl. diss., Univ. of Iowa, 1975. 329 pp. Abstracted in *DAI*, 36 (1975-76), 5342-A.
Uses a hybrid approach – formalistic plus the 'Geneva school' – to analyse *LR*'s dominant motifs of sensation and feeling, spatial

relations, dualism, and synthesis.

B1189   Thompson, Clifford R., Jr., 'Cervantine Motifs in the Short Stories of Leopoldo Alas', *REH*, 10 (1976), 391-403.
While giving examples of Cervantine dualities in other stories, C.T. focusses on 'Doña Berta' as the best example of Cervantine techniques in a short story. He cites the quixotic figure of Doña Berta herself, the opposition of past and present literary modes, and of the real and the ideal, as Cervantine motifs, and concludes that the 'ideal is reaffirmed rather than negated by the triumph of reality'.

B1190   ——, ' "Un documento" de Clarín: un paso hacia *La Regenta*', *Archivum*, 27-28 (1977-78), 65-69.
Points out parallel situations and characters, in particular, the conflict between spiritual and carnal desires in Cristina ('Un documento') and Ana Ozores.

B1191   ——, 'Egoism and Alienation in the Works of Leopoldo Alas', *RF*, 81 (1969), 193-203.
Both collective and individual egoism are intimately connected to the alienated state of the characters in LA's stories and novels.

B1192   ——, 'Evolution in the Short Stories of Clarín', *REH*, 18 (1984), 381-98.
Gives examples of how LA moves from satire to sympathy in his depiction of love and intellectual activity.

B1193   ——, 'Poetic Response in the Short Stories of Leopoldo Alas', *RomN*, 13 (1971-72), 272-75.
The poetry of LA's short stories is embedded primarily in the poetically idealistic attitudes of the main characters.

B1194   ——, 'A Thematic Study of the Short Stories of Leopoldo Alas', unpubl. diss., Harvard Univ., 1965. 224 pp.
Studies the major themes, problem of classification and chronology, problem of genre, naturalistic doctrine, and short-story tradition in nineteenth-century Spain. Stresses the theme of alienation in LA's stories.

B1195   Tolivar Alas, Ana Cristina, 'La música en *La Regenta*', *Los Cuadernos del Norte* (Oviedo), 5, No. 23 (Jan.-Feb. 1984), 70-76.

Catalogues references to popular and religious music, opera and the zarzuela, which produce 'una sensación de ahogo' in *LR*.

B1196   Tolivar Faes, J [osé Ramón], *Nombres y cosas de las calles de Oviedo* (Oviedo: Imp. la Carpeta, 1958), pp. 205-08, 357.
A sketch of LA and the street in Oviedo named after him; also of the street called 'Vetusta'.

B1197   Tomasso, Vicenzo de, *"Clarín" nella narrativa spagnola del secondo ottocento: sei studi su Leopoldo Alas* (Pisa: Pacini Editore, [1973]). 110 pp.
Except for the sections on Italy and *lo italiano* in LA's work and the presence of juridical terms in *SUH* and *LR*, these essays offer little new material to the Clarín scholar.

B1198   ——, 'Il significato dei riferimenti letterari ne *La Regenta* di Clarín', *Dialoghi* (Roma), 16, Nos. 1-3 (Jan.-June 1968), 40-60. Rpt. in B1197, pp. 23-46.
On the Cervantine theme of life versus literature in *LR*.

B1199   Torner, Fernando M., 'Nuestros propósitos', *Revista Popular* (Oviedo) (1.7.01), 2-3.
On LA's moral and artistic legacy and the necessity of perpetuating it – hence the special issue of *Revista Popular* dedicated to Clarín's memory.

B1200   Torre, Guillermo de, 'Clarín, crítico y novelista', in his *Del 98 al barroco* (Madrid: Gredos, 1969), pp. 265-81.
An appreciative, though somewhat rambling, look at the many talents of LA, as critic, novelist, and short-story writer.

B1201   ——, 'En el cincuentenario de Leopoldo Alas, "Clarín" ', *La Nación* (Buenos Aires) (14.10.51).
Words of homage.

B1202   ——, 'Presencia de "Clarín" ', *Archivum*, 2 (1952), 221-31.
Comments on the dual aspects of datedness and modernity in LA's writings; and draws parallels between LA and Unamuno.

B1203   ——, 'Unamuno y "Clarín" ', in his *La aventura y el orden* (Buenos Aires: Losada, 1943), pp. 51-60. Rpt. in his *Tríptico del sacrificio* (Buenos Aires: Losada, 1948), pp. 23-30;

and in his *La aventura estética de nuestra edad y otros ensayos* (Barcelona: Seix Barral, 1962), pp. 239-46.
Discusses the correspondence between LA and Unamuno.

B1204 Torre Callejo, Luz María de la, *Leopoldo Alas, Clarín, y su obra* (México: UNAM, 1965). 99 pp.
A published M.A. thesis (UNAM), which tells us nothing that we did not already know about LA.

B1205 Torrendell, J., *"Clarín" y su ensayo (Estudio crítico)* (Barcelona: López Editor, Librería Española, 1895). 70 pp.
Teresa, which J.T. categorizes as a naturalist example of the theater of ideas, failed mostly because of the public's bad taste, LA's enemies, and the play's lack of dramatic qualities.

B1206 Torrente Ballester, Gonzalo, *Literatura española contemporánea (1898-1936)* (Madrid: Afrodisio Aguado, 1949), pp. 126-41.
On LA as a critic, 'un arquetipo de lo que debe ser el crítico literario considerado como ser moral.' See also B1207.

B1207 ——, *Panorama de la literatura española contemporánea*, I, 2nd ed. (Madrid: Guadarrama, 1961), pp. 72-84.
An expanded version of B1206, with the addition of the section, 'Clarín, novelista'.

B1208 ——, 'La verdad como escándalo', *Los Cuadernos del Norte* (Oviedo), 5, No. 23 (Jan.-Feb. 1984), 25-28.
LA's iconoclastic vision of reality in *LR* was unacceptable to his contemporaries.

—— : See also Chacel, Rosa.

B1209 Torrente-Legazpi, Ramón Luis, 'Del ideal hispánico de "Clarín"', *EstLit*, No. 343 (7.5.66), 34.
Emphasizes LA's *hispanismo*.

B1210 Torres, David, 'Índice de la revista ilustrada *Arte y Letras* (Barcelona, 1882-83)', *Hispania* (U.S.A), 66 (1983), 345-47.
Discusses LA's role in *Arte y Letras*, his opinion of it, and his publications therein.

B1211 ——, 'Introducción', in *Los prólogos de Leopoldo Alas* (see Ab32), pp. 7-10.

B1212 ——, 'Noticia de otro juicio sobre la *Teresa* de Clarín', *Humanitas* (Nuevo León), 22 (1981), 177-80. Rpt. in *RL*, 44, No. 87 (1982), 141-44; and in *BIDEA*, 37, Nos 109-10 (1983), 589-93.
Rpts Luis Alberto's review (see B19).

B1212 bis ——, 'Presentación de los prólogos', in *Los prólogos de Leopoldo Alas* (see Ab32), pp. 13-51.

Torres Bernal, José de: See Antón del Olmet, Luis.

B1213 Torres Nebrera, Gregorio, 'Texto de "Clarín" ', in *Comentario lingüístico y literario de textos españoles*, by Manuel Ariza Viguera et al (Madrid: Alhambra, 1981), pp. 211-29.
A rather verbose treatment of 'El frío del Papa' as a pre-Unamunian text of religious crisis.

Tosal, José María: See Rodríguez, Carlos.

B1214 Traviesas, M. Miguel, 'Leopoldo Alas, profesor', *España*, No. 224 (24.7.19), 11-12.
'Para mí, el maestro era superior al literato (Clarín), con ser literato tan exquisito', writes M.T.

B1215 Tungeln, Annie Laurie Von, 'Pessimistic Tendencies of Leopoldo Alas', unpubl. M.A. thesis, Univ. of Oklahoma, 1931. 62 pp.
Concludes that LA is definitely a pessimist in all genres, including his criticism (of which only a part seems to have been read by this author).

B1216 Tuñón de Lara, Manuel, 'La España de Galdós y de "Clarín". Su obra y la sociedad española de la segunda mitad del siglo XIX', in his *Medio siglo de cultura española (1885-1936)*, 3rd ed. rev. (Madrid: Tecnos, 1977), pp. 19-36. 1st ed., 1970.
LA and Galdós are 'escritores que no se limitan a su "especialidad" ... "Clarín" y Galdós son, en ese sentido, *intelectuales*, es decir, no tratan de escindir los hechos que conocen, sino de ponerlos en relación unos con otros y de conocer también sus conexiones.'

B1217 Turin, Yvonne, *L'Éducation et l'école en Espagne de 1874 à 1902 (Libéralisme et tradition)* (Paris: Presses Universitaires de France, 1959), pp. 88-90.

Discusses the 1891 *Discurso* read at the Univ. de Oviedo (see Ab19).

B1218   Turner, Harriet S., 'Vigencia de Clarín: vistas retrospectivas en torno a *La Regenta*', *Arbor*, 116, No. 456 (Dec. 1983), 31-54.
An excellent overview of North American criticism of *LR*, from 1933-83, this essay also contains suggestive comments on the novel's self-reflexivity.

B1219   Tyrmand, Mary Ellen, 'Women and Society in the Nineteenth-Century Spanish Novel', unpubl. diss., Yale Univ., 1974. 175 pp. Abstracted in *DAI*, 35 (1974-75), 3774-A.
Studies six novels by Fernán Caballero, Valera, Galdós, and LA, to 'determine the interplay between character, society and destiny in the lives of Spanish women'.

B1220   Ullman, Pierre L., 'The Antifeminist Premises of Clarín's *Su único hijo*', *Estudos Ibero-Americanos*, 1 (July 1975), 57-91.
An attempt to view LA's non-misogynist antifeminism, which is based on the existence of two kinds of altruism, masculine and feminine, as a structuring principle in *SUH* (also in 'Doña Berta', *Teresa*, and *LR*). The application of LA's little-known article, 'Psicología del sexo', to *SUH* is also a stimulating approach. Though this is an interesting paper, the author tends to wander from his thesis and tries to be fashionably relevant.

B1221   ——, 'Clarín: ensayos, solos, paliques: a Question of Genre?', *Ensayistas*, Nos 14-15 (Mar. 1983), 113-19.
Concludes that it is probably useless to try to classify by sub-genres the various names LA gave his essays.

B1222   ——, 'Clarín's Androcratic Ethic and the Antiapocalyptic Structure of " ¡Adiós, Cordera! " ', in *The Analysis of Hispanic Texts: Current Trends in Methodology*, ed. Lisa E. Davis and Isabel C. Tarán. Second York Coll. Colloquium (New York: Bilingual Press, 1976), pp. 11-31.
Offers the somewhat labored thesis that 'the symbols of " ¡Adiós, Cordera! ", if analyzed anagogically, form themselves into an anti-apocalypse, that is, a triumph of the Dragon over the Lamb, of Satan over Christ, of the infernal over the divine trinity, and that the antiapocalypse is facilitated by the process of feminizing the trinity.'

B1223   Unamuno, Miguel de, 'La afanosa grandiosidad española',
Ahora (13.7.34), 5.
Praises 'Zurita' and recommends re-reading LA's work.

B1224   ——, 'Carta a Clarín', in his *Obras selectas*, 4th ed.
(Madrid: Plenitud, 1960), pp. 977-86. 1st ed., 1946.
Rpts letter dated 9.5.1900, which is also found in B15, pp. 84-100.

Urales, Federico [pseud.] : See Montseny y Carret, Juan.

Uría Ríu, Juan: See Anon., B1308.

B1225   Urmeneta, Fermín de, 'Sobre estética clariniana', *RIE*, 27
(1969), 255-61.
On the interrelatedness of characters and the symbolic use of repetition in ' ¡Adiós, Cordera! '

B1226   Valbuena Prat, Ángel, *Historia de la literatura española*,
6th ed., III (Barcelona: Gustavo Gili, 1960), pp. 451-53.
8th ed. (1968), pp. 446-48.
LA's sensibility, his appreciation of detail and *lo íntimo*, and his
critical reaction to Spain's problems prepare the ground for the
Generation of 1898.

B1227   ——, 'Modernismo y generación del 98 en la literatura
española', in *Historia general de las literaturas hispánicas*,
VI, *Literatura contemporánea*, ed. Guillermo Díaz-Plaja
(Barcelona: Vergara, 1967), pp. 70-71.
On LA as a precursor of the Generation of 1898.

B1228   Valdeavellano, Luis G. de, 'Clarín visto por Adolfo Posada',
Ínsula, No. 12 (Dec. 46), 2.
A favorable review of Posada's biography (B973).

B1229   Valdés, Juan Alonso, 'Prólogo', in *Siglo pasado* (see Ab25),
pp. 5-10.

B1230   Valdivia, Aniceto, 'Al Sr. D. Leopoldo Alas, renombrado
Clarín', *Madrid Cómico*, No. 68 (10.4.81), 6-7.
Rejects LA's opinion that Palacio Valdés's *El señorito Octavio* is
a good novel.

B1231   ——, 'Punto final', *Madrid Cómico*, No. 69 (17.4.81), 3.
An *ad hominem* attack on LA's intelligence.

B1232 Valentí Camp, Santiago, 'Leopoldo Alas (Clarín)', in his *Ideólogos, teorizantes y videntes* (Barcelona: Minerva, 1922), pp. 113-25.
Essentially a laudatory piece on LA's contribution to Spanish letters.

B1233 Valentí Fiol, Eduard, *El primer modernismo literario catalán y sus fundamentos ideológicos* (Barcelona: Ariel, 1973), pp. 61-78.
Author appears to place LA among religious *modernistas* although he notes his aversion to literary modernists.

B1234 Valera, Juan, *Ecos argentinos* (Madrid: Fernando Fe, 1901), pp. 14-15.
Comments on the many literary foes LA attracts.

B1235 Valis, Noël Maureen, *The Decadent Vision in Leopoldo Alas (A Study of La Regenta and Su único hijo)* (Baton Rouge: Louisiana State Univ. Press, 1981). 215 pp.
In LA, the idea of decadence, as depicted through a corrupt society and degenerate, weak-willed, or fragmented characters, functions as a unifying device in the novels. Although decadent themes, types, and leitmotifs pervade the whole of LA's novels, author does not suggest the notion of a decadent style, but rather the creation of a decadent vision, stimulated in large part by the reigning French literary movements, namely, naturalism and later the decadent movement proper.
Reviews: .1. Dial, John. *REH*, 17 (1983), 468-69.
.2. García Sarriá, Francisco. *BHS*, 59 (1982), 155-57.
.3. Hafter, Monroe Z. *KRQ*, 30 (1983), 109-10.
.4. Kronik, John W. *Hispania* (U.S.A.), 65 (1982), 463-64.
.5. Pérez Gallego, Cándido. *Arbor*, 115, No. 449 (1983), 143-44.
.6. Richmond, Carolyn. *Ínsula*, No. 418 (Sept. 1981), 5, 7.
.7. Rogers, Douglass M. *SAR*, 47, No. 2 (May 1982), 110-13.
.8. Round, Nicholas G. *MLR*, 79 (1984), 217-19.
.9. Sánchez, Elizabeth. *MFS*, 28 (1982), 335-37.

B1236 ——, 'Dos artículos olvidados sobre *La Regenta*, de Clarín', *BIDEA*, 37, Nos 109-10 (1983), 625-52.
Discusses and rpts two articles by Lara y Pedraja ('Orlando') and J.O. Picón. See B642, 961.

B1237 ——, 'Fermín de Pas: una flor del mal clariniana', *ETL*, 7 (1978-79), 31-36.

Analyses the long description of Fermín de Pas given in Ch. 1 of *LR*, and links its decadent motifs with the French literary interest in decadence.

B1238 ——, 'The Idea of Decadence in the Novels of Leopoldo Alas (Clarín)', unpubl. diss., Bryn Mawr Coll., 1975. 402 pp. Abstracted in *DAI*, 36 (1975-76), 6141-A.
See B1235, a revised and updated version of diss.

B1239 ——, 'The Landscape of the Soul in Clarín and Baudelaire', *RLC*, 54 (1980), 17-31.
By juxtaposing the troubled, inner being of the poet in *Les Fleurs du Mal* with the confused, anguished psyche of Ana Ozores in *LR*, one sees that LA has employed a spiritual and emotional geography of a soul in agony, which is correlated to a very physical landscape and climate.

B1240 ——, 'Leopoldo Alas y Zola: paralelismos y divergencias temáticos', *Anuario de Letras* (México), 17 (1979), 327-35.
Affinities and contrasts in Zola and LA in their treatment of the themes of fertility, maternity, sterility, corruption, and decay.

B1241 ——, 'Leopoldo Alas y los Goncourt: el alma neurótica', *Archivum*, 27-28 (1977-78), 51-63. Also in: *HisJ*, 1, No. 1 (Fall 1979), 27-35.
Examines the novelistic treatment of the themes of sensation, sexual frustration, and latent impulses of self-destruction in LA and the brothers Goncourt.

B1242 ——, 'Order and Meaning in Clarín's *La Regenta*', *Novel*, 16 (1983), 246-58.
LR as the great nineteenth-century novel of absence. Discusses the implications found in the fluctuation between connecting and disconnecting, in the tension between order and disorder, as the novel seems to rush toward entropy.

B1243 ——, 'El "Pipá" de Clarín y "El incendio" de Ana María Matute: una infancia traicionada', *Los Cuadernos del Norte* (Oviedo), 2, No. 7 (May-June 1981), 72-77.
Discusses characters, situations, and structure of the two stories, showing how in the tripartite movement reality—illusion—reality, the protagonists experience the destruction of their dreams through the element of fire.

B1244 ——, 'The Presence of *Nana* in Clarín's "La mosca sabia"',
in *La Chispa '83: Selected Proceedings*, ed. Gilbert Paolini
(New Orleans: Tulane Univ., 1983), pp. 287-96.
Interprets the story as a sly poke at Zola as the supreme theoretician
of the experimental novel.

B1245 ——, 'Romantic Reverberation in Clarín's *La Regenta*:
Hugo and the Clarinian Decay of Romanticism', *The
Comparatist*, 3 (1979), 40-52.
A discussion of Ch. 1 of *LR* and how LA refashions and refills an
older literary mold, the Romanticism of the archromantic, Victor
Hugo, by deliberately distorting the simpler lines of the 1832 novel,
Notre-Dame de Paris.

B1246 ——, 'A Spanish Decadent Hero: Clarín's Antonio Reyes
of "Una medianía"', *MLS*, 9, No. 2 (Spring 1979), 53-60.
Presents Antonio Reyes' character delineation as an example of the
successful blending of both the *fin de siècle* Spanish intellectual and
the typical decadent hero.

B1247 ——, ' "Tambor y gaita": Clarín's Last Project?', *RF*, 93
(1981), 397-402.
Discusses and rpts this fragment from a projected novel.

B1248 Valverde, José María, *Azorín* (Barcelona: Planeta, 1971),
pp. 34-35, 40-54.
Comments on LA's influence on Azorín and how the younger writer
emancipated himself from that influence, in particular, from LA's
style.

B1249 ——, ' "Clarín"', in his *Historia de la literatura universal*,
III, *Del romanticismo a nuestros días*, 4th ed. (Barcelona:
Planeta, 1973), pp. 166-67. 1st ed., 1968.
Notes in *LR* 'un voluntario desenfoque en el retrato de la protago-
nista'.

B1250 Vaquero, José Manuel, 'Proponen la celebración de un
simposio internacional sobre Clarín', *El País* (16.6.81).
Rpt. in B183, p. 28.
Details on the proposed symposium and the 1981 Clarín exhibit
in Oviedo.

B1251 Varela Jácome, Benito, 'Estructuración de *Su único hijo*', in his *Estructuras novelísticas del siglo XIX* (Barcelona: Aubí, 1974), pp. 185-213.

Uses a mainly structuralist approach to analyse *SUH*, which he calls a significant intellectual novel and the best novel of *interioridad* of its time.

B1252 ——, 'Estudio', in *Alas "Clarín"* (see Aa9), pp. 13-169.

B1253 *Vázquez Azpiri, Héctor, *Clarín* (Madrid: EPESA, 1970?). 140 pp.

Cited by B480, p. 293. This study is supposed to form part of the series, Grandes Escritores Contemporáneos, but I have been unable to find it. Was it ever published?

B1254 Vázquez de Prada y Grande, Rodrigo, '*La Regenta* cumple cien años', *Argumentos* (Madrid), 8, Nos 63-64 (1984), 4-7.

Calls *LR* 'una novela totalizadora', for which multiple readings can be made.

B1255 Vázquez-Zamora, R[afael], ' "Clarín", novelista', *Destino* (Barcelona), 2a época, No. 534 (11.10.47), 10-11.

Despite the excellence of his style, LA was a fanatic in his novels, says R.V.-Z.

B1256 ——, 'El látigo de "Clarín" ', *Destino* (Barcelona), 2a época, No. 535 (18.10.47), 11-12.

Discusses LA the critic, his combative spirit and intellectual perceptiveness. How would LA have been able today, asks the author, to insert his criticism within the very limited space of modern newspapers?

B1257 Vega, Ricardo de la, 'Al crítico señor de Clarín', *Madrid Cómico*, No. 6 (8.2.80), 7-8.

A satirical response to LA's negative comments on author's verse.

B1258 ——, 'A mi clarinito', *Madrid Cómico*, No. 13 (28.3.80), 5-6.

Continues the polemic on poetry, this time, on the question of the poetic meter, *sáficos adónicos*.

B1259 ——, 'A mi discípulo Clarinito. Punto final', *Madrid Cómico*, No. 8 (22.2.80), 4.

A response to LA's comment that the author misused a point of grammar.

B1260 ——, 'A mi querido discípulo en peluquería Clarín', *Madrid Cómico*, No. 7 (15.2.80), 6-7.
An *ad hominem* attack on LA's supposed ignorance of Greek, grammar, and theater.

B1261 Vega Pico, J., 'Personajes de "Clarín". Doña Berta en el mapa de Madrid', *Asturias* (Madrid), No. 13 (Apr. 1952), 15.
Recounts the story of 'Doña Berta'.

B1262 *Vela, Fernando, ' "Clarín" en Oviedo', *Diario de Madrid*, No. 4 (20.10.34).

B1263 ——, 'Un día de Clarín en Oviedo', in his *El grano de pimienta* (Buenos Aires: Austral, 1950), pp. 30-32.
An impressionistic, Azorín-like sketch, dated 1917, in which author visualizes a day in LA's life in Oviedo.

B1264 ——, 'Evocación de Ortega', *Sur*, No. 241 (July-Aug. 1956), 3-12.
Pp. 3-6 contain a personal reminiscence of LA and a comparison between LA and Ortega y Gasset.

B1265 ——, 'El monumento a "Clarín" ', *El Noroeste* (Gijón) (26.9.20).
The monument to LA should be intimate, not grandiose, in appearance.

B1266 ——, 'Del mundo y de la ciudad. La chimenea de leña', *El Noroeste* (Gijón) (11.4.17).
F.V. is attracted to LA's stories for the hints of autobiographical confession in them.

B1267 Velázquez Cueto, Gerardo, *Galdós y Clarín*, Cuadernos de Estudio, 17 (Madrid: Cincel, 1981). 86 pp.
Pp. 67-84 are devoted to LA. A tissue of other critics' opinions. The analysis of ' ¡Adiós, Cordera! ' on pp. 77-84 is a dreadful example of how not to do structuralist criticism.

B1268 Vida, Jerónimo, '*La Regenta*, de D. Leopoldo Alas (Clarín)', *Boletín de la Institución Libre de Enseñanza*, 9 (15.8.85), 246-48. Rpt. in B144, pp. 297-302.
A thoughtful review of *LR*, which the author considers, after *La desheredada*, 'la novela de más miga, más seria, más fundamental'.

Author then goes on to enumerate a number of defects in the novel: its excesses of characters and words, of description and analyses, the insufficiency of dialogue and dramatic movement.

B1269   Vidart, Luis, 'Las informaciones literarias de fin de siglo', *Blanco y Negro*, No. 14 (9.8.91), 214-16.
On *la novela novelesca* and the opinions of LA, Picón, and other writers.

B1270   Vigil, Manuel, 'Clarín, obrero', *Revista Popular* (Oviedo) (1.7.01), 20-21.
On LA's sympathy for the working classes in Asturias.

B1271   Vilanova, Antonio, '*La Regenta* de Clarín y la teoría hegeliana de los caracteres indecisos', *Ínsula*, No. 451 (June 1984), 1, 12-13.
Interesting article on the Hegelian influence upon the development of LA's deepening conception of character. Uses some of LA's early criticism to good effect here.

B1272   Villa Pastur, Jesús, 'Homenaje a "Clarín"', *La Voz de Asturias* (Oviedo) (20.12.52), 3.
A favorable review of B61.

B1273   ——, 'La novela en la generación del 68 y el P. Blanco García', *Archivum*, 2 (1952), 303-11.
For Blanco García, ' "Clarín" era una espina clavada en el corazón del fraile agustino'.

B1274   Villán, Javier, 'Álvaro Custodio, de la Barraca y el Teatro Clásico de México al Escorial', *El Correo de Zamora* (23.9.83).
The director discusses *LR*'s modernity. See Aj4.

B1275   ——, '*La Regenta*, cien años después', *La Nueva España* (Oviedo) (11.9.83), 29.
Comments favorably on Álvaro Custodio's ability to synthesize into two and a half hours the stage production of *LR*. See Aj4.

Villavicencio, Laura N.: See Núñez de Villavicencio, Laura.

B1276   *Vincent, Gabriel, 'Structure et tonalité des contes de Leopoldo Alas', Diplôme, ref. 21-p-42, Biblioteca del Instituto Hispánico (Paris, n.d.).
Cited by Ferreras, B410, p. 222.

B1277 *Vincent, Jacqueline, '*Madame Bovary* et *La Regenta*',
Diplôme, Biblioteca del Instituto Hispánico (Paris, n.d.).
Cited by Ferreras, B410, p. 219.

B1278 Violón [pseud.], 'Carta abierta a D. Leopoldo Alas
(Clarín)', *Barcelona Cómica*, 4, No. 126 (25.11.91), 7,
10.
LA is 'un crítico mediano' and 'un novelista insoportable'.

B1279 Visser, Annemarie, 'A Vision of Spanish Intellectuals in
Leopoldo Alas' Short Stories', unpubl. M.A. thesis, Vanderbilt Univ., 1977. 112 pp.
On LA's ridicule of the pseudo-intellectual of Krausist and positivist
persuasion.

B1280 Wagner, Miriam, '*La Regenta*: Metaphor and Meaning',
unpubl. diss., Cornell Univ., 1972. 183 pp. Abstracted
in *DAI*, 33 (1972-73), 5204-A.
Studies implicit and explicit metaphor in *LR*, in particular, those
images of hunting, war, and resistance to enclosure which reveal
a Darwinian influence. See also B1022-23.

B1281 Warren, L.A., 'Clarín (Leopoldo Alas)', in his *Modern
Spanish Literature*, I (New York: Brentano's, 1929), pp.
172-80.
LR is 'one of the great novels of the century' for its 'keen observation, sharp wit, and a great intellectual power of analysis'.

B1282 Weber, Frances Wyers, 'The Dynamics of Motif in Leopoldo
Alas' *La Regenta*', *RR*, 57 (1966), 188-99.
A solid article on the 'interweaving of inner and outer realities, of
sentimental conflict and social satire in terms of the thematic dualities or tensions that give the work its form.'

B1283 ——, 'Ideology and Religious Parody in the Novels of
Leopoldo Alas', *BHS*, 43 (1966), 197-208. Spanish version
in B144, pp. 119-36. Extracted in B1297, pp. 590-94.
A good study. F.W.W. analyses the parody of values in LA's novels
not as an attack on religion or other ideals, but as the expression
of 'the futility of all efforts to live solely by abstractions, of all
attempts to deny man's compositeness.'

B1284 Weiner, Hadassah Ruth, 'Cinco breves apuntaciones sobre

La Regenta', Los Cuadernos del Norte (Oviedo), 5, No. 23 (Jan.-Feb. 1984), 30-33.
On the title; secondary characters; omniscient narrator; landscape; and indecisive temperaments in *LR*.

B1285 ——, 'Crítica y creación: dos dimensiones de la novelística de Clarín', unpubl. diss., Indiana Univ., 1973. 184 pp. Abstracted in *DAI*, 34 (1973-74), 1942-A.
On the integralistic vision of LA in his two novels, i.e., the unity of objectives of both critic and novelist in *SUH* and *LR*.

B1286 ——, 'Integralismo de Clarín: los "interiores ahumados"', *Los Cuadernos del Norte* (Oviedo), 2, No. 7 (May-June 1981), 84-93.
A review of LA's ideas on the novel, especially his emphasis on the study of 'the smoky interiors' of characters, social groups, and settings, and the importance of composition, or form, in the novel.

B1287 ——, '*Madame Bovary* et *La Regenta*. Étude comparative', in *Bulletin 1976-1977. Société des Professeurs Français en Amérique*, pp. 65-79.
Establishes a comparison between the ballroom scenes and the opera and theater scenes in the two novels. Cites only Clavería and Bonafoux as critical antecedents.

B1288 ——, '*La Regenta* y *Su único hijo*: revisión del estilo personal de Clarín', *Torre*, 24, Nos 93-94 (July-Dec. 1976), 67-83.
Studies some structural similarities, such as the opening pages, the organization of some of the chapters, plot development, and characters. In their endings, however, we see that *LR* 'es un drama entero con prólogo, varias jornadas, epílogo' while *SUH* 'nos deja cuando cae el telón después del primer acto'.

B1289 ——, '*Su único hijo*: desequilibrio y exaltación', *BIDEA*, 30 (1976), 431-47.
Both characters and structure in *SUH* reflect an imbalance and excess which appear to be sought deliberately by LA.

B1290 *Wesley, Howard David, '"Clarín" and Pérez de Ayala', unpubl. M.A. thesis, Univ. of Texas-Austin, 1937.

B1291 Wesseling, Pieter, 'Structure and its Implications in Leopoldo Alas' *La Regenta*', *HR*, 51 (1983), 393-408.

Convincingly argues that the structure of *LR* is based on the pendulum, though at times the article seems too schematic and a bit inflated; two unnecessary diagrams.

B1292 Wiltrout, Ann, 'El cosmos de *La Regenta* y el mundo de su autor', *Archivum*, 21 (1971), 47-64.
A rehash of earlier judgements, this paper offers nothing new and sometimes jumps without transitions from one loose point to another.

B1293 Wolfe, Daniel Michael, 'Cleric-Woman Relationship in *Pepita Jiménez* and *La Regenta*', unpubl. M.A. thesis, Univ. of Virginia, 1975. 73 pp.
Emphasizes the spirit-flesh conflict.

B1294 X., 'Crítica de teatros. Opiniones de "Clarín". Coincidencia notable. *María Rosa* y los críticos', *El Correo* (13.1.95).
Publishes excerpts from LA's 'Revista literaria' (*Las Novedades* (New York), (1.12.94).

B1295 Yglesia, Ángela de la, '*La Regenta*, un parto difícil', *Blanco y Negro*, No. 3277 (22.2.75), 14-15.
In an interview, the actress Emma Penella (Ana Ozores in the film version of *LR*) explains why it took two years to make the film (censorship, personal problems, etc.). See Aj3.

Ynduráin Hernández, Francisco: See Anon., B1329.

B1296 *Zaldívar, A., 'Evocación de "Clarín"', *Norte* (Buenos Aires), 25, No. 153 (1957).
Cited by Ortiz Aponte, B890, p. 196.

Zaloña Bances, José: See Anon., B1310.

B1297 Zavala, Iris M., ed., *Romanticismo y realismo (Historia y crítica de la literatura española*, ed. Francisco Rico, V) (Barcelona: Grijalbo, 1982), pp. 563-622.
Contains introduction (pp. 563-68) and bibliography (pp. 568-71); and rpts extracts of B13, 113, 145, 205, 281, 564, 861, 1034, 1161, 1283.

——: See also Blanco Aguinaga, Carlos.

Zeda [pseud.]: See Fernández Villegas, Francisco.

B1298 Zuleta, Emilia de, *Historia de la crítica española*

contemporánea (Madrid: Gredos, 1966), pp. 66-77.
LA's ideas on criticism, the novel, naturalism, poetry; and his position in Spanish criticism.

B1299   Zulueta, Carmen de, *Navarro Ledesma, el hombre y su tiempo* (Madrid: Alfaguara, 1968), pp. 9, 40-41, 68-69, 128-31.
On Navarro Ledesma's opinion of LA's work and the feud between N.L. and LA. Also cites a letter from LA to N.L. (dated 22.8.89).

B1300   *Anon., 'Acta', *El Carbayón* (Oviedo) (2.10.95). Rpt. by Gómez-Santos, B514, pp. 124-25.
On the LA-Arturo de Armada dispute over the Spanish Navy.

B1301   ——, 'Actualidades', *Blanco y Negro*, No. 529 (22.6.01), n. pag.
An obituary.

B1302   ——, 'Alas y Canella', *Asturias Semanal*, No. 349 (14-21. 2.76), 2.
Compares the view of Oviedo given in *LR* and in Canella's *El libro de Oviedo*.

B1303   ——, 'Asociación de Amigos del Real Coliseo Carlos III. Noticias teatrales. Estreno de *La Regenta*, el primero de septiembre', *Gaceta del Coliseo* (San Lorenzo del Escorial), 5, No. 43 (July 1983), 5.
On A. Custodio's dramatic adaptation of *LR* (see Aj4) and its cast.

B1304   ——, 'Ateneo. – Leopoldo Alas', *El Correo* (6.3.86).
On LA's lecture on Alcalá Galiano.

B1305   ——, 'El banquete a Clarín', *El Progreso*, 1 (21.11.97).
On a banquet given at the café Inglés and organized by *El Progreso*.

B1306   ——, 'El catedrático señor Montero Díaz, inauguró ayer en la Universidad el curso de conferencias dedicado a estudiar a "Clarín" ', *La Nueva España* (Oviedo) (18.11.52), 5.
A summary of Montero Díaz's talk on LA's philosophy.

B1307   ——, 'Centenario de *La Regenta*', *Información Cultural* (Madrid), No. 13 (June 1984), 16-17.

Talks about the re-evaluation and commemoration of *LR* on its hundreth birthday.

B1308   ——, 'El ciclo de conferencias del centenario de "Clarín". "El Oviedo de Clarín", por el catedrático don Juan Uría Ríu', *La Nueva España* (Oviedo) (16.12.52), 4.
Reviews and summarizes Uría Ríu's talk on LA, in which he describes the Oviedo of Clarín's time and of his novels.

B1309   ——, 'El ciclo de conferencias en el centenario de "Clarín". "Clarín", novelista. -- Por don José María Roca Franquesa', *La Nueva España* (Oviedo) (22.11.52), 6.
LR is an excellent novel, says R.F. in his talk (summarized here), but morally pernicious. Also notes the possible influence of Zola's *La Conquête de Plassans* on *LR*.

B1310   ——, 'El ciclo de conferencias en el centenario de "Clarín". "Don Leopoldo Alas, visto por un alumno", por el profesor don José Zaloña Bances', *La Nueva España* (Oviedo) (4.12.52), 4.
A summary of a talk given on LA's brilliant teaching and his ability to poeticize special moments.

B1311   ——, 'Clarín', *Arte y Letras* (Barcelona), 2 (23.6.01), 362.
An obituary.

B1312   ——, 'Clarín', in *Avecilla* (see Ad23), pp. 3-4.

B1313   ——, ' "Clarín" en América', *Nuestro Tiempo*, 1 (1901), 366-68.
Comments on the high esteem in which Latin Americans held LA.

B1314   ——, ' "Clarín" homenajeado por el Ayuntamiento', *La Voz de Asturias* (Oviedo) (14.6.81). Rpt. in B183, pp. 17-18.
Details of the June 13, 1981 homage and exhibit in Oviedo.

B1315   *——, 'Clarín honra de Asturias y de España. Una caricatura de Pérez de Ayala y una opinión de "Azorín" ', *La Revista de la Sociedad Popular "Santa Susana"* (Oviedo) (1935).

B1315 bis ——, ' "Clarín" (Leopoldo Alas)', in *Pipá* (see Ad21), pp. 3-6.

B1316 ——, 'Clarín (Leopoldo Alas y Ureña, llamado)', in *Gran Enciclopedia Larousse*, II (Barcelona: Planeta, 1967), pp. 1004-05.
Gives ideological formation of LA, as well as other details.

B1317 ——, ' "Clarín", recuperado en el LXXX aniversario de su muerte', *El Libro Español*, 24, No. 282 (June 1981), 247-48.
Comments on the recent upsurge in critical interest in LA.

B1318 ——, 'Clarín, seud. de Leopoldo Alas Ureña', in *Diccionario enciclopédico Salvat Universal*, VII (Barcelona: Salvat, 1969), p. 102.
Gives a good analysis of *LR*.

B1319 ——, 'Clarín vive', *La Nueva España* (Oviedo) (13.6.81). Rpt. in B183, p. 15.
On the eightieth anniversary of LA's death.

B1320 ——, ' "Clarín" y su busto', *EstLit*, No. 396 (18.5.68), 13.
The bust of LA, which had been removed from Oviedo's main park, the Campo de San Francisco, in 1936, has been reinstalled.

B1321 ——, 'Clarinistas de todo el mundo estudian en Barcelona la literatura de Leopoldo Alas', *El País* (20.3.84), 26. Rpt. in *El País, Edición Internacional* (26.3.84), 20; and in *Spain: Boletín Cultural*, No. 30 (April 1984), 29.
On a special *LR* symposium given at the Univ. de Barcelona.

B1322 ——, 'Contra Rodó. Don José Batlle y Ordóñez le niega estilo. Fulmina a *Ariel*. El juicio de "Clarín" ', *El País* (Montevideo) (23.2.20).
Uses LA's favorable judgement of Rodó to combat J.B.'s negative view.

B1323 *——, 'Las cosas en su punto', *Región* (Oviedo) (26.4.52).
Cited by Martínez Cachero, B714, p. 91.

B1324 ——, 'Una cuestión con don Juan Menéndez Pidal', *El Carbayón* (Oviedo) (26.10.83). Rpt. by Gómez-Santos, B514, pp. 113-14.
A response to a satirical article on LA by J. Menéndez Pidal in *El Trasgo*. See also B619.

B1325   ——, 'Del ciclo de conferencias dedicado a "Clarín".
Disertó ayer el catedrático de la Universidad de Murcia,
don Mariano Baquero Goyanes, sobre "la técnica narrativa
de Clarín" ', *La Nueva España* (Oviedo) (17.12.52), 4.
A résumé of Baquero Goyanes's talk on LA's narrative techniques
(use of dialogue, description, rhythm, landscape, and psychological
perspectivism).

B1326   ——, 'Del ciclo de conferencias en el centenario de "Clarín". "Clarín", catedrático universitario, por el catedrático
don José Aparicio Díaz', *La Nueva España* (Oviedo) (12.
12.52), 4.
In his talk, Aparicio Díaz analyses LA's doctoral thesis and his prologue to *La lucha por el derecho.*

B1327   ——, 'Del ciclo de conferencias en el centenario de Clarín.
"Clarín, crítico de su tiempo", por el decano de la Facultad
de Filosofía y Letras, D. Emiliano Díaz Echarri', *La Nueva
España* (Oviedo) (28.11.52), 4.
This summary of Díaz Echarri's talk notes the emphasis on LA's
excellence as a critic, although *LR* is criticized as immoral.

B1328   ——, 'Del ciclo de conferencias en el centenario de "Clarín". "Clarín", en el lenguaje – Por don Emilio Alarcos
Llorach', *La Nueva España* (Oviedo) (25.11.52), 5.
Alarcos Llorach spoke of LA's concept of language and the social
versus academic use of language.

B1329   ——, 'Del ciclo de conferencias en el centenario de "Clarín". "Las corrientes literarias en la época de 'Clarín' ",
por don Francisco Ynduráin Hernández, de la Universidad
de Zaragoza', *La Nueva España* (Oviedo) (11.12.52), 5.
On Ynduráin's discussion of possible influences on LA.

B1330   ——, 'D. Leopoldo Alas', *El Español* (13.6.01).
An obituary.

B1331   ——, 'D. Leopoldo Alas (Clarín)', *El Correo* (13.6.01).
An obituary.

B1332   ——, 'D. Leopoldo Alas (Clarín)', *El Correo* (14.6.01).
Details of LA's death.

B1333 ——, 'D. Leopoldo Alas (Clarín)', *La Ilustración Artística* (Barcelona), 20 (24.6.01), 415, 418.
An obituary.

B1334 ——, 'Don Leopoldo Alas (Clarín)', *Nuevo Mundo*, 4, No. 202 (17.11.97).
On LA's popularity and his temperament as a critic.

B1335 ——, 'El drama de Alas en Barcelona', *El Carbayón* (Oviedo) (21.6.95).
An article on the successful first night of *Teresa* in Barcelona.

B1336 ——, 'Ecos teatrales', *La Dinastía* (Barcelona) (16.6.95).
On the performance of *Teresa* in Barcelona.

B1337 ——, 'En honor de Leopoldo Alas (Clarín)', *Nuevo Mundo*, 9, No. 459 (24.10.02).
Remarks on the marble tablet dedicated to LA in his classroom at the Univ. de Oviedo.

B1338 ——, 'Entierro de D. Leopoldo Alas', *El Correo* (15.6.01).
On LA's burial.

B1339 ——, 'Espíritu y letras en los hombres asturianos', *Asturias* (Madrid: Centro Asturiano de Madrid), 11, No. 56 (Dec. 1961), n. pag.
LA is cited as an example of 'el intelectualismo apasionado' of Asturias.

B1340 ——, 'Expediente relativo a la publicación de la biografía de "Clarín"', no. 9347, 1952-53, Diputación Provincial de Oviedo, Archivo.
An interesting series of documents detailing the publication of Gómez-Santos's biography (B514). Contains an evaluation of the MS, requested revisions, questions on possible Church censorship, and the financing of the book.

B1341 ——, 'El filósofo de Vetusta', *La Balesquida*, 2, No. 2 (1931), 19.
A poetic homage to LA (dated Spring 1901).

B1342 *——, 'Fray Candil y Clarín', *El Fígaro* (La Habana) (10. 4.92), 6.
Cited by Barinaga, B132, p. 321.

B1343 ——, 'Hispanistas de Estados Unidos quieren organizar un congreso internacional sobre "Clarín" ', *La Nueva España* (Oviedo) (10.11.83), 23.
Details of the proposed Oct. 1985 conference in Athens, Ga.

B1344 *——, 'Honrando la memoria de un ilustre profesor', *El Carbayón* (Oviedo) (5.5.31).

B1345 ——, 'Hoy se clausura la Exposición de "Clarín", en el Ayuntamiento', *La Nueva España* (Oviedo) (20.6.81). Rpt. in B183, p. 18.
The exhibit provoked people's interest in LA.

B1346 ——, 'La huelga de Gijón', *Nuestro Tiempo*, 1 (1901), 582-91.
Quotes LA and cites his role as mediator in the strike.

B1347 ——, 'Imágenes de la vida y de la obra de Clarín'.
A television screenplay, on the life and times of LA, deposited in the Biblioteca Nacional (n.p., n.d.). 70 pp. Internal evidence indicates this televised biography was probably produced in the 1960s.

B1348 ——, 'Jorge Guillén: me gustaría conocer la historia del procesamiento del hijo de Clarín', *Asturias Semanal*, No. 386 (6-13.11.76), 42.
On Guillén's correspondence with J.A. Cabezas, in which he asks for details on LA's son and his death in 1937.

B1349 *——, 'Un juicio oportuno: la opinión de Leopoldo Alas', *La Campaña* (Río Negro, Uruguay) (30.6.97).

B1350 ——, 'Leopoldo Alas', *El Imparcial* (6.3.02).
Praises LA's role as a mediator in the Gijón strike and urges that his articles on the strike be rpt.

B1351 ——, 'Leopoldo Alas', *Madrid Cómico*, No. 21 (15.6.01), 190.
An obituary.

B1352 ——, 'Leopoldo Alas (Clarín)', *El Liberal* (14.6.01).
An obituary.

B1353 ——, 'Leopoldo Alas (Clarín)', *Nuevo Mundo*, 8, No. 389 (19.6.01), 67.
An obituary.

B1354 ——, 'Leopoldo Alas. Los funerales', *El Español* (15.6.01).
Details of LA's burial.

B1355 ——, 'Libros nuevos', *El Imparcial* (24.12.88).
A brief, favorable review of *Mezclilla.*

B1356 ——, 'Libros nuevos. *Solos de "Clarín"'*, *El Correo* (2.10.91).
A favorable review of the 4th ed.

B1357 *——, 'Una necrología', *El Carbayón* (Oviedo) (14.6.01).
Gómez-Santos (B514, pp. 69-70) also notes and rpts from the same
newspaper the description of LA's funeral (*El Carbayón*, 15.6.01).

B1358 ——, 'NO a *La Regenta* cinematográfica', *Asturias Semanal*,
No. 152 (29.4.72), 12-15.
Twelve Asturian intellectuals interviewed generally concur that only
a great director, such as Visconti or Buñuel, could make a first-rate
film version of *LR*. See Aj3.

B1359 *——, 'Nuestro artículo en el centenario de "Clarín"', *El
Pregonero de San Juan* (Mieres) (June 1952), 6.

B1360 ——, 'Palique', in *Gran Enciclopedia Larousse*, VIII (see
B1316), p. 61.
Introductory material.

B1361 ——, 'Pedro Olea: no tengo nada contra el cine de consumo,
si es digno y honrado', *La Nueva España* (Oviedo) (21.4.72),
11.
More on *LR* as projected film. 'Si hiciera *La Regenta* sería absoluta-
mente fiel a "Clarín"', says the director Olea. An interview. See Aj3.

B1362 ——, 'El primer drama de "Clarín"', *El Carbayón* (Oviedo)
(28.3.95).
Reviewer notes that the Madrid journals did not give detailed analyses
of *Teresa.*

B1363 ——, 'Prólogo', in *La Regenta* (see Ac4), I, pp. 22-30.

B1364 ——, '*La Regenta*', in *Gran Enciclopedia Larousse*, VIII
(see B1316), pp. 1006-07.
Introductory material.

B1365 ——, '*La Regenta*, Don Rafael Lapesa, *La Nueva España*

de Oviedo y *Pasquín'*, *Gaceta del Coliseo* (San Lorenzo del Escorial), 5, No. 47 (Oct. 1983), 7-8.
On the stage adaptation of *LR* and its critical reception (see Aj4).

B1366   ——, 'Reseña de la colocación de dos lápidas para honrar la memoria del catedrático D. Leopoldo Alas', *Anales de la Universidad de Oviedo*, 2 (1902-03), 312-14.
Details on the two marble tablets dedicated to LA in Oviedo, one placed in his classroom at the university, and the other indicating a street named after him.

B1367   ——, *'La Revista Nacional* y Clarín. Elogio de Rodó', *La Tribuna Popular* (Montevideo) (14.6.97).
Juxtaposes Antonio de Valbuena's negative view of *La Revista Nacional* and LA's favorable opinion of it and of Rodó.

B1368   ——, 'Un Roman espagnol', *Le Temps* (Paris) (11.10.86), n. pag.
Favorable review of *LR*.

B1369   ——, 'Se celebró el ochenta aniversario de la muerte de Leopoldo Alas "Clarín"', *La Nueva España* (Oviedo) (14. 6.81). Rpt. in B183, p. 16.
On the 13 June ceremony of homage and the proposed 1984 Clarín Symposium in Oviedo.

B1370   ——, 'Se conmemoró el ochenta aniversario de la muerte de Clarín', *Región* (Oviedo) (14.6.81). Rpt. in B183, p. 17.
Reports on the 13 June, 1981 act of homage and exhibit of *clariniana*.

B1371   ——, 'Sería un lugar de poesía', *Asturias Gráfica* (Sept. 1920), n. pag.
On the need for a monument dedicated to LA and placed in the park of Oviedo.

B1372   ——, '75 Aniversario de la muerte de "Clarín"', *Asturias Semanal*, No. 366 (19-26.6.76), 32-33.
To celebrate the 75th anniversary of LA's death, the journal gives a résumé of what Clarín's colleagues and friends said of him in *El Progreso de Asturias*, 1, No. 65 (16.6.01). Notes opinions of Félix Aramburu, Gumersindo Azcárate, Adolfo Buylla, Adolfo Posada,

Rogelio Jove, Rafael Altamira, Melquíades Álvarez, and Fermín Canella.

B1373 ——, '*Su único hijo*', *El Liberal* (5.7.91).
Gives a favorable review and an excerpt from the novel.

B1374 ——, 'Teatro español', *La Iberia* (21.3.95).
A very unfavorable review of *Teresa*, 'un cuadro tenebroso, lúgubre, repugnante y plagado de exageración.'

B1375 *——, '[*Teresa*]', *El Carbayón* (Oviedo) (13.4.96).

B1376 ——, '[*Teresa*]', *El Día* (21.3.95).
A review.

B1377 *——, '[*Teresa*]', *Juan Rana* (10.6.97).
Cited by Romero, Ae4, p. 64.

B1378 *——, '[*Teresa*]', *Juan Rana* (27.7.97).
Cited by Romero, Ae4, p. 64.

B1379 ——, 'The Toads of Vetusta', *TLS* (London) (12.1.67), 26.
In setting up a creative tension between the author and his material in *LR*, LA succeeds in writing an admirably complex and restrained novel on 'the disgusting existence of the toad-like inhabitants of Vetusta'. A review of the 1966 Alianza ed. (Ac7).

B1380 *——, 'Ya estuvo bien', *Región* (Oviedo) (27.4.52).
Cited by Martínez Cachero, B714, p. 92.

B1381   Abellán, Manuel L., 'Clarín: la inversión de paradigmas
ideológicos como recurso literario. (A propósito de "La
conversión de Chiripa")', *Diálogos Hispánicos de Amsterdam
(Narrativa de la Restauración)*, No. 4 (1984), 97-108.
Uses 'genetic structuralism' in an attempt to analyse the story's
ideological and structural ironic inversions. Critical jargon and
pretension obscure the point of this article.

B1382   Alarcos Llorach, Emilio, ' "Clarín" y la lengua', in his *Cajón
de sastre asturiano*, I, Colección Popular, 51 (Salinas,
Asturias: Ayalga, 1980), pp. 92-110.
Examines LA's opinions on current language use, academy norms,
and use of regional speech such as *el bable*.

——: See also B1447.

B1383   Alonso, Pedro Pablo, 'Dionisio Gamallo: "La Iglesia Cató-
lica estafa a la humanidad en las cuestiones sexuales" ',
La Nueva España (Oviedo) (1.12.84), 6.
Reports on papers given at the Oviedo Symposium ('Clarín y *La
Regenta* en su tiempo', 26 Nov.-1 Dec. 1984): those of Gamallo
Fierros ('*La Regenta* a través de cartas de la Pardo Bazán a "Clarín" '),
Álvaro Custodio ('El sentido dramático de *La Regenta*'), Carolyn
Richmond ('Análisis de un personaje secundario de *La Regenta*:
Don Saturnino Bermúdez'), Noël Valis ('Sobre la última frase de *La
Regenta*'), and Concepción Núñez Rey ('*La Regenta* y *O primo
Basilio*').

B1384   ——. 'En el año 1987 se publicará la primera versión de *La
Regenta* en francés', *La Nueva España* (Oviedo) (27.11.84), 36.
Yvan Lissorgues and Jean-François Botrel will head a team of French
scholars in the translation of *LR*, to be published by Arthème Fayard.

B1385   ——, 'Grossi: "Clarín defendío en el Ayuntamiento sus ideas
republicanas y anticlericales" ', *La Nueva España* (Oviedo)
(28.11.84), 6.
Reviews Rodrigo Grossi's paper – ' "Clarín" concejal ... y algunos sucesos
de la ciudad de Oviedo' – delivered at the 1984 Oviedo Symposium.

B1386   ——, 'Harriet Turner: " ' ¡Adiós, Cordera!' tiene una técnica
de insólita modernidad" ', *La Nueva España* (Oviedo) (29.11.84),
6.

Discusses Turner's paper given at the 1984 Symposium, on textual
self-reflexivity found in ' ¡Adiós, Cordera! '.

B1387 ——, 'Leopoldo Alas y *La Regenta* protagonizan desde
ayer la vida cultural de Oviedo', *La Nueva España* (Oviedo)
(27.11.84), 5.
On the inauguration of the 1984 Symposium; and papers by Martínez
Cachero ('Recepción de *La Regenta* "in vita" Leopoldo Alas') and
Juan Antonio Cabezas ('Los últimos años de "Clarín" ').

B1388 ——, 'Lissorgues: 'En Leopoldo Alas destaca su honradez
intelectual" ', *La Nueva España* (Oviedo) (28.11.84), 6.
Reviews papers given at the 1984 Symposium: those of Yvan
Lissorgues (' "Clarín" y el movimiento obrero de 1890 a 1901'),
Carmen Bobes ('El valor sémico del tiempo en *La Regenta*'), and
Antonio Masip ('El deporte en *La Regenta*').

B1389 ——, 'Riopérez y Milá: "Azorín fue pionero en la defensa
de la obra de Leopoldo Alas" ', *La Nueva España* (Oviedo)
(29.11.84), 6.
On Santiago Riopérez y Milá's paper at the 1984 Symposium, in
which he gives more details on the LA-Azorín relationship.

B1390 ——, 'Vilanova: "*La Regenta* analiza un temperamento
apasionado y sensual" ', *La Nueva España* (Oviedo) (29.
11.84), 6.
Discusses papers given by Ricardo Gullón and Antonio Vilanova at
the 1984 Symposium.

Alperi, Víctor: See B1447.

Álvarez Calleja, José: See Martínez Cachero, José María, B14.

B1391 *Álvarez Vara, Ignacio, 'La Regenta de la Mancha: la crítica
empieza a comparar a Clarín con Cervantes', *Cambio 16*,
No. 645 (1984), 128, 130.

B1392 *Andreu Valdés, Martín, 'Más detalles acerca del sentimiento
religioso de "Clarín" ', *Región* (Oviedo) (21.5.67).

B1393 *——, 'El sentimiento religioso de "Clarín" ', *Región* (Oviedo)
(15.3.67).

Arce, Evaristo: See B1447.

Argüelles, Juan Benito: See B1431, 1447.

B1394 *Barcia Trelles, Augusto, *Leopoldo Alas "Clarín"* (Buenos Aires: Centro Asturiano de Buenos Aires, 1952). 20 pp.
Personal reminiscences by one of LA's former students, according to Martínez Cachero, B1429, p. 68.

B1395 *Blasco, Eusebio, [Necrología], *Relieves* (Madrid), No. 138 (21.6.01).
Remembers LA as a 'tyrant' in his day, but respects his talents, according to Martínez Cachero, B1429, p. 46.

B1396 Bobes Naves, María del Carmen, 'Recursos sintácticos en la primera parte de *La Regenta*. La sintaxis literaria: historia y discurso', in *III Simposio de Lengua y Literatura Españolas para Profesores de Bachillerato* (Oviedo: Univ., 1983), pp. 25-39.
A semiotic analysis, in which the author concludes that Ana's story is the most complex, coherent and comprehensive in *LR*. Also makes some interesting comments on the structural function of confession in the novel.

———: See also B1388.

B1397 *Busto, Marino, 'Leopoldo Alas "Clarín" y Guimarán de Carreño', *El Noroeste* (Gijón) (31.12.78).

Cabezas, Juan Antonio: See B1387, 1447.

B1398 *Cabo Martínez, María Rosa, 'Homenaje a Leopoldo Alas "Clarín" con motivo del primer Centenario de la publicación de su novela *La Regenta*', *Magister* (Revista de la Escuela Universitaria de Magisterio de Oviedo), No. 2 (1984), 231-36.

B1399 Campo, Pilar, 'El colectivo Casona estrenó *Teresa* en Oviedo', *La Voz de Asturias* (Oviedo) (1.12.84), 40.
Discusses the 30 Nov. 1984 theatrical production of *Teresa* (see Ae1).

B1400 ———, '400 especialistas analizan, en Oviedo, la obra de Leopoldo Alas "Clarín" ', *La Voz de Asturias* (Oviedo) (27.11. 84), 40.
On Martínez Cachero's paper, 'Recepción de *La Regenta* "in vita" Leopoldo Alas', given at the 1984 Symposium.

B1401   ——, 'Discusiones en torno a la personalidad de Ana Ozores', *La Voz de Asturias* (Oviedo) (29.11.84), 18.
Reports on Antonio Vilanova's paper, 'La Regenta entre la ley natural y el deber moral', given at the 1984 Symposium.

B1402   ——, 'Presentados varios estudios sobre la figura de "Clarín"', *La Voz de Asturias* (Oviedo) (28.11.84), 21.
Reports on papers given at the 1984 Symposium: those of José María Izquierdo Rojo ('Historia clínica de Leopoldo Alas'), Victoriano Rivas Andrés ('"Me nacieron en Zamora": circunstancias y puntualizaciones'), and Antonio Masip Hidalgo ('El deporte en *La Regenta*').

B1403   ——, '*La Regenta* en las cartas de Emilia Pardo Bazán a "Clarín"', *La Voz de Asturias* (Oviedo) (1.12.84), 18.
On two papers given at the 1984 Symposium: those of Dionisio Gamallo Fierros ('*La Regenta* a través de cartas de la Pardo Bazán a "Clarín"') and Álvaro Custodio ('El sentido dramático de *La Regenta*').

B1404   Cándido [pseud.], 'Clarín y la burguesía', *La Nueva España* (Oviedo) (27.11.84), 2.
An editorial, in which C. discusses the significance of LA's critical treatment of the Spanish bourgeoisie in *LR*.

Cecchini Estrada, Carlos: See B1447.

Cordero, Lorenzo: See B1447.

Cueto Alas, Juan: See B1447.

Custodio, Álvaro: See B1383, 1403.

B1405   *Díaz, Edmundo, [Necrología], *El Nalón* (Muros de Pravia), No. 105 (15.6.01), 2.

B1406   Fernández, Carmen, 'Introducción', in *La Regenta* (see Ac23), pp. 9-25.

Fernández Álvarez, Faustino: See B1447.

Fernández Álvarez, Rafael: See B1447.

Fernández Buelta, José: See Anon., B1306, 1308-10, 1325-29.
According to Martínez Cachero, B1429, p. 61, these articles were written by J.F.B.

B1407 Fernández de la Llana, Juan [pseud.: Juan Santana], 'Un recuerdo a "Clarín"', *La Balesquida. Programa Oficial de Fiestas* (Oviedo) (1984), n. pag.
Rpts article originally printed as *'Clarín, [¿]taurófobo o no?', *Región* (Oviedo) (19.7.63). Thinks LA might have been an *aficionado*.

B1408 Fernández Gutiérrez, José María, Francisco Mundi Pedret, Ramón Oteo Sans, & Sara Pujol Russell, 'Historia de las ediciones de *La Regenta*', *Cuadernos de la Facultad de Letras de Tarragona* (Fall, 1984). [8 pp.]
Gives a detailed description of eds published during LA's lifetime, and information on later eds.

B1409 Fernández Rodríguez-Avello, Manuel, 'Clarín y el billete de cuarenta duros', *Vetusta* (Oviedo), No. 2 (July 1984), 3.
On the banknote nicknamed *el Carbayón*, which was issued in 1984 with a portrait of LA; and on LA's economic difficulties.

———: See also B1447.

B1410 *Fries, F.R., [Epilogue and notes], in *Die Präsidentin* (see Ai22).

B1411 Gamallo Fierros, Dionisio, 'El itinerario espiritual de Clarín', *La Voz de Asturias* (Oviedo) (29.11.84), 20-21.
Discusses LA's religious crisis and rpts two poems – 'Fragmentos de un incendio' and 'De "La Torre"' – originally published in *La Gran Vía* (13.1.95).

B1412 ———, 'Laverde en Compostela', *BBMP*, 37 (1961), 232-33, 236-37, 240-41.
Cites generously from Pardo Bazán's letters to LA on the subject of writing an *Historia de la literatura española*.

———: See also B1383, 1403.

B1413 García, Soledad Miranda, *Pluma y altar en el XIX: de Galdós al cura Santa Cruz* (Madrid: Ediciones Pegaso, 1983), pp. 165-66, 183-84, 301-04 *et passim*.
On religious types in *LR*; and 'la religiosidad de la élite'.

García-Alcalde, Guillermo: See B1447.

B1414 García de Castro, Ramón, *Semblanza intelectual del pensador asturiano Estanislao Sánchez-Calvo (1842-1895)* (Oviedo: IDEA, 1982), pp. 16-17.
On the friendship between LA and Sánchez-Calvo.

García de la Concha, Víctor: See B1447.

B1415 García Domínguez, Elías, 'Los cuentos de Clarín', in *Cuentos morales* (see Ad43), pp. v-ix.

Gómez Ojea, Carmen: See B1447.

B1416 Gómez-Santos, Marino, 'La casa solariega de Clarín', *¿Qué Pasa?* (Madrid), No. 207 (June 1984), 4-5.
Anecdotal details on the Guimarán summer home.

González, Ángel: See B1447.

B1417 González Herrán, José Manuel, *La obra de Pereda ante la crítica literaria de su tiempo*. Colección Pronillo 2 (Santander: Ayuntamiento and Ediciones de Librería Estudio, 1983). 525 pp.
See *Índice onomástico* for references to LA's views of Pereda's work.

González Orejas, Francisco: See B1447.

Gracia Noriega, José Ignacio: See B1447.

B1418 Grossi Fernández, Rodrigo, 'Algunos motivos asturianos en Clarín', in *III Simposio de Lengua y Literatura para Profesores de Bachillerato* (Oviedo: Univ., 1983), pp. 119-29.
Lists terms taken from *el bable*, Asturian patronymics and toponyms, found in LA's fiction.

B1419 ——, '¿Vetusta = Oviedo?', *Vetusta* (Oviedo), No. 2 (July 1984), 8.
Notes the universality of Vetusta and the symbolism of names in *LR*.

——: See also B1385.

Gullón, Ricardo: See B1390.

Izquierdo Rojo, José María: See B1402.

B1420 J.L.F., 'Reposición de la placa a "Clarín" en la Facultad de

Derecho', *La Voz de Asturias* (Oviedo) (1.12.84), 18.
Reports on the ceremony in which a plaque in memory of LA was reinstalled at the University.

Lissorgues, Yvan: See B1388.

B1421 Llorente Herrero, Pilar, & Feliciano Páez-Camino Arias, 'Galdós y Clarín en la clase de historia', *Cuadernos de Pedagogía* (Barcelona), 10, No. 119 (Nov. 1984), 29-32.
Schematizes *LR* into various themes, for pre-university classroom presentation.

Lombardía, Miguel Ángel: See B1447.

B1422 *López, Francisco, '*La Regenta* levanta ampollas. Conversación con Andrés Amorós, crítico literario', *Argumentos* (Madrid), 4, No. 45 (1981), 54-57.

B1423 M.S., 'Profeta en Vetusta', *El País* (3.12.84), 31.
LA has been 'rehabilitated' in Oviedo by the Nov. 1984 Symposium.

B1424 *Martínez Cachero, José María, 'La actitud anti-modernista del crítico "Clarín"', *Anales de Literatura Española* (Univ. de Alicante), No. 2 (1983), 383-98. Rpt. in B1429, pp. 207-24.
Confirms LA's *anti-modernista* stance, which M.C. attributes to 'una inadecuación o falta de correspondencia entre la insoslayable realidad literaria del Modernismo y el ánimo de Leopoldo Alas'.

B1425 ——, 'Cien años de *La Regenta*', *Boletín Informativo. Fundación Juan March*, No. 143 (Dec. 1984), 30-34.
Gives an overview of themes discussed in a series of lectures at the Fundación Juan March in Oct. 1984: *LR* as a *roman à clé*; provincial mores; the critical reception of *LR*; and novelistic settings.

B1426 ——, '"Clarín"', in *Gran Enciclopedia Gallega*, VI (Santiago de Compostela: Silverio Cañada, 1977), pp. 197-98. Rpt. in B1429, pp. 139-44, as '"Clarín" y Galicia'.
On LA's literary relationship with Luis Taboada, Valle-Inclán, Pardo Bazán, and Emilio Fernández Vaamonde.

B1427 *——, 'Las desventuras de un busto', *El Alcázar* (Madrid) (5.6.62).

B1428   *——, 'Leopoldo Alas, vecino de Oviedo', *La Nueva España*
(Oviedo) (27.3, 3.4.83). Rpt. in B1429, pp. 33-42.
Recounts LA's home life in Oviedo and his relationship with the
Univ. de Oviedo, the Casino, and the Ayuntamiento de Oviedo.

B1429   ——, *Las palabras y los días de Leopoldo Alas (Miscelánea
de estudios sobre "Clarín")* (Oviedo: IDEA, 1984). 325 pp.
Rpts B709, 710, 712, 714, 718, 724, 729, 731, 732, 734, 736, 743,
1424, 1426, 1428; and extracts from B721, 722.

B1430   ——, 'Pequeña historia (bibliográfica) de una gran novela',
El Libro Español, Nos 314-15 (Aug.-Sept. 1984), 77-80.
Discusses various eds of *LR*, such as the first, popular and critical
eds, and translations.

B1431   ——, Juan Benito Argüelles, & José Álvarez Calleja, *La
Regenta 1884-1984. Exposición bibliográfica y documental*
(Oviedo: Caja de Ahorros de Asturias, 1984). 23 pp.
Describes the contents of the exhibition, shown in Oviedo, Gijón,
and Madrid; the major characters of *LR*; the various eds of *LR*.
With a chronology of LA.

——: See also B1387, 1400.

Masip Hidalgo, Antonio: See B1388, 1402, 1447.

Medio, Dolores: See B1447.

B1432   Millás, Jaime, 'Un pulpo de muchos brazos', *El País* (17.
6.84).
On Ac20.

B1433   Miquis, Alejandro, 'La semana teatral', *Nuevo Mundo* (25.
6.08), n. pag.
Talks of *Teresa* as an example of the theater of ideas. 'En *Teresa*
está el germen abortado de una copiosa dramaturgia....'

B1434   Morales Saro, María Cruz, 'Oviedo y Vetusta', *Vetusta*
(Oviedo), No. 6 (Nov. 1984), 12-13.
Contrasts views on architecture and urbanism in LA and Fermín
Canella.

Mundi Pedret, Francisco: See Fernández Gutiérrez, José
María.

B1435 Narbona Jiménez, Antonio, 'Leopoldo Alas "Clarín":
Solos de Clarín', in *Textos hispánicos comentados*, ed.
Antonio Narbona Jiménez (Córdoba: Univ., 1984), pp.
135-47.
A semantic and syntactic analysis of the 'proceso reductor y distor-
sionante' found in the first paragraph of 'La mosca sabia'.

B1436 Navarro Adriaensens, José M., 'Leopoldo Alas y su actitud
ante la lengua', *Anales de Literatura Española* (Univ. de
Alicante), No. 2 (1983), 399-407.
Concludes that LA, while he generally follows the norms of the
Academia, is also aware of the unstable conditions of language use.

Núñez Rey, Concepción: See B1383.

B1437 *Ochoa, Juan, [*Mezclilla*], *El Atlántico* (Santander) (25.2.89).
Cited by Torres, Ab32, p. 41.

Oteo Sans, Ramón: See Fernández Gutiérrez, José María.

Ovín de la Vega, José Manuel: See B1447.

B1438 *Padrós de Palacios, Esteban, 'Introducción', in *La Regenta*
(see Ac24).

Páez-Camino Arias, Feliciano: See Llorente Herrero, Pilar.

Plans, Juan José: See B1447.

Poblet Vega-Arango, Fernando: See B1447.

B1439 Pons, F., 'El grupo "Casona" presenta un interesante mon-
taje de la obra de Clarín, *Teresa*', *La Nueva España* (Oviedo)
(1.12.84), 34.
On the 30 Nov. presentation of *Teresa* (see Ae1).

Pujol Russell, Sara: See Fernández Gutiérrez, José María.

B1440 Richmond, Carolyn, ' "Las dos cajas" de Clarín y otras dos
de Marsillach', *HR*, 52 (1984), 459-75.
Joaquín Marsillach's 'El entierro de un violín' (1883), rpt here, as
a probable source for LA's story.

——: See also B1383.

Riopérez y Milá, Santiago: See B1389.

Rivas Andrés, Victoriano: See B1402.

B1441   Sanroma Aldea, José, 'Introducción', in *Adiós, Cordera y otros cuentos* (see Ad41), pp. 9-25.

Santana, Juan [pseud.] : See Fernández de la Llana, Juan.

B1442   Serna, David, '1984, el año de Clarín', *Hoja del Lunes* (Oviedo) (26.11.84), 27.
On the Oviedo Symposium and the newly-acquired significance of *LR.*

Silva y Cienfuegos-Jovellanos, Pedro de: See B1447.

B1443   Somovilla, Miguel, 'Especialistas en la obra de Leopoldo Alas se reúnen en el centenario de *La Regenta*', *El País* (26.11.84), 30.
Details of the Oviedo Symposium.

Taibo I, Paco Ignacio: See B1447.

B1444   Tolivar Faes, José Ramón, 'Don Ramón García-Alas y su disertación acerca del establecimiento de la primitiva diócesis de esta región', *BIDEA*, 33, No. 98 (1979), 573-97.
Biobibliographical details on LA's paternal grandfather.

Turner, Harriet: See B1386.

B1445   Uría Ríos, Paloma, ' "El entierro civil de *La Regenta* era el entierro de Ríos" ', *Ástura*, 2 (1984), 65-71.
Convincing details of the similarities between Santos Barinaga's burial in *LR* and the real-life civil interment of republican Juan González Ríos in 1884.

Valis, Noël M.: See B1383

B1446   Varela Jácome, Benito, 'Leopoldo Alas "Clarín", *La Regenta*', in *Nuevas técnicas de análisis de textos*, by B.V.J., Ángeles Cardona de Gibert, & Xavier Fages Gironella (Madrid: Bruño, 1980), pp. 347-65.
Semiotic analysis of the final scene, highlighting its conflictive structure. Unilluminating.

B1447   *VVAA, *"La Regenta" cien años después* (Oviedo, 1984).
With artwork by Miguel Ángel Lombardía; and the collaboration

of Emilio Alarcos Llorach, Evaristo Arce, Víctor Alperi, Juan Benito Argüelles, Lorenzo Cordero, Carlos Cecchini Estrada, Juan Antonio Cabezas, Juan Cueto Alas, Faustino Fernández Álvarez, Rafael Fernández Álvarez, Manuel Fernández Avello, Guillermo García-Alcalde, Carmen Gómez Ojea, Francisco González Orejas, José Ignacio Gracia Noriega, Ángel González, Víctor García de la Concha, Miguel Ángel Lombardía, Dolores Medio, Antonio Masip, Juan José Plans, José Manuel Ovín de la Vega, Fernando Poblet Vega-Arango, Pedro de Silva y Cienfuegos-Jovellanos, and Paco Ignacio Taibo I.

Vilanova, Antonio: See B1390, 1401.

B1448   Yllán Calderón, Esperanza, 'Cánovas, visto por "Clarín" y Galdós', *Cuadernos de Historia Moderna y Contemporánea*, 1 (1980), 111-22.
Reviews LA's harsh treatment of the politician-statesman in *Cánovas y su tiempo*.

B1449   Anon., 'Los especialistas califican a *La Regenta* como la mejor novela en castellano del siglo XIX', *El País* (3.12.84), 31. Rpt. in *El País, Edición Internacional* (10.12.84), 20.
Reviews some of the highlights of the 1984 Symposium.

B1450   ——, 'Leopoldo Alas, "el hombre de la mano tendida"', *La Nueva España* (Oviedo) (23.12.76).
On LA's son and the portrait which forty years after his death graces the halls of the Univ. de Oviedo.

B1451   ——, 'Medalla conmemorativa del centenario de *La Regenta*', *La Nueva España* (Oviedo) (27.11.84), 3.
Details on a commemorative medal presented by the Ayuntamiento de Oviedo.

B1452   *——, [Necrología], *Caras y Caretas* (Buenos Aires), No. 142 (22.6.01).

of; and Dualism, use of

Economic position: Af1, 7; Ag1; B191-92, 204, 206, 939, 1086, 1409

Editions, status of: B1130, 1408, 1430-31

Education, views on: Ab19, 22, 31; Ag20; see also Educator, under Alas, Leopoldo

Educator: Ad5; B6, 40-42, 87, 270, 286, 324-25, 359, 520, 584, 599, 657, 756, 761, 795, 937, 971-72, 1104, 1214, 1217, 1310; see also Education, views on, under Alas, Leopoldo

Eightieth anniversary: B183, 393, 724, 917, 1165, 1250, 1314, 1317, 1319, 1345, 1369, 1370

English, difficulties with: Af17

Exhibit of *clariniana*: B1314, 1345, 1370, 1431

Galician writers, relationship with: B1426

Gambling, love of: B43, 949

Games, obsession with: B938, 949

Gijón strike, role in: B1092, 1346, 1350; see also Working classes, relationship with, under Alas, Leopoldo

Grammar, concern with: Ab16; Af5, 26; B178, 299, 468, 962, 999, 1117, 1259

hispanismo: B194, 1209

History, conception of: B656; see also History, use of

Homage volumes: B61, 64, 91-92, 183 291, 296-97, 606-08, 990, 1018, 1199, 1272, 1372

Humor: B37, 43, 245, 301-02, 304, 525, 541, 628

Ideology: Ab28-31; Ac19; Ad5; B15-16, 160, 126, 219, 241, 287, 321, 401, 477-78, 561, 646, 777, 780, 925-26, 984, 1216-17, 1283, 1316, 1381, 1385

Illness, preoccupation with: Af1, 23, 32

Influences on: B218, 496, 571-72, 622, 776, 1046, 1125, 1309, 1329; see also Non-Hispanic writers, relationship to, under Alas, Leopoldo

Journalist: Ab28, 30-31; B197, 619, 663-64, 892, 1101

Language, use of: Ab22; B560, 794, 853, 925-26, 1070, 1328, 1382, 1436

Latin-American writers, attitude toward: Af29-30; Ag22; B86, 294 313, 549, 593, 942, 944-45, 1061

Latin-American reaction to: B1060-61, 1178-79, 1313

Law, concept of: Ab6; B6, 223, 324, 765; see also Juridical, motif of

Literary critic: Ab27, 29; B145, 149, 199, 216, 221, 268, 337, 350-52, 368, 414-16, 468-69, 474, 503 505, 509, 521-22, 535, 544, 563, 603, 626, 710-11, 754, 756, 761, 766, 791, 811, 829, 836, 914, 922, 933, 956, 960, 1062, 1068, 1088, 1104, 1150, 1154, 1158, 1200, 1206-07, 1215, 1221, 1256, 1285, 1294, 1298, 1327, 1334

Literary development: Ad19; B66, 760

Marriage: B58, 445

Maternal, obsession with: Af28; B164, 363, 502, 1053; see also Maternity, theme of; Virgin Mary, preoccupation with, under Alas, Leopoldo

Medal, commemorative: B1451

Modernity: Ai6; B119, 401, 562, 631, 633, 811, 1113, 1147, 1202, 1274

Monument to: B18, 249, 449, 475, 1265, 1320, 1337, 1366, 1371, 1420, 1427

Moral sensibility: Ac11-12; B589, 604, 771, 897, 1104, 1166

INDEX OF ALAS'S WORKS

INDEX OF LITERARY FIGURES

INDEX OF SCHOLARS AND CRITICS

Bonet, Laureano, Ab23.1, 29.1, 30.2;
Ac2, 21; Ad39.3; Ag24; B723.1,
952
Boni, Marco, Ai24.1
Bonilla, Lucía Dolores, Ah10
Borgers, Oscar, B541.4
Botrel, Jean-François, Ab28, 30.3; Af8;
B188, 287, 1384
Bravo, María-Elena, Ai7.1
Bravo-Villasante, Carmen, Af23
Brent, Albert, B1125-26
Brooks, Nancy C., Ah15
Brooks, Walter, Ai8, 10
Brown, G.G., Ab27.1; Ad31; B149.1,
861.1, 1095.2
Buceta, Erasmo, Ah23
Bull, William E., B211.2, 626, 1125
Burell, Consuelo, Ah22
Bustillo, Eduardo, B426, 734
Buylla, Adolfo: See Álvarez Buylla,
Adolfo

C.V., Ac5.1
Cabal, C., B514.2
Cabezas, Juan Antonio, Aa5; B890,
1348, 1387, 1447
Camus, Alfredo, Ab20; B630
Canals, Salvador, B479, 734
Canella [y Secades], Fermín, Ah16;
B796, 907, 1302, 1372, 1434
Cano, José Luis, B460.3
Cano, Leopoldo, Ab2; B1014
Carandell, José María, Ah13
Carenas, Francisco, B887
Carr, Raymond, Ai6.1
Casalduero, Joaquín, B82
Caso González, José, Ad28.3
Castañón, José Manuel, Ah18
Caudel, Francisco, Ac12.2
Cavalheiro, Edgard, Ai25
Cavia, Mariano de, Ab12
Cecchini Estrada, Carlos, B1447
Cejador y Frauca, Julio, Ah62; B447

Cerezales, Manuel, Ac28.6
Cerra, L., B480.2
Cesareo, G.A., B30
Chamberlin, Vernon A., B626
Chandler, Richard E., Ah47
Chaves, Teresa L., Ah15
Cheyne, G.J.G., Ad31.1
Cimorra, Clemente, Ah5
Clark, Barret H., Ai10
Clavería, Carlos, B1287
Colford, William E., Ai12
Colón, Isabel, Ac28.7
Comas, Antonio, Ac25
Cordero, Lorenzo, Ab28.1; B1447
Cortón, Antonio, B102
Cossío, Francisco de, B1091
Cossío, José María de, Af3
Crow, John A., Ah25
Cuervo, Rufino José, Af5
Cuesta, José Victoriano de la, Af6;
B662
Cueto Alas, Juan, Ab28.2; Ac18;
B1447
Custodio, Álvaro, Aj4; B429, 1274-
75, 1303, 1383, 1403; see also
La Regenta (play version)

DaSilva, Zenia, Ai15
D'Auria, Riccardo, Ab29.2
Davis, Gifford, B149.2
Davis, Lisa E., B699, 1222
Debicki, Andrew P., B149.3
Dial, John, B1235.1
Díaz, Janet W., B480.3, 861.2
Díaz, José María, Ab2
Díaz-Caneja, Juan, B935
Díaz Echarri, Emiliano, B1327
Díaz Ordóñez, Víctor, Ab20
Díaz-Plaja, Fernando, Ah59
Díaz-Plaja, Guillermo, Ah7, 48; B124,
1227
Díez Borque, José María, Ab23.2, 27.2,
27.3; B409, 480.4

Peña y Goñi, Antonio, B1117
Pérez Echevarría, Francisco, Ab2
Pérez Gallego, Cándido, B1235.5
Pérez Petit, Víctor, Af30; B942, 944-45
Pikhart, Antonín, Af26; Ai2, 4; B574
Pincus Sigele, Rizel, B82, 678
Pino, Juan del, B139.1
Plácido [pseud.]: See Heras, Dionisio
   de las
Plans, Juan José, B1447
Plinio, B410.1, 477.1
Poblet Vega-Arango, Fernando, B1447
Pokhlebkin, R., Ai27-28
Porto, Juan Antonio, Aj3
Porto-Pompiani, González, B152
Posada, Adolfo, Ab22, 32; Ad16; Ag11,
   20; B54, 370, 609, 630, 641, 1228,
   1372
Primo de Rivera, José Antonio, B1143;
   see also *falangismo*
Propp, Vladímir, B1069

Quiroga Clerigo, Manuel, B861.3
Quirós Linares, Francisco, B12

R.G. [Ricardo Gullón?], B211.5, 973.2
Ragucci, Rodolfo M., Af5; Ah8, 55
Ramos-Gascón, Antonio, Ab29; Ad2;
   Af36; B199, 750
Rand, Marguerite C., B541.10
Reiss, Katharine, Ai23
Resnick, Seymour, Ai11
Révah, I.S., B514.6
Revilla, Manuel de la, Ab5, 7; B105
Reyes Nevares, Salvador, Aa7
Richmond, Carolyn, Ab31.2; Ac11.1,
   20, 28; Ad39; B196, 198, 387,
   930, 1235.6, 1383
Rico, Eduardo G., Ad28.7
Rico, Francisco, B1297
Río, Amelia A. del, Ah6
Río, Ángel de, Ah6
Riopérez y Milá, Santiago, B1389

Rivas Andrés, Victoriano, B1402
Robin, Claire-Nicolle, Ai20
Roca Franquesa, José María, B1309
Rocamora, Pedro: See Cerezales, Manuel
Rodríguez Monegal, Emir, B1060, 1062
Rodríguez Serra, Bernardo, Af31; Ag12
Rogers, Douglass M., Ab15; B1235.7
Romea, Julián, B485
Romera Castillo, José, B723.2
Romero, Leonardo, Ae2, 4
Romero Márquez, Antonio, B53.1
Rossi, Giuseppe Carlo, B61.1
Rössner, Michael, B1157
Round, Nicholas, G., B1235.8
Rubia Barcia, José, B807
Rubín, Pío: See González Rubín, Pío
Ruiz de la Peña, Juan Ignacio, Ah27;
   B293
Ruiz y Benítez de Lugo, Ricardo, Ah56;
   B637
Rutherford, John, Ac11.2, 12.4; Ai6;
   B480.5, 695, 723.3, 861.4

S.S., Ad25
Sabatier, Paul, Ab25
Sáinz de Robles, Federico Carlos, Aa8;
   Ad24; Ah3
Sáinz Rodríguez, Pedro, B1105-06
Salanova Matas, Ernesto, Ac28.12
Sánchez, Elizabeth D., B1235.9
Sánchez Arnòsi, Milagros, B144.1
Sánchez-Calvo, Estanislao, B236, 1414
Sánchez de Castro, Francisco, Ab2
Sánchez Pérez, Antonio, B731
Sánchez Reyes, Enrique, Af17; Ah50
Santullano, Luis, Ad23; B211.6, 218.1
Sarmiento, Edward, B541.11
Sarrailh, Jean, Ah42; B932
Savine, Albert, Ab16
Schwartz, Kessel, Ah47
Seco Serrano, Carlos, B145.1
Sela, Aniceto, B242
Senna, Carl, Ai6.3

RESEARCH BIBLIOGRAPHIES & CHECKLISTS
Edited by
A.D. Deyermond, J.R. Little and J.E. Varey

RESEARCH BIBLIOGRAPHIES & CHECKLISTS

RCB

General editors

A.D. Deyermond, J.R. Little and J.E. Varey

RESEARCH BIBLIOGRAPHIES & CHECKLISTS